Financially Free

Add $20,000 (or More) per Year
to Your Income Through
Part-Time Real Estate Investing

Marc Garrison

SIMON AND SCHUSTER · NEW YORK

This publication is designed to provide accurate and authoritative information, not legal advice. Before acting on any suggestion presented in this book, legal or other professional assistance may be advisable.

Published by Simon and Schuster
A Division of Simon & Schuster, Inc.
Simon & Schuster Building
Rockefeller Center
1230 Avenue of the Americas
New York, New York 10020

SIMON AND SCHUSTER and colophon are registered trademarks of Simon & Schuster, Inc.
Designed by Irving Perkins Associates
Manufactured in the United States of America
10 9 8 7 6 5 4 3 2 1

Library of Congress Cataloging in Publication Data
Garrison, Marc.
    Financially free.

    Includes index.
    1. Real estate investment—United States.
I. Title.
HD1382.5.G37   1986   332.63'24   86-6761
ISBN: 0-671-61731-1

Contents

PART IV: TEN KEYS TO SUCCESS— POINTS AND PITFALLS

PART V: MORE THAN WEALTH

To my wife, DeAnn, my friend and blessing. Your laughter and love drive winter away from any heart.

To my son, Ryan, my "buddy." I stand in awe at your young spirit, while still a child it stands so tall. You truly personify love.

To my daughter, Kelly, my funny little girl. Your smile and giggle remove the troubles of any day.

To my newborn son, Hunter, so long in coming. Neither of us could wait; you still remember—it's in your eyes. I look forward to getting to know you again.

To my friends who are still waiting. I welcome and await the treasures you will bring.

To my father, James. You taught me how to work, and how to savor life. I humbly thank you for those priceless gifts.

To my mother, Sharon, always by my side, never a complaint. How beautiful a day can be when you touch it.

To my brothers and sister, Kenneth, James, and Karie. Family are people before whom you may think out loud. Thank you for that, but most of all for your love and support.

To my outlaws, Devere, Ruth, Lyle, Bruce, Anita, Susan, and Lisa. I couldn't ask for a better second family. You make me proud to be related to each one of you.

To Brent DeMille, Bob Allen, and Stephen Wayner. Your friendship and support have given me the courage to pursue my dreams. It is with gratefulness that I call each one of you my friend.

To my working editor, Bruce C. Erb. Endless nights, mountains of notes, real sweat, anger (from crashed disks and the pressure), frustration, and your deep friendship have made this book possible.

To each of you, thanks is not enough. Maybe love is, and perhaps a trip with me sometime to Disneyworld or Mexico.

Introduction
by Robert G. Allen

A couple of years ago I bought a house—as an investment, of course—from a young investor. Not yet twenty-five, he had already achieved an almost unheard-of level of financial freedom through real estate investing. The interesting part was how he had done it. Starting his investing career when he was twenty-two years old, he had bought and sold real estate in his spare time, using his own unique, fast-track techniques. When I met him he was just entering the very same M.B.A. program from which I had graduated—and he was paying for it with profits from his real estate investments.

Since that time I have enjoyed watching Marc grow and develop. He completed his master of business administration degree; he bought and sold several million dollars' worth of real estate in his spare time; he traveled across the nation teaching thousands of eager investors the basic tools for finding good deals (and has become one of the top-rated real estate speakers today); and now he has written what I consider to be the best A-to-Z investment book I've read in years—the very book you're holding in your hands.

I'm very glad Marc took the time to put his unique ideas into print. As you'll see, he has taken much of the confusion out of real estate investing by reducing the entire process of buying and selling to basic building blocks. If making millions in real estate has seemed like an impossible magic trick until now, you'll see that, like a stage magician, once you've learned a few simple techniques there's no mystery in it for you; it only *looks* like magic. I like the fact that Marc teaches only what he's learned through experience, actually buying and selling real estate—without any formal training—in the turbulent market of the '80s.

9

I also thoroughly enjoy and believe in Marc's three plans for success. You can choose your own pathway: investing only a little at a time, to provide cash flow for today; part-time investing, to build up equity and provide for future security; or full-time, to create the wealth you've only dreamed of until now.

Marc is a good friend, a shrewd investor, an excellent educator, and a *very* good writer. He's right when he says, "Real estate investing is the safest, surest road to financial freedom." Let him show you how to get started down that road—and become financially free!

Prologue

The following story is hard-core American reality. It is a true story not just of this couple, but of hundreds of thousands of other American couples whose dreams never seem to turn out. The names have been changed at the request of those involved.

Jim Cooper was the all-American boy in high school, and Heather Holiday was his all-American cheerleader sweetheart. When they married a year after graduation in the little white chapel on the edge of town, the entire world lay at their feet; their goals were hazy and their dreams somewhat vague, but there was no doubting that they would succeed. One thing was sure: they wouldn't end up like their own parents, working all week to make ends meet and fighting all night when they didn't.

During the first few months of bliss, plans were laid and promises made, and Jim went right to work, forty hours a week, thrilled to be a thread in the fabric of America. He picked up a couple of night classes at the local college, and dreamed of law school and a high-paying career. Heather had to work also, but that was okay; a lot of wives have to work, and My! they thought, look at all the money we're making.

The dreams are fresh, and the sweet smell of potential success fills their home. Anything is possible, and the future holds incredible promise. There's no doubt that the Coopers will be living proof that the American Dream is alive and well.

The honeymoon wasn't really over until the expenses finally caught up and then passed the income. Work suddenly wasn't so much fun, Jim decided, when you had no choice.

Before they were ready, the Coopers found themselves expecting the first of a new generation. Mixed in with the happiness was a little regret, a touch of worry, and the low-grade fever of envy, as they watched old friends climb the ladder of success. Somehow the plans seemed to be getting derailed, and it was maddeningly difficult to see just what was going wrong.

Of course Heather had to quit working for a while (modern science hasn't figured a way around *that* yet), but Jim got a raise, and they had some money saved. Well, a little anyway (where did it all go?). Jim's father-in-law offered him a few extra hours helping in the factory downtown. Jim found himself awake one midnight morning, contemplating the future. The factory job paid well; Heather would never have to work again. Besides, school seemed to be taking forever, and he couldn't even remember why he wanted to be a lawyer. A foreman can make pretty good money these days . . .

So they lowered their hopes a notch or two and tried to ignore a growing discontent.

Babies aren't free, and with Heather out of work Jim took on a little overtime each week, to make ends meet. He didn't regret a penny of it; the extra hours at work were well worth the effort every time he picked up his little girl and held her close. But late one night, holding his gurgling bundle of innocence above her crib, he felt a stab of genuine fear: the trainload of dreams was seriously jumping the track, and it was getting more and more unlikely that he could get it back.

The Coopers found themselves spending a little more each month than they made. Not much, of course. They could still make the minimum payments on the Sears bill, and Visa didn't ask for much either. It would be quite a while before all the cards are charged up to the limit, and by then Jim would be making even more money.

They put off the plans for the cute little house with the homemade curtains, the white picket fence, and the rose garden. Going out to dinner meant hamburger and fries in a booth by the window, watching the cars go by. Surprisingly, accepting fate wasn't that hard. They consoled themselves with the thought that money can't buy happiness, and they blended themselves into the background of middle-class America.

One very late night, Jim sat at the kitchen table, trying to concentrate on the task of paying the bills. Giving up, he pushed the stack of bills aside and rested his head on his arm, listening to the stillness of the summer night. A year on the job and a quick promotion to foreman, and they were *still* barely getting by. He was working like a dog, but Heather had stopped noticing months before. He couldn't figure out what was wrong with her; she spent all day doing nothing but watching soap operas and changing diapers and *eating*, but you'd think she was picked on or something, the way she complained. He was sure he still loved her, but he had wanted so much more. He dropped the pen, clicked off the light, and stumbled to bed.

The old dreams are fading fast, becoming ethereal fantasies. Dreams of law school, a home, luxury, and leisure are put away in the same attic as the childhood dreams of growing up and being a fireman or a cowboy or a princess.

The dreams have begun to die.

A few years pass; the couple voted most likely to succeed now live the very lives they swore to avoid at all costs.

The frustration they both feel flares up at times, especially when the credit cards are all charged to the limit, the savings account is empty, and the checking account is overdrawn again. Heather reminds Jim of the promises and dreams he shared with her when they were first married. She can't understand why her life has little in common with the one she envisioned at the altar.

Jim begins to resent his family for being the reason he never made it to law school. That lazy wife of his, who can't control her appetite or her children, is more of a nuisance every day. She's the one who spends all the money, isn't she? And the kids ... It breaks his heart to watch them grow up from such a distance. He *tried* to stay close, but somehow things got away from him. His little girl is ready to start school and he's hardly had time to get to know her. He has a son now—he wants so desperately to take him fishing in a few years—but the little guy is almost two, and Jim never seems to have enough time to play with him. This whole family of strangers is little more now than a financial ball and chain, keeping him from the success he deserves.

The dreams are dead.

PART I

The Foundation

Dreams Die First

*I finally know what distinguishes man
from other beasts: financial worries.*
    —JULES RENARD

There is one attribute that we all share, one gift, one spark of divinity that separates us from all other creations. We can *dream*. Some of us dream of having a career that allows us to expand our technical and intellectual abilities. Or we may dream of having an impact on this world by making new discoveries in science or medicine, or simply by teaching young children to read. We may want to create works of art or literature, be the best parents possible, serve our churches, or just enjoy outdoor sports. We may just want to have the cute little home with the homemade curtains, or we may dream of untold wealth, Rolls-Royces and Lear jets.

Whatever our dreams are, they give zest and savor to our lives. This ability to dream will be the catalyst for achievement, growth, and happiness in our lives—as long as we keep those dreams alive.

Dreams don't die until reality sinks its cold, black claws into them and starts to tear them away from us. Few of us fight very hard or for very long to hold onto those dreams, preferring to follow the example of everyone around us and acquiesce to a cruel fate. We don't feel cheated; after all, that's life, right?

Wrong.

Jim and Heather's story is not too far from reality, is it? Millions of Americans are living—or are destined to live—the same subtle nightmare of debt, despair, and dying dreams. If you recognize yourself in the story, I don't have to convince you that you need more from life—that you need to invest.

But there are also thousands—maybe hundreds of thousands— of Americans for whom this tragic tale simply doesn't hold true. They (you?) are perfectly happy with their work. They enjoy every minute of it, they feel like they are accomplishing something worthwhile, and they are making more than enough money to get by. If you are a member of this elite club, do you really need to invest? Why should you consider investing in real estate?

First, because it is unlikely—in spite of your dream job and personal satisfaction—that you are as financially secure as you would like to be. Sure, if you were rich you wouldn't do anything differently than you do now, but you would have the satisfaction of knowing that you were independent from the need to earn a living. If you think work is fun now, imagine how much more you would love it if there was absolutely no financial pressure.

Second, because there is a dark cloud looming ahead that you might not have noticed: retirement. We'll talk about your future in more detail by and by, and I'll give you some statistics on retirement, inflation, and your future that should scare you into immediate action. Whether you love or hate your current vocation, whether you are flat broke or filthy rich, your future is, at best, uncertain. Real estate investing can take away that uncertainty.

Even if you are exactly where you always wanted to be, doing what you always wanted to do, don't try to tell me you don't have any unfulfilled dreams. It's our nature, isn't it? Well, I've found through personal experience that real estate investing will allow you to fulfill your dreams.

Let me tell you a little about myself. Several years ago I was working as an electrical foreman on a major industrial construction project. Because of the demands placed on me by my wonderful, high-paying job, I would be away from my wife and two children for weeks on end. The job demanded eleven to twelve hours a day, seven days a week.

Of course, not all jobs require your presence every day. But I'm sure you've experienced the same feelings that were driving me crazy and slowly destroying my dreams. My personal life was inconsequential to the company, and when I confronted them about some time off they always laughed and said, "Sure . . . just don't bother coming back." After work at nights I would call my family and listen to their voices. I would feel tears of pain as I heard the small, distant voices of my son, my daughter, and my wife. It seemed as though they were a million miles away and I was in prison.

After hanging up I would hate myself. I didn't know who to blame. I had worked so hard to get a technical degree and an electrical license. I was making excellent money, but not really enough for the sacrifice of listening to my kids crying for their daddy. While sitting in the "man camp" (the live-in camp inhabited by a thousand roughneck men and a few even rougher women), alone, night after night, I began to review my life.

I had been raised in an excellent family. What we lacked financially my parents more than made up with love. That may sound trite to the cynical "me generation," but we had the kind of family closeness and pride that at one time set this country apart from most of the world and that no fortune or lack of fortune could destroy.

I grew up in the Los Angeles area of Southern California, in a neighborhood not noted as a tourist attraction. I began working as an electrician for a member of my church the summer I was fourteen.

One of the dreams that I always had was to go to college. The realities of life made it obvious that if I wanted to go, the only one who could raise the tuition would be me, literally by the sweat of my brow.

In high school, I worked hard to get good grades. After graduation I continued working and immediately began going to college part-time. After serving two years as a missionary for my church in Sweden, I found myself back in the work-full-time, go-to-school-part-time routine, catching only one or two classes per semester. Some rudimentary arithmetic told me that at this rate I would graduate by the time I was forty-five years old.

Thinking back on that period in my life, I am grateful to the bosses who allowed me to work and study. I have to admit that without their patience and support I might have quit school then and there. But I think I worked extra hard for them, so they tolerated my studying during breaks and lunch and rushing off to class instead of staying after work to talk.

It was about this time that I reached a magical point, a turning point that must be reached by all people who want to be in control of their lives. That is the point where they pick up the reins and decide that they are the masters of their own destiny.

It happened when I was twenty-two years old. I had been married only three months, still working and going to school, when I was involved in a car accident. It was nothing especially traumatic; it was one of those run-of-the-mill accidents that don't even make it into the papers. But it caused me to consider my own mortality and think about my life. I looked back at what I had accomplished and where I was headed, and I didn't like what I saw. I had a dream of finishing college, of owning my own home, of having enough income so that my wife wasn't forced to work a job she didn't like, of getting a pilot's license, and of having the freedom to do what I really wanted. I wasn't asking for a lot, but no matter how I looked at it, the common denominator in each of these goals was money.

I had tried working overtime as a method of increasing cash flow, but all that ever seemed to do for me was to help me pay more taxes and to cause family problems. Life wasn't fun when it meant getting up before the sun, dropping my wife off at work, driving to my job, working the day, picking up my wife on the way home, getting a quick bite to eat and a quick kiss, and then driving to a second job and working until the sun was somewhere over China. Life seemed like a marathon dance with no prize for the winners. Every Friday as we sat together doing our finances, we saw that once again we had spent every cent we had earned.

During this time I began an intensive study of the investment world. I reviewed every type of investment that was open to us. I had met several real estate investors while working as an electrician and decided to include real estate in my study. After several months I began to notice that real estate was that perfect investment for someone, like myself, who didn't have a lot of cash or credit.

I decided to get involved by going out and looking at properties. This was the learning period, the period people fear most, when I made at least ten mistakes a day just to keep in shape. But it paid off. Before I knew it I was making money from my real estate investments. With the extra income I was soon earning from my real estate investing I was able to finish a technical degree and get a state electrical license and the dream job (or so I thought).

Now, as I sat alone in the man camp, I realized that my "dream job" was the job that was tearing me apart. For years I had worked to get to the point I was—electrical foreman (lots of power and prestige there, let me tell you) on one of the highest-paying heavy industrial construction projects in the nation.

How did it make me feel? I felt mad at myself. I felt that all my work had been in vain. I saw that the dream I had worked so hard to achieve was nothing but a lie. The position, the pay, and the prestige carried a price that I was unwilling to pay.

I was walking down a dark road, day and night, down a road that got further and further from any light. It was the same road most of my friends were walking, and maybe the same road you're on now.

I looked back once in a while and watched as my family became, in the words of Carl Sandburg, far and wee. And I was losing the opportunity to invest in real estate. Real estate had been just a tool to get some money to pay for college. Now that I didn't even have the time to invest, I could see how investing could change my life.

Alone at nights, on the job, I began to plan.

I'll never forget the day I quit my job (yes, take this job and shove it!) and started a four-week vacation with my family, driving almost five thousand miles throughout the western United States. The trip wasn't just for fun, however; it was to plan out my strategy. I was committing myself to a life where I would be able to say no to a job that I did not like or that violated my principles.

I began my plan by enrolling in school to finish another degree and then an M.B.A. (master of business administration). During this period of rebirth, I would use my extra time to invest in real estate.

It didn't take long for me to see that I could make far more money as an investor than as an electrician, or even as a college graduate, and at the same time I could be my own boss. The last year of my M.B.A. program, the career guidance counselor called me in to ask what the problem was; all the other M.B.A. candidates were scrambling for jobs. I politely explained that I already had enough work to keep me busy and that the degree was simply to fulfill my desire for knowledge. I'm afraid for a second the counselor was ready to call security; she had a crazy man in her office.

Today I can afford to continue my education without my wife's having to take a job. I can get as many doctorates as I want or pursue any other endeavors I desire. I've found that school is a million times more fun when the pressure to succeed comes from within and has nothing to do with proving myself to IBM. Is that freedom? It sure is. It's the same kind of freedom that I want you to enjoy.

The income has allowed me much more than just school and survival. During last summer I was able to travel with my wife for an unforgettable trip throughout Europe. This summer we visited New Orleans, Washington, D.C., Boston, Plymouth Rock, and the entire Pacific coast from Southern California to Canada. Next summer, it's back to Sweden. More important than being able to enjoy my family on some great vacation, I don't find myself lying awake nights worrying about where I am going to get the money to fix the car. Instead I have problems like what to do with the $3,500 check I will receive next week from the sale of a property. I have begun to realize that through real estate investing *anyone* can achieve his or her financial goals.

I get excited when I discuss the possibilities that real estate investing offers. I don't want to sound like a housewife captured on a hidden camera in a Tide commercial, but investing really *has* changed my life. It has allowed me to fulfill dreams that I once thought were dead forever.

Let's talk for a minute about *your* dreams. What is it you really want? Would you really love to be independently wealthy, able to do whatever you want, whenever you want to do it? Do you want to join the ranks of the leisure class? Or would you rather have a little extra income and a secure retirement plan? Perhaps you really want nothing more than to have all the toys that money can buy. The first time I drove a Mercedes Benz to school it was a heady feeling. And I enjoy the comforts of a nice house nestled away at the foot of a mountain. But millionaires eventually grow tired of toys, and you will need something more someday. Having a billion dollars and being able to satisfy every whim may sound exciting now, but I have to warn you about something. If you eat prime rib for dinner every night, it soon tastes like cardboard.

U.S. News and World Report did a study about those people whom a lot of us envy, the one-in-a-million person who is the epitome of success: the self-made millionaire. An interesting part of their study concerned how each of these individuals had become millionaires. No matter what your goals are, the self-made millionaires have an excellent lesson for each of us who has a desire to be something more than "one of the crowd."

In interviews, these millionaires again and again stressed the same factors that had led to their success: drive, determination, and discipline; tenacity, readiness for opportunity, and *educated persistence*. I love the last expression—educated persistence—because it sums everything else up, wrapping it up and tying it with a bow the color of sweat. It is an expression I try to live by every day. The combination of constantly educating yourself and *never* giving up practically assures success.

If I can develop in you that one quality, any level of financial success you desire will be assured, because everything else will fall into place if you refuse to give up and never stop learning.

So let's work on education and then on persistence, you and I. Let's examine what you need to know to become financially independent, and then put it to work—every day for the rest of your life.

If you stick with me to the end of the book, I'll give you a healthy dose of education. And since I can't stand over your shoulder and coach you, I'll put you in touch with experts in your hometown who can help you *for free!*

Teaching you persistence is a bit tougher; I hope I can instill the right balance of desire for success and fear of poverty to get you going, but keeping you going will be the real challenge. Persistence is a rare quality; it's often the difference between success and failure. When Sir Winston Churchill, very near the end of his illustrious life, was invited to address the prep school he had attended as a boy, his entire speech—the sum total of all his experience—was this: "Never, ever, ever, ever give up!" We'll talk more about persistence as we go along—a lot.

Education, persistence, and . . . courage. Many eager would-be investors can't wait to get out and start making their fortunes—until they run headfirst into their own fears. If you are letting fear keep you from success, now is the time to develop the necessary risk-taking courage.

I would love to have a nice plaque in my office with these words engraved on it: "Fear is the mind-killer." Fear paralyzes the mind and freezes the blood.

The first time you call a homeowner about the ad he placed in the paper to sell his home, your hand is likely to tremble and your voice to quaver. That's okay; every single one of us has to go through the same experience when we start out. The first time you hand a written offer to a seller, the pages may be shaking like a fistful of drying autumn leaves. So what? There is no other way to succeed as an investor.

I know several very successful investors. Many of them, eschewing the life of the idle rich, have dedicated their lives to teaching others—through books, workshops, and seminars. They all have favorite stories about how they got started and how they overcame their fears.

Take a friend of mine, Bob Allen, author of the best-selling books, *Nothing Down* and *Creating Wealth*. After graduating from an M.B.A. program near the bottom of his class, he hit the job market, ready for the exciting world of big business. It wasn't until the world of big business slapped him in the face that Bob encountered failure, frustration, and fear.

Today Bob is especially proud of one of his books. It is a leather-bound book, appropriately entitled *The Many Failures of Robert G. Allen*. It contains rejection letters from nearly every major (and more than one minor) company in the United States. It is a unique collection, a slice of Americana, with samples from almost every state. Nobody, but nobody, wanted Bob. He had graduated from an excellent, highly regarded graduate program, and the business world was telling him that he was a failure—before giving him a chance to prove he could be a success. Yet he hung in there and finally found a publisher.

So why is Bob Allen a multimillionaire today? *Educated persistence,* and overcoming his fears. Bob's motivation for investing in real estate was simple—hunger. It was Hobson's choice: Do or die. Make or break. Sink or swim. Pick your own expression; he simply knew that he *had* to make it on his own, and he did.

Bob had dreams. You have dreams. Bob educated himself. Have you? Bob persisted, in the face of fear and fatigue. What have you done so far? Bob set goals; he wrote them down on paper and concentrated his efforts on accomplishing them. With his dreams as a catalyst, Bob set goals that would turn those dreams into reality. Why should you do any differently?

* * *

There really isn't a special class of people destined for success. Nobody has ever had their dreams turned into reality by fate alone. But there is only a handful of people who are willing to persist, to educate themselves, and to overcome their fears and conquer their failures. And you can do every one of those things if your desire for success is strong enough, and if you have the right kind of education.

I'm amazed, as I travel across the country talking to investors, that so many Americans feel sorry for themselves because they weren't born rich. They seem to be totally unaware that they live in one of the few countries in the world where desire and hard, smart work can mean success. I am glad that I live in America. I am glad that it is the world's largest school of hard knocks. If it weren't so, I would still be working from paycheck to paycheck.

Do you know who I feel the most sorry for? I feel sorry for the rich kids, born with silver spoons in their mouths. They have never known the hunger for achievement; most of them don't have enough motivation to blow out a match.

You envy their lifestyle? They have never had a dream, and their upbringing has been remarkably similar to the fat, fleshy pigs down on Uncle Zack's farm. At least Uncle Zack's pigs serve some purpose.

It really doesn't matter where you are now, or whether you are happy or miserable in your work, or how fat your bank account is today. You still need to plan for the future; you need to find peace and financial security in a turbulent economy; and you have unfulfilled dreams that want so much to be reawakened and satisfied.

Be grateful for your hunger, for your unfulfilled dreams. Without them you would sit listlessly, watching the world go by. Don't let them die just yet.

If you have dreams that are either dying or dead, poisoned by reality, bring them back to life. Now is the time to be the master of your own destiny. If you aren't yet convinced that you need to invest, the next chapter should do the trick. Whatever your dreams, turn the page, follow me, and let me teach you how to be financially free.

CHAPTER 2

Golden Handcuffs and Social Insecurity

We forge the chains that bind us.
—CHARLES DICKENS

You may have heard the expression "golden handcuffs." You may be wearing golden handcuffs now, without even being aware that they are restricting your every movement. We are creatures with an incredible ability to adapt yourselves to our environment. We take jobs that tie us down for most of our lives and never seem to notice that they are keeping us from everything we ever wanted to do. We hope for a bright future without making any actual plans for extricating ourselves from a dismal present.

There are undoubtedly worse feelings in the world than the one that comes with realizing you are trapped for life in a job that doesn't pay you enough or that you hate, but I am hard-pressed to imagine what they are. I suppose being sentenced to solitary confinement for life would run a close second, but at least then you would most likely have done something to deserve the sentence.

But you've done everything they said would bring you success, and yet here you are, for what seems like an eternity, chained to a desk or to a machine, barely making enough to get by.

Golden handcuffs with velvet linings. A job that pays enough to take care of all the bills, with just enough left over for one or two weeks' vacation every year. A good job, that offers excellent insurance benefits for the family. A company plan that assures a small pension upon retirement. What more could you want?

But they're still called golden handcuffs, because before you know it you can't quit even if you wanted to. What would you do? Who'd pay the MasterCard bill, and what would your in-laws

26

say? What would your spouse say? The golden handcuffs are now latched so tightly that you've lost most of the feeling of American initiative and independence you dimly remember having. Most of the time you don't even notice you're wearing them.

For some, these handcuffs are a blessing. They absolutely love working for someone else and being part of a large corporate organization. They thrill at the team spirit and the enormous potential for major group accomplishment. I am not anti-job, but let me prove a point.

The disadvantage of working forty years for someone else comes when you take home your pay. After a week of working— even at work you thoroughly enjoy—it's back into the eight-year-old station wagon with the McDonald's Quarter Pounder boxes scattered in the back and the Big Gulp spill on the front seat. As you pull away from the office, content with your work, you pass the executive parking lot and admire the sleek lines of the CEO's Mercedes Benz.

Why is the feeling of oppression so common? For most people, it's not the job itself but the *lack of choice* that causes job depression. It's the feeling that you're trapped, stuck in your job forever and always two weeks from bankruptcy. If you didn't *have* to work you'd probably love your job. But knowing that when the alarm clock rings you have little choice but to get up and face another workday is bound to be depressing.

It's possible to keep your job *and* invest part-time. It is within your reach to earn $20,000 or more a year through part-time real estate investing. Or, what the heck, just put a few thousand extra dollars in your pocket now and then. For the minority of workers who love every day on the job, why not have the best of both worlds?

For the 99.9 percent of the workers who don't make it into upper management, the golden handcuffs that come with working for someone else are laced with a slow-acting poison. One that works its way into their skin and finds its way into their dreams, killing them gently and oh so slowly.

My personal experience might be similar to yours. When I worked as an electrician on a job site, I met a lot of interesting people. Many of them had spent thirty years or more working one electrical job after another. They were wed to their work, and it was a rocky marriage at best. But it was life; what else did they have? They had no hopes and no dreams. All they had was an old, beat-up pair of golden handcuffs, and a promise that was burned into their minds each day: that if they quit performing (got old, got weak, got sick) they would be laid off or fired. (Sound familiar?) That was it, no roses and no watch; they were canned and their positions filled by younger, quicker workers eager for their jobs.

And no matter how much you love your work, your time is just not your own; most jobs require that you be in a certain place at a certain time every day, Monday through Friday.

I compare that with the one-time-only experience I enjoyed recently: my son's first day of school. I was the only father out of 153 parents who showed up for that special day. As I sat on a chair made for a six-year-old backside and looked out through my knees at the teacher, I noticed some of the women were pointing at me. As I left, I heard one of the mothers whisper to another, "he must be unemployed."

The experience of having the time to do something like I did that day may not seem like much, but think about it. You are either there or you miss out forever. There is no second first day of school, just as there is no second first kiss or second first anything. If I had still been working at my high-paying job, I would have missed the experience. I might not have minded much. It would have been just one more pinprick in my dreams, draining them slowly of life.

How many people are able to go with their children on the first day of school? Just to be with them and see that little boy or girl start a new phase of life? Too many working parents are too securely attached to their desks and typewriters, to their cash registers and welding torches—fettered by golden handcuffs.

There are almost as many pairs of these shiny handcuffs as there are employed people in America. You are probably wearing a pair right now. Jim and Heather Cooper slipped into a bright and shiny pair one day and never got free. Most people stop looking for a key, learning to enjoy the "security" the bracelets offer. Just like the lifers in prison who, when released on parole at sixty-five, immediately do something—anything—to get back inside where it is safe.

Some of the shackles are 24-karat gold. I know a man who is a well paid and highly respected lawyer. Specializing in civil litigation, he has made a name for himself in the legal arena. What does he want to do? He wants to make tables and dressers and children's toy boxes. He loves wood. I have seen beautiful, intricate works of superb craftsmanship that his skilled hands have produced. The man wants nothing more than to be a carpenter. I asked this man one day why he didn't pursue his love. His answer? He couldn't afford it. There were too many bills to pay, the kids needed braces, and his wife needed the new fur coat that he had promised her. He is wearing a 24-karat pair of handcuffs, and he has thrown away the key. The way he could afford to do what he wants to do is through real estate investing. He could easily work as a carpenter and rely on investing for the needed income.

I have helped a man who loves to design computer games get started in real estate investing. He quit his job working in a warehouse and formed his own company, which designs computer games. So far he hasn't made a dime off the games. How does he live? He invests in real estate. His program of real estate investment literally supports his dream. He is wealthier than most millionaires; he can do what he really enjoys doing.

That is the point of this book. *To make money in real estate you don't have to quit your job and invest full-time.* Your job can continue to provide the basic necessities—the bills, the braces, the car payments—and at night and on weekends you can, with very little time and effort, realize fantastic financial benefits working just a few hours a week in real estate investing. If you've read other investment books, you realize that many methods demand seven days a week, twelve hours a day. I believe that most people just want some extra money and time so they can enjoy living. Using the plan in this book, you will be able to achieve your financial dreams. And it's basic multiplication: if you increase tenfold the time you put into investing, your results will be ten times greater. But that's your choice.

Real estate investing isn't the only way to break free, but I sincerely believe it is the best way. It is safe, requires little starting capital, and is not shrouded by the impenetrable cloak of mystery that surrounds most forms of investment. Real estate is a basic, necessary commodity. As an investment it has worked better, for more people, than any other means of achieving financial freedom. In the next chapter we will compare real estate to other means of unlocking the golden handcuffs that bind you to your present life. When you see the possibilities there, you will be ready to learn the basic keys to wealth.

If you like working for someone else, that's great. But there are alternatives to an eight-hour-a-day, five-days-a-week, till-you-can't-work-anymore existence. *You can have the best of both worlds.*

Create your own wealth. Then, when you are lying on the beach on some tropical isle or relaxing by the fire in your cabin after a hard day on the slopes, you will know that you are not spoiled; you have earned your rewards.

"Marc," I can hear you saying, "you're way off base. I'm not wearing handcuffs at all." (That is you talking, isn't it?) "Not only do I love my work, but I also set my own hours and I make a good living. I live like a king or queen (or at least a prince or princess) and I put $2,000 into my IRA every year. I really don't need to invest in real estate at all."

Let me tell you something. You are on a cruise ship right now, on your way to a foreign land. You probably think that it will be paradise, and it may well be—if you plan well enough for the trip. Your destination: the Republic of Retirees. Your cruise ship: the USS *Inflation*.

Unfortunately, millions of people started out on the same cruise with the same plans. They thought that they had plenty of provisions for the trip, and the cruise itself was so much fun that they almost forgot where they were going. And they certainly didn't take into consideration the fact that the fare for the USS *Inflation* is very, very high. When they were dropped quite suddenly on the shores of their new country, it was a shock to find out that paradise wasn't such a hot deal when the only diet they could afford was bread and water.

If you are still working, you have time—ten, twenty, thirty years or more—before your ship will pull into port. What are your plans for that day?

Most Americans have three sources of income when their working years come to an end: their savings, a pension plan, and Social Security. We all have a tendency to assume that the combination of those three will be enough to take care of us for the rest of our lives. But every shred of evidence points in the opposite direction.

It's shocking how few people even think about retirement in more than a wistful fashion before it hits them. It's too easy to imagine that when that someday comes we'll all grab our fishing rods and knitting needles and enjoy a well-earned rest. The tragedies we see around us—hundreds of thousands of elderly people living in run-down, lonely apartments, kept company only by Bob Barker and Johnny Carson; horror stories of retirees freezing to death in winter because the gas company shut off their heat, or eating canned dog food because they can't afford the price of a TV dinner—affect us in about the same fashion as a roadside accident. It's always someone else; *we* certainly won't end up in the same fix.

Recent statistics show that out of 100 Americans age sixty-five and over, eighty-three have annual incomes of less than $2,500. Eleven of those 100 have incomes between $2,500 and $5,000, and only 6 have incomes in excess of $5,000. The most shocking fact for me is that only 15 out of 100 have more than $250 cash.

It is terribly (and I do mean *terribly*) surprising that so many retirees are in such sad financial shape, when they should be protected by their . . .

SAVINGS

How much will you be able to save between now and the day of your retirement party? Can you *really* put $2,000 into your Individual Retirement Account every year? How about $1,000, or even $500? Here's an easy mental exercise to keep you awake: Decide at what age you want to retire. Subtract your current age (no cheating; if you're over thirty-nine, admit it). Now you know how much time you have left. Use your years-to-retirement figure to find out how much that savings account will add up to when you are ready to use it.

In this table I am assuming that you are going to be earning 11 percent interest on your IRA. If you think 11 percent is too optimistic and perhaps 7 or 8 percent is much closer to the mark, get in touch with your local banker. He or she will be happy to show

COMPOUNDED VALUES OF IRA SAVINGS ACCOUNTS
AT 11 PERCENT

| Years to | annual deposit amounts | | | |
Retirement	$500	$1,000	$1,500	$2,000
·5	3,113.90	6,227.80	9,341.70	12,445.60
10	8,361.00	16,722.01	25,083.01	33,444.02
15	17,202.68	34,405.36	51,608.04	68,810.72
20	32,101.42	64,202.83	96,304.25	128,405.66
25	57,206.65	114,413.31	171,619.96	228,826.61
30	99,510.44	199,020.88	298,531.32	398,041.76
40	290,913.03	581,826.07	872,739.10	1,163,652.13

Example: If you began a $1,000-a-year savings plan at age 40 with annual deposits until retiring at age 65, you'd have 25 years to make your deposits. To calculate the value of your IRA at retirement, find the $1,000 annual deposit column and go down till you come across the figure that corresponds to 25 years. This amount ($114,413.31) represents the value of your $1,000-a-year IRA with 25 annual deposits at 11 percent interest.

you what your account would be worth by the time you retire at whatever percentage you think is reasonable.

At first glance you think, that's not bad at all; what's the problem? I've got a pension coming too.

PENSIONS

Many employers offer some kind of pension plan. These plans vary greatly, and you should know what your company offers. As a general rule, your pension will be 25 to 35 percent of your ending gross salary. If, for example, you are earning $35,000 a year when you retire and your company pays 30 percent, your pension will be $10,500 a year for the rest of your life. (Be aware that most likely your spouse will get nothing from your pension after you die if you happen to depart for the great beyond before he or she does.) Add that to your savings and at first glance the picture still seems rosy.

We know we can depend on our savings, pensions, and . . .

SOCIAL SECURITY

Good old Uncle Sam—bless his generous heart. Was there ever a more *giving* uncle born? He promises that if we will help out the elderly while we are young he will make sure that our children and grandchildren do the same for us. Ain't that a heartwarming promise?

The sad truth is that when the Social Security system was instituted there were about a dozen workers for every retired person. The extra burden on each tax payer was light and the benefits were terrific. Today, as you are well aware, Social Security takes a big bite out of every paycheck. The problem is the shift in the population. We live longer, we retire earlier, and there are more and more retirees every year in relation to the number of workers.

You see, we had this thing called the baby boom. From the end of World War II until about 1962 there were a whole bunch of babies born. So many, in fact, that it caused quite a bulge in the overall population curve. We baby boomers are moving through time like a watermelon through a boa constrictor, and we are not putting forth much of an effort to provide a generation of workers to support us when the time comes.

According to current government statistics, there are presently five workers for every Social Security recipient. The same research shows that within fifteen years the ratio of workers paying into the system to those receiving Social Security benefits will drop to two to one. Since Social Security is a pay-as-you-go program, that means simply that two employed members of the American work force will be responsible for paying the full bill for one recipient.

Projections show that, to maintain current benefits, as much as a 50 percent Social Security tax will be required on the gross monthly salary of each member of the work force. Other options include raising the eligibility age of Social Security recipients to seventy-two, or dropping the program altogether.

In light of such figures I don't put much faith in the Social Security system. I honestly believe that when the burden finally gets heavy enough on the workers they will revolt—politically—and we will see the end of the program. That's especially frightening in light of the fact that for the great majority of Americans the most important form of household wealth is the anticipated Social Security retirement benefits. In 1971 alone, the aggregate value of these annuities was approximately $2 trillion or some 60 percent of other household assets. You don't need to be a Rhodes scholar to figure out that there are a few major cracks in the dike.

I prefer to call this program *Social Insecurity*. In fact, the back of my business card looks like this:

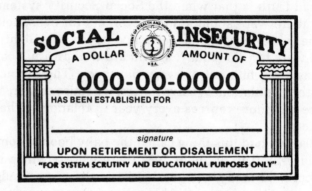

If you would like a copy of my Social Insecurity card, send $1.00 (for postage and handling) to M. S. Garrison and Company, P.O. Box 1096, Orem, Utah 84057. My office staff will send a copy out for you right away. I like to carry a copy of this full-color Social Insecurity card in my wallet as a constant reminder of why we should be investing.

It's unfortunate that so many have put so much faith in such a weak system. In an article by Martin Feldstein which appeared in the *Journal of Political Economy,* it was reported that the anticipation of receiving Social Security benefits reduces personal savings by as much as 50 percent. People simply say to themselves, "Why save? The government will take care of me." And they go about spending every cent they have.

My advice is to assume, for safety's sake, that we are looking at the imminent demise of the Social Security system. I may be wrong, but *please* don't bank on it. It would be far wiser to plan on not having it and then be pleasantly surprised with some extra money for shuffleboard chalk or bingo if they happen to find a way to make the money presses turn that much faster.

* * *

Gee whiz, with savings, plus pension, plus (cross your fingers) Social Security, you will have it made, won't you? Well then, why are so many of our own parents having such a tough time today?

Low Savings

We Americans are terrible when it comes to saving for a rainy day, aren't we? We believe firmly in the power of conspicuous consumption, and as a populace we sock away about 5 percent of our money in the bank. Compared with the Japanese (20 percent), we are incredible spendthrifts. The party on the cruise ship is so much fun that we simply forget to save for our final destination.

Inflation

This is the real monster. No matter how hard we are battered by inflation, we still fail to recognize just how devastating it can be in the long run.

Inflation has been likened to a pickpocket that quietly slips your wallet from your pocket, takes a dollar or two out, and then puts the wallet back without your ever noticing. But in the long run, inflation is anything but gentle. It kicks your legs out from under you, socks you in the jaw, knees you in the kidneys, and

A REALISTIC LOOK AT INFLATION: PAST, PRESENT, AND FUTURE

Item	1965	1985	1995	2005
single-family house	$19,950.00	$69,100.00	$160,607.00	$373,298.00
economy 4-door car	2,900.00	7,100.00	11,350.00	16,585.00
refrigerator	470.00	530.00	630.00	725.00
man's suit	140.00	268.00	399.00	610.00
car ins. premium	93.00	270.00	560.00	1,031.00
electric bill	12.00	48.00	87.00	170.00
dinner out (for two)	12.00	21.00	48.00	74.00
paperback book	1.05	3.50	5.70	10.12
movie ticket	.95	4.50	9.50	16.00
candy bar	.05	.35	.81	1.89
first-class stamp	.04	.22	.51	1.19

then takes your wallet, your watch, your wedding ring, and the fillings in your teeth . . . and then kicks your dog on the way out the door.

Yes, if you are frugal and put aside a thousand or more every year, you will have a half million dollars by the time you retire— but so what? Ten thousand dollars a month isn't much when a Big Mac and a Coke cost $45.79.

Remember the IRA that you are investing in, and how much we decided it would be worth by the time you retire? Well, plug that amount into this table for an eye-opener. This is what your bank account will be worth in terms of today's buying power:

PRESENT VALUES OF IRA/SAVINGS AND FUTURE VALUES IN REAL DOLLAR TERMS WITH 7 PERCENT INFLATION

	Projected dollar amounts of IRA/savings deposits			
Years	$100,000	$250,000	$500,000	$1,000,000
5	$71,298.62	$178,246.54	$356,493.09	$712,986.18
10	$50,834.93	$127,087.32	$254,174.65	$508,349.29
15	$36,244.60	$90,611.50	$181,223.01	$362,446.02
20	$25,841.90	$64,604.75	$129,209.50	$258,419.00
25	$18,424.92	$46,062.29	$92,124.59	$184,249.18
30	$13,136.71	$32,841.78	$65,683.56	$131,367.12
35	$9,366.29	$23,415.73	$46,831.47	$93,662.94
40	$6,678.04	$16,695.10	$33,390.19	$66,780.38

Example: The value of the thousand-dollar-a-year IRA deposit ($1,000 a year for 25 years at 11 percent interest) would be a little over $100,000 in nominal terms. To determine the actual present value of that sum, look under the $100,000 column and go down to the number opposite 25 years. The value of that $100,000 25 years from now would only be $18,424.92 in real dollar terms. In plain English, that means $100,000 dollars will buy you then only what $18,000 will buy you now!

I am using an average inflation rate of 7 percent in this table. The actual rate may be higher or lower; only the future knows. If I had to make a guess, I'd bet that it will be even higher, but I don't want to be labeled a pessimist.

* * *

Meet George. George is thirty-five. He's married, he's completely happy with his job as an engineer, and he has a couple of cars, a nice house, $600 in the family checking account, and 1.6 children. He now makes $29,000 a year. You can't get much more middle-class than George, and that suits him just fine.

George and his wife (Mrs. George, he sometimes calls her) are going to start putting away $2,000 a year into their IRA every year from now until they retire. George wants to retire when he's sixty-five. He wants to travel with Mrs. George. His company offers excellent benefits and will pay him 33 percent of his ending salary as a pension. Everything is right on schedule and George is happy.

Lucky George.

George has thirty more working years. When he retires, here is what he has to look forward to:

Savings account/IRA $398,041.76

George has figured out that if he and his wife live to be eighty-five (she's the same age; they were childhood sweethearts), they can withdraw $49,984.35 every year for the last twenty years before they will deplete their savings, which they hope will still be earning 11 percent interest. That gives them the following annual retirement income:

Savings account	$49,984.35
Pension plan (George's ending gross salary is $125,336—too bad he *still* is barely getting by.)	41,360.88
Social Security (The program collapsed in 1999.)	.00
Total	$91,345.23

That's not too bad at all, is it? In fact, they can really travel in style with that kind of money—if there is no inflation for the next twenty-seven years and none for the remaining twenty years after that.

But if we experience a mild, 7 percent average inflation rate,

that $91,345.23 shrinks to $11,999.76 by George's sixty-fifth birth-
day, and all the way down to $3,100.97 by the time he reaches
eighty-five! That's only $3,100.97 annual income in terms of
today's buying power! Can you live on $258.41 a month today? If
he is unfortunate enough to live longer than that, his entire savings will be exhausted—and so will he.

Poor George.

By the time I move into the Seizure World retirement home, I
want to own it. How about you? I do not want to depend on wel-
fare to support me. Savings, pensions, and Social Security just
aren't enough. You *must* invest. If you are thoroughly convinced—enough to *do* something about it—then read on. If not, I
have a homework assignment for you. Visit the nearest retirement home or the poorest section of one-bedroom apartments in
town. Ask the residents what they think about investing. If they
could relive their lives, knowing what they know now, would
they have done anything differently? When you have their answers, come back and read on.

CHAPTER 3

Where to Now, Saint Peter?

*We do not see the lens through
which we look.*
    —RUTH BENEDICT

Harry was basically a good man all his life. He worked hard
to earn his reward, and as he drew his last breath he fancied he
saw at the end of a long, dark tunnel a brilliant light—heaven. At
last, after laboring for almost a century, he had broken the bonds
of mortality.

When he arrived at the pearly gates, Saint Peter himself
greeted Harry and welcomed him graciously into a spacious
room, decorated in sculptured marble and pure gold. Even the
lighting was, well, heavenly. There were doors on every side
leading out, and each was unmarked; there was no indication
where any door would lead.

Harry turned and asked, "Where to now, Saint Peter?"

"I don't know," was the answer. "I've never gotten beyond the
gate myself."

It must be painfully evident at this point that you need to do
something now to provide for your financial future. The question
is, what? Which way do you go, once you have broken free;
which door do you open? How will you provide the income to retire and fulfill your dreams? The doors are open; it's up to you.
There are a million ways to invest, and it seems I have tried about
half of them.

Let me tell you about some of my experiences.

When I was ready to start my career as an investor, I was faced with a plethora of choices. Should I invest in stocks, or bonds, or gold and silver? Maybe I should invest in real estate, or in Cousin Eddie's yogurt and pickle shop.

What makes any investment the best? The proper combination of risk and return to fit your personality and goals. The concept of risk and return includes these factors:

- loss of principal
- loss of income
- inflation
- management
- timing risk
- liquidity risk
- cash flow
- tax shelter
- equity buildup
- control

Investing in a Chicago family-run business or maybe buying a stake in the future of "Golden Glitter Movies" will offer an incredible return on your investment, but the risks—such as loss of principal or management difficulties—might outweigh the benefits.

The stock and commodities markets are only slightly less risky. I think that instead of three-piece suits, Wall Street brokers ought to wear visors perched on their heads and garters on their sleeves. They could stand in the pit and cry, "Hurry, hurry, step right up, folks, place your bets. Hey, hey, fella, step right up and buy some pork bellies, buy a little XYZ for the missus, it's a sure bet. Hurry, hurry; everybody's a winner!"

True, millions have been made on Wall Street, but millions upon millions have been lost.

What about gold and silver? At least the supply can't be controlled, and rarity means value, right? True, but the value is strictly a matter of collective personal opinion, especially today, when neither gold nor silver is used as a form of currency in our economy. And in a paper economy, the value of precious metals is never a sure bet.

Last year I bought a considerable number of one-ounce silver bars as a hedge against inflation. These silver bars were of the highest quality. My purchase price was the best I could get, "spot" (which is the going price of the metal at a given time if traded in large lots), plus a small commission to the trader.

I was guaranteed in investment magazine articles that silver was ready to skyrocket. The traders said it was a sure thing. The only sure thing that I had was a certainty that no one knows what the price is going to be next week. In fact the price of precious metals is like the random movements of a three-year-old child: it just runs around with no predictability. Even the "experts" have no more luck than TV weathermen or government economists.

My "premium silver" is now worth about 60 percent of what I paid for it. Why? What did I do to lower its price, and what can I do to increase the price? Polish it, fix it up, advertise it to the right people? Or do I just have to sit and wait till some mythical market force or rumor of war drives the price up?

You're absolutely right, I have no control, I have to sit and wait. I am not in the driver's seat with this one. You don't have to take my word for it; history is evidence enough. The prices have never been predictable, and those who have tried to outguess the market have always lost sooner or later. Today's market will find itself in tomorrow's history book—a book nobody can write yet.

So you cannot control risk or return with stocks, bonds, precious metals, or other commodity markets. What does that leave you with? Oh sure, if you want to avoid risk entirely you can always invest in an IRA, mutual fund, or some high-paying savings account. They are practically risk-free. But they are also practically return-free as well, in that most seem only to keep pace with inflation.

Right before I quit my job I decided to jump onto the IRA bandwagon. After a lot of study I chose the "hottest," most secure mutual fund available. (A mutual fund is a stock portfolio in which an investor buys shares of the portfolio. This portfolio is managed, along certain guidelines, by a managing committee.)

My choice was one that had appreciated more than 35 percent each year for the previous five years. I couldn't go wrong. My stockbroker had this fund as his own personal IRA and it was his "sure winning pick." Today, several years later, I am proud to tell you that after fund expenses, fees, etc., my investment is now worth about 90 percent of my original investment. How could this be? It was a sure winner. Again, the only answer is, I didn't have control.

I've left out one investment that has turned paupers into princes: the sole proprietorship. Ray Kroc took a small hamburger stand in California and turned it into the largest fast-food chain in the world: McDonald's. Unfortunately, for every one phenomenal success there are a thousand heartbreaking failures. The failure rate for small businesses, according to the U.S. Department of Commerce, varies from 60 percent to 80 percent, *every year.*

ANALYZING AN INVESTMENT

Let me suggest the following format for you to use in analyzing any investments—before you sink one dime into them.

Take the ten risk/return factors mentioned at the beginning of the chapter and run the proposed investment through each of them. Let's look at each in more detail:

Loss of Principal

With any investment there is a possibility that you'll lose your investment. Buy gold at the wrong time and you might lose most of your investment overnight. (The price might drop from $700 dollars an ounce down to $320. Sound impossible? It wouldn't be the first time.) An insured savings account, on the other hand, will insure your investment against loss. Buying a chunk of real estate blindly, with no consideration as to its true market value or salability, is highly risky; real estate bought prudently, after a careful market analysis, will be sheltered from this problem.

Loss of Income

Many investments offer some income. Stocks generally pay dividends; passbooks pay interest; precious metals offer no income whatsoever until they are sold. The risk of losing this income varies with each investment. With the savings account the risk is minimal. Real estate usually depends on rental income and tax benefits, and an unexpected vacancy or unanticipated repair will cause a loss of projected income.

Inflation

How much is the investment affected by inflation? A single year of double-digit inflation will ravage a 5 percent passbook. In fact, any investment that doesn't increase in value by at least the same percentage as the inflation rate is losing true value. Here real estate outshines all other investments; since World War II, real estate has kept up with inflation. In fact, it has often outdistanced inflation. That's why, when inflation was raging in the '70s, real estate prices were also skyrocketing. Those who bought real estate at the time are still congratulating themselves on their keen foresight and vacationing in Hawaii.

Management

How difficult will your investment be to manage? Are there any hidden costs? Real estate is one of the few investments that require management, and for many potential investors this single drawback is enough to keep them from getting involved. Do not invest in real estate without carefully planning its management. Later in this book we'll take a much closer look at property management and discuss ways to lighten this burden.

Timing Risk

When you buy is often as important as what you buy. This is especially true of commodities, stocks, and precious metals. In real estate the days of "buy anything and hold on" are gone—for now, at least. Timing is crucial. The trusty savings account is nearly immune to timing risk; no matter when you open your account, you'll earn the same low interest rate.

Liquidity Risk

Liquidity is a measure of an investor's ability to easily sell or transfer title to an asset. Investing in dollar bills might have no other benefit, but it certainly passes this test. A certificate of deposit will offer a higher interest rate, but it is quite illiquid in comparison to a regular savings account. Real estate is quite illiquid; in most cases you'll have a long-range plan for your property, rather than expecting to sell it on a moment's notice. Gold is highly liquid, as are stocks.

Cash Flow

Does the investment offer an income stream? This is another aspect of the income factor examined above. Gold, as was pointed out, has no risk of income loss—because it offers no income! The savings account is essentially risk-free, but the cash flow leaves a lot to be desired. Real estate is a winner here. It offers rental income, which can be substantial in some cases, and it offers a tremendous source of income in the form of tax savings.

Tax Shelter

Continuing on the subject of tax savings, real estate is one of the greatest tax shelters available. Investment properties can be depreciated; that is, the owner can claim that the property is losing value every year and get a deduction based on that loss, in spite of the fact that it is actually *increasing* in value constantly! The only logic behind this is that it is a government program.

Additionally, the profit on the sale of real estate that has been held for more than six months is taxed at a much lower rate than ordinary income. Other investments can't make the same claim. The income from most of them, in fact, is taxed as ordinary income.

Equity Buildup

Also called appreciation, this is the consideration that mirrors the risk of losing principal. While there is little chance of losing the principal invested in the savings account, there is also no increase in its value other than the interest paid. Gold may double, triple, or increase in value even ten times. That is, it *may* increase in value. The chance of a remarkable increase is there, but determining its likelihood will require a crystal ball. Real estate's track record is excellent in this regard. A sharp investor can even find a good deal in which the sellers are willing to walk away from part or all of their equity. That means instant equity buildup. I can think of a recent property that I purchased that instantly added $75,000 to my net worth statement. Finding such diamonds in the rough will be fully covered later.

Control

How well can you control the risk and return of your investment? With most investments you have no control. You throw your money down on the table and watch it closely, hoping you picked a winner. Even with a safe investment, such as a savings account, you have no control. You play by the bank's rules and earn the interest rate they're willing to pay.

Real estate again stands out. You can control the risk and return by learning the market well enough to buy only good deals. If you can buy a house worth $85,000 for $75,000, you are surely controlling both. The risk and return are not dictated by ten thousand other people buying the same house.

As you can see, the idea of risk and return is really a double-edged sword. In most investments you sacrifice safety and security for the possibility of a high return. Or if you can't sleep nights worrying about the risks involved, you sacrifice any return above the inflation rate. I challenge you to run through this type of analysis with every investment you can think of: precious metals, penny stocks, futures, growth stocks. Then relate the results to your present financial situation. Investing in metals, stocks, or most other popular vehicles *can* be quite rewarding. In fact, for a balanced portfolio, I suggest having your eggs in several baskets—once you have a few dozen eggs to work with. But for most people, whose balance sheets list desire as their greatest asset, diversification simply won't generate wealth.

There is an investment, available to those of us who have many nonmaterial assets, that offers both high return *and* control of risk. You know what comes next: the *only* investment that can provide all of the things that we have talked about as being necessary, such as cash income, low risk, tax benefits, and growth for the future. *Real estate.*

If there is one thing that separates real estate from all other investments, it is the amount of control that you have over your money. You control the risk *and* the return. Almost every variable that will affect your investment is forseeable, with enough homework on your part.

You can control the price, and by studying market values or by having a piece of property appraised, you are able to determine exactly how good your deal is. Compare that with stock prices, which are determined solely by the aggregate opinion of a fickle public or the manipulation of some Wall Street imp.

Great, so I can control risk; what about return? I'm glad I asked. Just today I received a $3,500 annual second mortgage payment on a property that I purchased a while back with less money than most people spend on Christmas presents for their children. When I first saw that property it was really a mess. The family was apparently so poor that they couldn't afford a litter box for the cat, and since they also couldn't afford toys, the kids had used the windows for target practice. Instead of looking at it as a disaster, I thought about a couple of nights' work. After negotiating a purchase agreement, my wife and children went over there and *worked.*

At the same time, I was running an ad in the paper to sell it. Several days before closing the house ourselves, we had signed a sales agreement with another young family. As it turned out, we discounted the price to allow them to finish some of the painting.

After we closed the property, we walked away with an immediate net profit of over 300 percent on the money we put into it. If we add in the annual second mortgage payments that we are getting, our return on our money will be in excess of 1,400 percent within five years of our investment. But if we figure that we received our down payment back plus several thousand more within days of our closing, our return really has to be counted as infinity.

Let me put this another way. Would you put up $1,000 if you could get $5,000 cash back within two weeks and $3,000 a year for five years? Well, it beats selling soap or brushes door-to-door.

It is legal, it is a way to help other families get into homes, and it is a fantastic way to provide for your own income, security, and retirement. It's also fun to get a $3,000 shot in the arm once a year.

When you finish this book you will know how to do this—no kidding.

As we get into more specific numbers situations and talk about how to shop for wholesale bargains in real estate, you will see the returns that you can get *while maintaining complete control.*

Why is real estate such an incredible combination of low risk and high return? Because it is a stable, basic commodity. Its price is not subject to the daily whims of a few powerful men or thousands of *scared* investors. An old, battered house has more intrinsic value than a stack of gold. It has value, in and of itself, like a can of beans in grandma's pantry. Its value is determined partly by how it sparkles when it is polished, but mostly by its value in use and its necessity and scarcity (alias supply and demand). And scarcity is assured: they just aren't making any more land.

Because of its unique place in the economy, real estate has rules all its own. You just don't play the real estate game the same way you play the stock market.

Try this: Call a stockbroker and tell him you would like to invest. Be sure to insist that you must be allowed to buy your stock with little or no money down, and tell him you need to have your investment generating income every month. Tell him that you want enough income from your stock to make the payments on your investment, with enough left over so that you can pocket $100 every month. And before you buy, tell him that you don't want to pay the market price. You will buy only stock that is far below market value. Oh, yes, and tell him you want to be able to double your initial investment within the first month or two.

Now put the phone down and call the fire department. Have them send a couple of paramedics over to the stockbroker's office right away. Tell them there is a possible heart attack or stroke victim.

If I'm making real estate sound like the ultimate investment for everyone, then I must be doing something right. "But Marc," you think, "if buying and selling a little dirt is so great, why isn't everyone investing in real estate?" I have often wondered about that, and I have come up with three common reasons:

1. **Laziness.** It takes more than a phone call to a banker or stockbroker—it takes work. It takes hours of study and

hundreds of phone calls. It requires Saturday and Sunday drives, and countless disappointments, delays, and dead-ends. Successful real estate investing will cut into your TV time, and for many people giving up those "M*A*S*H" reruns is simply too high a price to pay.

2. **Ignorance.** Most people are unaware that they can buy real estate wholesale and sell it retail. They don't realize that enormous profits can be (and are) enjoyed with a little judicious buying and selling coupled with educated persistence.

3. **Fear.** Nothing can destroy a promising career as a real estate investor quite like fear. Fear is the mind-killer. I've seen seminar junkies who attend every convention, seminar, and workshop that comes to town, like kids at the circus. They know as much about buying houses as most of the speakers, and yet they wait, thinking that they will buy that first property after the *next* seminar. They are so afraid of failure, or of other people, that they never make one offer. They are afraid to make that jump.

If I can convince you to overcome your fears, to educate yourself, and to commit yourself to the work that success requires, there is no way you can fail.

Now you've heard the boring details of investing and reasons why you should invest. Now I'll let you in on the secret: the *fun* stuff!

By shopping in the wholesale housing market (which you will learn to do), I recently purchased another home, putting only $1,400 down and assuming an 11.5 percent FHA loan. I sold that home one week before I actually closed, for $14,500 more than my own purchase price. When I sold the home, I received a $5,000 down payment from the buyer. When I closed the deal I put $3,000 in my pocket after paying the $1,400 to my seller and my share of the closing costs. And for the next five years I will get payments of almost $2,000 per year on the second mortgage I hold. This one is fun—in fact they all are!

As a real estate investor and consultant I hear stories every day that put my own best deals to shame. You'll read about a few of them as we go along, but what I would really love is to get a letter from you someday telling me a story like the one I just related to you. What I don't want to read is a letter from you saying that you're retired and living as over 90 percent of our retired citizens do, dependent on their families and the government to support them and rescue them from poverty. No company, and certainly no government bureaucracy, can offer the retirement income that real estate can.

Before we leave this chapter, let's talk a little more about courage. If you never develop the risk-taking courage that is required, you'll never even make an offer on a property.

When do we lose that courage? We had it as babies, when we took those first stumbling steps. Each of us got up on our wobbly legs ... and down we went. I think the difference then—why most of us didn't give up—was that our efforts, and initial failures, were met with enthusiastic praise from loving parents. They knew what we were capable of.

I *know* what you can do with investing.

All you need to do is develop risk-taking courage. Let me share four secrets I have discovered for overcoming those fears that are holding you back:

1. *Reward yourself* for taking risks. For example, make a written offer for a house (after I have taught you how). Then treat yourself to something small, whether your offer is accepted or not. We all need the occasional pat on the back just for trying, even if it is our own hand that does the patting.
2. *List all the rewards* that you might receive if you take the risk and succeed. When you consider making that offer, think about the money you can make fixing the house up and selling it. Listing the rewards will instill the confidence you will need when doubt creeps in.
3. *Realize that failure is only the first step to success.* Thomas Edison burned up yards of filament, spending countless hours without sleep—until failure paid off. Every worthwhile success was preceded by failure.
4. *Prepare for the worst and plan for the best.* List every problem that might crop up if you take the risk, and prepare yourself accordingly. If the worst thing that could happen is a fire, have a fire extinguisher handy. But at the same time, plan for the best. Preparing for failure is not the same as planning for failure. *Plan for success.*

   With this courage you are ready to be shown the road map for reaching financial freedom through real estate investment. These keys and tools have been discovered through thousands of hours of study, investing, and *mistakes*. This book has been written to help you get to your goal fast without having to suffer through the mistakes I have made. It is a pleasure for me to share this with you.

—PART II—

Real Estate Tools

CHAPTER 4

The Principles of Real Estate Investing

Every expert started out the same way—by learning the basics.
—RYAN MARC GARRISON

We are going to be looking at real estate as the ultimate investment. But before we can look at the details of a real estate transaction, or even discuss any type of property in detail, we need to understand the subject of real estate itself. What is real estate? What laws govern its sale, or its lease? This is the dry, admittedly boring stuff, and if you already understand it thoroughly, jump ahead. No, on second thought, stay with me; the review can't hurt, and it can always help.

Let's start with the obvious question: What is real estate? Understand first that real estate, unlike most other "investments," is more than a store of wealth; it is a tangible asset, a worthwhile, usable commodity. Real estate is a commodity in the same sense that a stereo is. It is purchased, used, enjoyed, and sold. Unlike the stereo, though, real estate is comprised of two major components: the land itself and man-made improvements affixed to the land. And, of course, the legal aspects of real estate ownership are slightly more complicated than ownership of a stereo.

The land consists of the surface area of the real estate purchase and, when legally specified, the mineral rights and air rights. The mineral rights are the rights of the owner to use and enjoy the space below the surface of the earth. Theoretically, this space is like an inverted pyramid that starts on the surface and extends to the center of the earth (about 4,000 miles), but in practice the rights generally extend no more than 50,000 feet. (Do you need more than that?)

The air rights apply to the legally specified three-dimensional area that extends 1,500 feet above the property. The federal and local governments may limit the height of air rights by enacting and enforcing building height restrictions and by designating certain airspace as public property for use by aircraft.

Improvements include the buildings, structures, and other man-made additions such as driveways, irrigation canals, and fences. These improvements take two forms: improvements on the land and improvements to the land. The first includes all types of permanent man-made structures, and improvements to the land are changes made in the physical condition of the land itself, such as grading, utility lines, and the construction of access roads that make the land suitable for a use.

The laws governing the ownership of land dictate that the owner has a "bundle of rights." These rights include the right to possess the property, use the property, enjoy the property, exclude others from using it, sell the property, and give it away. These rights are intangible factors that pertain to the land and on-site improvements and are guaranteed by law. The government, through its police powers, can enact laws that not only protect the landowner from the rest of the public, but the public from the landowner; what the law giveth it can take away, and the law can give and take any rights it deems are in the best interest of the public. That means if Farmer Brown wants to change his new suburban home into a slaughterhouse, he may be prevented from doing so by local government zoning ordinances.

Legal restrictions on a person's rights to a property are generally placed so that the property owner *and* the neighbors may each enjoy the "highest and best use" possible from their properties. Other restrictions on ownership include easements, which guarantee access across your property to another landowner or to a public utility, and the law of eminent domain, which allows properties to be purchased by the government at a fair market value to allow for improvements deemed advantageous to the public interest.

Property is possessed in two basic forms: freehold and less-than-freehold estates. A freehold estate is what you think of as ownership; the property is held for an indefinite period of time by the possessor. The less-than-freehold estate is common in tenant-landlord relations, where the possessor is given the right by the owner to possess and use the land for a period of time. It is also called a leasehold.

Stop here for a second and review. Make sure you understand the vocabulary presented so far; reread if necessary, because we're about to tackle another string of new terms and every one of them may be important to you shortly.

FORMS AND RIGHTS OF OWNERSHIP

The ways of holding property in freehold estate are sole ownership, tenancy in common, joint tenancy, community property, tenancy by the entireties, real estate investment trusts, partnerships, corporations, or a combination of the above. A basic knowledge of these forms of ownership is absolutely necessary for anyone interested in real estate investing.

Sole Ownership

When one individual owns the property, without any co-owners, he is said to have sole ownership. He can buy, sell, trade, or do anything else that he sees fit—within the limits of the law. He alone is responsible for the debts of the property and the taxes owed on the property and any income from the property.

The alternative to sole ownership is co-ownership, in which a freehold estate is shared by more than one individual. They may hold the property as tenants in common, as joint tenants, as a trust, partnership, or corporation (see explanations below). The method of ownership chosen will determine the tax consequences and the right of survivorship for the owners.

Tenancy in Common

When two or more persons own a property, they may choose to do so as tenants in common. Under this arrangement, each person owns an undivided interest—a fraction—in the property. Each owner has the right to sell, trade, or give away his interest in the property, without the permission of the other owners.

If one of the owners dies, his ownership interest passes on to his heirs. This is an important consideration, because if, for example, you owned a piece of property with your best friend as tenants in common, and your friend died, you would suddenly be faced with a new co-owner—one you might not get along with too well.

Tenants in common do not necessarily share the property equally. They can agree to hold any portion they choose. Three partners can each hold one third, or one partner may own half and the other two share the remaining half, or any other division they may agree to.

Since each partner owns his own share separately, he is also responsible for a proportional share of property repairs, taxes, mortgage payments, etc. And he is entitled to a proportional share of any income derived from the property.

One problem tenants in common face is the possibility of disagreement among the partners. If the difficulty cannot be solved outside a courtroom, any one of the partners may file a suit against the others, demanding that the property be physically divided or sold. Also, if one of the partners files for bankruptcy, the bankruptcy court can sell the property to satisfy debts. Each of the other partners will receive his proportionate share of the proceeds, but they have no say in the matter of the sale.

Joint Tenancy

When two or more persons own a piece of property as joint tenants, they have equal rights in the property and they all have the right of survivorship. They have an equal voice in the disposition of the property, and they share its income equally.

For a joint tenancy to occur, four "unities" must occur: unity of time, unity of title, unity of possession, and unity of interest. Unity of time means that every co-owner acquires his ownership at the same time. Unity of title means that there is only one title to the property and that each owner has a share of it. Unity of possession means that each owner has an equal share in the possession of the property. Unity of interest means that each owner has an equal interest in the property. If there are two owners, each has a one-half interest; if there are four owners, each has a one-fourth interest.

Joint tenancy is popular, especially among married couples, because of the right of survivorship. If one owner dies, his rights are extinguished and the property ownership goes directly to the surviving owners. This eliminates the problems that are encountered in a tenancy in common when one owner dies, leaving his share of the property to heirs.

Community Property

Some states apply the law of community property to husbands and wives. California (my old home state) is one such state, and the community property fights around Beverly Hills and Hollywood are staggering. Some of the other states that are governed by the rules of community property are Arizona, Idaho, Louisiana, Nevada, New Mexico, Texas, and Washington. Check with a local attorney to see if your state has a community property law.

Simply put, the idea behind community property is that each spouse is entitled to one half of everything acquired during the marriage. Unlike tenancy by the entireties, the rights of survivorship vary from one state to the next. You should find out the laws in your own state when you are considering the purchase of real property.

Tenancy by the Entireties

This is similar to joint tenancy in that the co-owners have the right to survivorship. But only a husband and wife can be tenants by the entireties. It is a doctrine applied in states that do not recognize community property. In this form of co-ownership, the husband and wife are considered to be one legal entity, not two separate owners. As long as they are both alive, they act as one owner. Both of their signatures must appear on the deed in order to convey title.

A tenancy by the entireties faces a problem when there is marital trouble. This form of co-ownership can only be severed by agreement between the two parties, and in the case of divorce both must agree on the division of the property.

Real Estate Investment Trusts

REITs are formed by groups of investors (usually more than a hundred), who put their money into a common pot, called a trust, which is managed by trust officers. The investors are called beneficiaries, and their interest in the investment is similar to that of shareholders in a corporation.

Partnerships

Co-owners may choose to form a partnership for the purpose of buying a property. They may do so as a general partnership, in which case each partner has say in the management of the partnership. But each partner also has an unlimited financial responsibility to the partnership. He may be sued for every last dime of his own personal wealth to satisfy the debts of the partnership.

The alternative is a limited partnership, in which the general partners have full control over the property, make all of the management decisions of the partnership, and accept the full financial responsibility, while the limited partners only provide investment capital and share the profits. The advantage to the limited partners is easy to see: they have little or no management hassles, and their losses are limited to the extent of their investment. The only problem that plagues limited partnerships is that it is difficult to ensure the honesty of the general partners, and the limited partners can easily be taken for a ride.

Corporations

A corporation is a separate legal entity in the eyes of the law. That is the most important difference between a corporation and a partnership: it exists independently of its owners. They can come and go, trading and selling their interest (in the form of stock), but the corporation goes on. It is responsible for its own taxes and its own financial obligations. The shareholders cannot be sued for the debts of the corporation.

The problem with a corporation is that it must pay income tax before distributing profits to the owners, who then must pay taxes on their income. The double taxation takes away profit that would have been shared by the owners in a partnership.

If you are considering purchasing property with another person, check with a real estate attorney first (you can find them in the yellow pages under *Lawyers,* or get a recommendation from a title officer, a banker, or another investor). It is vital that you understand the laws in your own state before you make such a decision.

I know that studying page after page of definitions isn't nearly as much fun as, say, reading this week's issue of *TV Guide.* But then it's unlikely that anything you read in *TV Guide* will help you invest in real estate, right? Before we continue, read the following list of terms. How many can you define for yourself? If you need to review, do so now.

    land
    air rights
    mineral rights
    improvements to the land
    improvements on the land
    zoning
    easements
    eminent domain
    freehold estate
    less-than-freehold estate
    leasehold
    sole ownership
    tenancy in common
    joint tenancy
    community property
    tenancy by the entireties
    real estate investment trusts (REITs)
    partnerships
    corporations

In the back of this book there is a reference guide to terms, which have been extracted from *The Real Estate Greenbook.*

Several years ago I began putting together a complete real estate encyclopedia and reference guide. It has been published by the National Committee for Real Estate Investment. If you come across any terms that you are unfamiliar with, please take time to look them up.

THE BEST INVESTMENTS

You now understand the basic rights of ownership, and the forms such ownership can take. Let's consider next the different types of real estate investments. You can claim to be a real estate investor whether you buy an acre of swampland in Florida or the Taj Mahal. But which is the best investment for *you*, and why?

Real estate includes all of the following:

Raw land: Undeveloped real estate. Examples would be rangeland or, in a city, empty fields that don't have improvements such as utility hookups or curb and gutter.

Developed land: Land that has been improved and is either already built on or ready to be built on.

Apartments: A building with rooms or individual dwelling units that people live in but do not own. Payment is made by the tenant to the landlord (owner or his representative), usually on a monthly basis.

Mobile home: A personal residence, considered to be private property, that is not permanently attached to the land and may be moved to another location or mobile home site.

Condominium: Typically, condominiums are multi-unit housing complexes where individual, apartmentlike units are purchased instead of rented. Each condominium owner has his or her own deed or mortgage. Typically, owners of these housing units are required to pay a monthly common fee, which pays for all outside maintenance, lawn care, and common utility fees.

Co-op: Similar to a condominium, but ownership exists in shares of the total building, not in one specific unit. As a member of a co-op, you are assigned one specific living unit within a complex.

Residential property: Property or land that is zoned by the local government agencies to be used for single-family homes or other living quarters.

Hotel or motel: A property where individual sleeping rooms or suites are rented by the night.

Commercial property: Property that is specifically zoned by the local government authorities for commercial uses such as shopping centers, stores, and laundries.

Industrial property: Property that is specifically zoned by the local government authorities for industrial uses such as manufacturing and processing plants.

Of these many types of investments, only two are really ideal for the beginning investor: single-family homes and apartments. Mobile homes and raw land rarely if ever return even the original investment, and commercial and industrial properties are expensive and very complicated investments.

Nearly 80 percent of all real estate transactions take place in the lower-middle range of house prices. Specifically, the average home in this range is a three-bedroom, two-bathroom house with a carport or garage and approximately 1,100 square feet. Why are these bread-and-butter houses such hot sellers? Because they are the transition houses for people moving up and down the financial ladder of life. They are usually the starter homes for up-and-coming couples, and they are the lifelong homes for the blue-collar backbone of America. In chapter 5 we will talk about the specifics of how to find these bargain properties.

This area of real estate investing has several advantages. First, these units represent the bottom end of the housing market. The sale prices are low, the down payments are usually low, and the demand is high. These homes can be diamonds in the rough. By putting in some minimal fix-up and cleaning, you can resell them at fantastic profits.

Rental properties—small apartments and single-family homes that you rent out—are good investments because there is always a shortage of housing and there are always people who can afford to rent but cannot afford to buy a home. Because of the high price of home ownership, and the fact that it is generally undertaken with borrowed funds, there will always be renters, those who are afraid of the financial obligation or unwilling to leverage themselves into ownership.

The main advantage that real estate offers is leverage. Using a small amount of money—or even *no* money, in a few cases—you can buy real estate worth tens of thousands of dollars. In this book you will learn the basics of using leverage: how to find the deals that allow you to invest little or none of your own money and yet reap tremendous rewards.

The second advantage is the price appreciation that occurs in real estate, whether it is through inflation, or fixing up, or just the fact that buyers and sellers are working in an imperfect market, usually with only a hazy knowledge as to the real value of property. The house that you bought yesterday for $60,000 may be worth $65,000 to another person. Find that person and you've made $5,000.

Price is also boosted by the simple law of supply and demand. The supply of housing is growing slowly, and the population is mushrooming, through both the constant flow of immigrants looking for the promised land and our reliance on the old-fashioned way of enlarging our own families. As long as demand for housing continues to outrun supply (and do you see it doing anything else?), prices will keep going up.

Other factors which affect the price of real estate are the general economic condition of the community, the condition of the surrounding neighborhood, the actual condition of the property, the terms (this includes the available financing, the time period involved, owner financing, down payment, and other factors), the legal rights inherent in the transfer of the property, the income-producing capability of the property, and its perceived future value.

One of the most interesting characteristics of real estate is the concept of "fixity." Unlike two cans of beans, two similar real estate investments can't be compared side by side. The investment is fixed; it is permanently attached. To compare two investments you need to use some specialized valuation techniques. A system of determining value in real estate will be discussed in chapter 11.

The tax advantages of real estate are staggering. You can own a rental unit, collect rent, pay operating expenses and loan payments, and come out with a positive cash flow, and then still get a tax break on the fifteenth of April. Uncle Sam allows you to claim a loss in the value of the improvements. This loan is called depreciation, and it is used to offset your income, lessening your tax obligation. It's interesting that you are allowed to depreciate the property at the same time it is actually appreciating, but that's just Uncle Sam's way of encouraging us to invest in real estate. You are also allowed to deduct operating expenses, which further reduces your income (for tax purposes).

Below is a sample cash flow statement, showing how much money you actually need. Below that is an income statement for the IRS, which takes operating losses and depreciation into account. You can see that even though you put money in your pocket, the IRS is going to allow you to claim a loss—which is deductible—on your 1040, and reduce your taxes accordingly.

Cash Flow Statement

gross income	$4,000
less operating expenses	−250
net operating income	3,750
less loan payments	−3,250
cash flow	$500

Profit and Loss Statement for IRS

gross income	$4,000
less operating expenses	−250
net operating income	3,750
less interest charge	−2,750
taxable income before depreciation	1,000
less depreciation	−2,500
taxable income (loss)	−$1,500

Of course, besides the advantages of preferred tax treatment, appreciation, and leverage, there is also monthly income that can be made, using a few simple methods of buying, renting, managing, and selling that I will be showing you throughout the book.

You now know what real estate is, how it is owned, what rights an owner has over his real estate, the different types of real estate, which real estate investments are the best, and the advantages of owning real estate. We can begin the next part of your education: how to buy real estate.

—— CHAPTER 5 ——————————————

Tools for Buying Real Estate

*If the only tool you have is a
hammer, you tend to see every
problem as a nail.*
   —ABRAHAM MASLOW

Reread the quote above. It's one of my favorites, because it is *so* true. In real estate investing, the beginner is often taught only one or two methods for finding good deals. And that's too bad, because with only a couple of tools you are extremely limited. Many real estate writers, in fact, pass over this subject entirely, concentrating on such things as how to structure financing, or how to negotiate a seller to death, when what you really need first are a few methods for *finding* those fantastic deals that will make your fortune.

In this chapter we will look closely at ten ways to find the best properties at the best prices. I must have tried a hundred ways myself by now, and these are by far the most effective. Here are the top ten on my real estate investor's hit parade for finding good deals in real estate:

1. Classified ad—"For Sale by Owner"
2. Advertising for sellers
3. Realtors
4. Word-of-mouth advertising
5. "Farming"
6. Empties
7. "For rent" ads
8. Foreclosure—before the auction
9. Foreclosure—at the auction
10. Foreclosure—after the auction

There are many more methods for finding good deals, but these are the quickest, surest, safest, and easiest that I have found. As you study each one, try it on for size—in your mind—and decide whether or not it's the one for you. Some of the methods I use the most may not fit you any better than my size 13 shoes would, so don't assume they will all work for you. Instead, consider choosing the five tools that seem to "fit" you best. Don't just choose one. Several weeks ago I chartered a boat out of Ilwaco, Washington, for a day of salmon fishing. As I sat bobbing up and down in that boat, I wished that I could have had more than one line in the water. The lesson holds true with real estate investing. Have at least five tools working at all times, finding real estate bargains for you.

Before we get into specifics, let's look for a minute at the whole concept of good deals. It is obvious that a good deal in real estate is one that will provide you with an opportunity to buy low and sell high or to have rental income in excess of mortgage payments. But what seller in his or her right mind would sell a home or rental below its market value? And if there is already a positive cash flow, why would they sell at all? It would seem that the only way you can find a really good deal is to find a really crazy seller.

Not so. Every day there are many sellers who are truly motivated to sell and who are willing to accept less than full value for their property. The reasons vary, from the owner who has been transferred and only has a few weeks to sell, to the out-of-work owner facing foreclosure. And there are always a few sellers who insist on selling "by owner"and who undervalue their property, accepting a low offer.

Of course we're talking about a minority. Out of the thousands of homes that go up for sale every day, only about 5 to 15 percent will be sold substantially below their market value. It will be your challenge to find them. That's the name of the investing game. The methods I'm offering are simply ways that I have found to narrow the search.

1. THE CLASSIFIED AD

This is number one because it is the Old Faithful of the investing world. It is the first and last method that most investors rely on for finding properties. And like most tried-and-true methods, it is popular because it *works*.

If you grab today's paper right now (go ahead, I'll wait), you'll find a section in the classified ads that says "Real Estate for Sale" or something to that effect. Within these few pages of hard-to-read print await dozens of bargain properties. A typical ad might read:

> **BY OWNER.** Nice 3 bdrm 2 bth w/fplc & AC. Assumable
> FHA 11% $20,000 down. Call 444-7891

How much of the above ad did you understand? Translated, it means: Home for sale by owner (not through a real estate agency). Nice (could mean anything) three bedrooms, two bathrooms, a fireplace and air conditioner. There is an existing FHA loan (we'll discuss loans in detail later) with an interest rate of 11 percent that can be taken over by the buyer. The seller wants at least $20,000 in cash.

That ad wouldn't be very enticing, but consider this one:

> **TRANSFERRED.** Must sell. Present all offers. Negotiable
> down. Assumable 11% FHA. Call 444-7891

Now here's an enticing ad. This seller is admitting that a real problem exists. He or she is being transferred out of the area, and if the house cannot be sold, there may be serious financial difficulties. Every line cries for help, and every investor who can read between the lines will run to the nearest telephone.

This person really wants to sell! Look at the phone number in this ad and in the other. Aren't they the same? If you were keeping track of these ads, and saw the first one on May first and the second one on June first, wouldn't you draw a pretty quick conclusion? Here is an owner who is really ready to sell!

One of your goals as you begin your investing career is to learn property values as quickly as possible. This is one of the best ways of doing so. Keep track of the ads you make calls on, and you'll find that after researching the classified ads for weeks and making telephone calls on the most promising ads, you will develop an excellent feel for values.

Also, you will become an expert at reading between the lines. For example, *nice* often means "average to poor," and *a fixer-*

upper usually means "a real rat's nest that needs major renovation."

The challenge and the fun behind using classifieds is that they are like a boring old black-and-white film. You have to sift through a lot of boring black and white to find something really good. And when it's good, it's great. To find the great ones you have to learn to recognize hidden clues. I called on an ad recently that said in the heading, "Illness forces sale." I asked the seller what type of illness was forcing the sale, he replied that he was just sick of the property. Good deals are found in the classified ads.

Let's examine some of those clues. The key phrases that you should look for include:

> low down
> anxious
> flexible terms
> desperate
> owner will carry
> nothing down
> will trade
> transferred
> death in family
> must sell
> foreclosure
> kick me, I'm down

These things do appear! I have seen every one of them at one time or another, and they were like a red flag waving in front of me.

There are other clues; each ad has its own hidden messages. An ad can tell you many things, sometimes in very subtle ways. There are several more points to keep in mind as you read through your paper:

1. Flowery, poetic ads usually do not indicate a flexible or motivated seller or a don't-wanter.
2. Just because a seller does seem to be flexible, the property is not necessarily a good deal. Call and check on it personally before you invest your time in driving out to see it.
3. When an ad indicates that you will be dealing through a

Realtor, you should be aware that a commission of 6 percent to 8 percent of the selling price will be involved.

4. When a seller publishes his terms, he is saying, "This is what I would like, but what will you give me?"

5. Look for ads with long-distance phone numbers. These ads are placed by people who have inherited homes, have been transferred, or are the trustees for an estate. These people tend to be extremely motivated sellers. (But remember to call them collect!)

To help you learn how to read between the lines of classified ads, I have prepared a self-test that includes sample ads. This ad-scanning practice will help you sift through the hundreds of ads that you may be reading, saving you hundreds of hours that would otherwise be wasted calling the wrong sellers.

Ad-Scanning Exercise

Of all the ways for finding good deals in real estate, nothing beats the classified ad for the beginning investor. This is the meeting place for do-it-yourself buyers and sellers. Owners who don't want to put their homes into the hands of real estate agents really have few options for finding buyers. They can put a sign on the front lawn, but it is the one or two inches of newspaper space that will sell their homes.

You, as an investor, must learn the fine art of reading between only a couple of lines and trying to get the whole story. By trying the following exercise you should get a good idea of how well you read ads.

Rarely will you find an ad like the following:

> Little or nothing down. No qualifying, assumable loan,
> positive cash flow. Call 373-2343

If it were that easy, everyone would be investing in real estate. However, a little practice and you will be able to sift through a dozen ads in minutes.

In each of the following examples, rate them on a scale of A to D, as follows:

A Excellent possibility, to be called immediately. Probably includes a few key phrases, such as "nothing down" or "desperate seller."

B Definitely worth calling, but possibly not a real good bargain. Seller seems anxious, but price is high or down payment is too high.

C Probably worth following up, but somewhat unlikely as a good deal. Price too high, some inflexibility. Properties sold by a realty company are often in this category.

D Not worth dialing the phone. Seller obviously is looking for a homeowner willing to pay top dollar, not an investor. No anxiety is apparent.

1. ____Anxious owner. 6-plex, $89,000, $8,000 down. Owner will carry contract. 888-9090

2. ____Desperate owner facing foreclosure. Make up back payments, take over loan. 777-8080.

3. ____For sale by owner. 2 bdrm 2 bth. $69,000 firm, $20,-000 down. 666-7070

4. ____Lease option. 3-year option, $1,000 down. Payments $600. 555-6060

5. ____Nice 3 bdrm. 2 bth in good location $68,000, $20,000 down. 444-5050

6. ____4 bdrm—will trade equity, possible no down. willing to consider all offers. 333-4040

7. ____low down, assumable loan, 3 bdrm. 2 bath $68,000. 222-3030

8. ____9% assumable loan, 2 bdrm. $59,000 firm, $7,000 down. 111-2020

9. ____beautiful 3 bdrm $87,000, $12,000 down. owner/agent. 222-1010

10. ____townhome for sale. excellent tax shelter. $93,000 firm. Mtn. View Realty 333-2020

11. ____For sale by owner. 4 bdrm, 3 bth. $95,000, $10,000 down. Will carry contract. 444-3030

12. ____nice 3 brm. in exc. cond. $88,000, $8,000 down, payments $850. will consider all offers. 555-4040

Here is how I would rate these ads:

1) B The down payment is high relative to the sales price.
2) A Call right away. If you understand the foreclosure process you might be able to do really well with this one.
3) D The down payment is way too high.
4) B A lease with option to buy is an agreement whereby you rent the property from the seller but agree upon a

sales price and terms for some time in the future. Usually part of your rental (lease) goes toward the purchase of the property. This situation sounds pretty good.

5) D Again, too much money up front.

6) A This person is desperate: "willing to consider all offers," "will trade equity." Call on this one right away.

7) A Low down, assumable loan, nice basic house. Give it a call.

8) B Assumable loan, but higher down. Give it a call when you can.

9) D This home is being sold by an experienced real estate agent (owner/agent). It doesn't have one sign of motivation.

10) D Again, no signs of motivation. Be leary of investments that are being sold as tax shelters. They are usually high-priced.

11) C The words "will carry contract" give some hope to this ad. You might want to give them a call.

12) B "Will consider all offers" jumps out and hits me. It conflicts with the high down, but these people may be willing to negotiate.

Here's your score:

12 correct: Outstanding; start calling.
9–11: Very good.
6–8: Pretty good; you'll get much better with practice.
less than 5: Practice makes perfect. Make some phone calls and you'll get a better picture quickly.

Remember, educated persistence is the key to success. Don't give up if you're having trouble identifying the good ads right now. Pick up your own newspaper and scan the ads. Start making those phone calls and finding the good deals. Later on I'll be giving you a form you can use when you make the phone calls that will further simplify the process and identify the best opportunities.

Recently a friend of mine received a call from his friend who said he had set a goal to buy his first property within two weeks.

Unfortunately, he couldn't seem to find any desperately motivated sellers in the newspaper. My friend had to chuckle as he
heard this because he had just returned from buying two properties that had both been listed in the paper for two days. This is the
ad that he had seen:

> Two 1 bdrm. 4-plexes. $160,000 both. $7,000 down. Take
> over payments. Positive cash flow. Call 375-9660.

With one glance he had been able to see that the down payment was less than 5 percent of the asking price, and that the
asking price was much below the probable market value of such a
property. He quickly called the seller to find out more. In the conversation that followed, he learned that the seller had just gotten
the property out of a foreclosure and that it needed a great deal of
work.

My friend learned what the seller's needs were and, after examining the property, made an offer. The terms that were agreed
on were excellent: $1,000 down (remember the seller had asked
for $7,000), an assumable mortgage of $150,000 with payments of
$1,150 per month (the rents from both buildings together would
total $1,500 per month). The grounds needed cleaning and the ex-
terior of the building needed new paint, repairs that would cost
$1,000. The seller was overjoyed to sell the property; he was tired
of it!

Out of all the ways for finding good deals, finding homes for
sale by owner (called FSBOs, and pronounced *fizboes*) through
the classified ads is one of the most rewarding. But what's the
problem? This method requires an extraordinary amount of time,
and a lot of persistence.

Let me leave you with a hint that has saved me thousands of
hours in using classified ads. When I first started using ads I read
them every day. It really got tiring. After about two years I began
to notice some trends. I realized that over 90 percent of the for-
sale-by-owner ads start on Thursdays and Sundays. I started
calling only on those two days, for three reasons. First, other investors in the area will no doubt be making calls, and I want to be
the first one through the door. Second, by only calling two days a
week, I save myself several hours that would otherwise be

wasted looking for new ads. And last, by hitting the paper only two days a week, I don't get burned out on reading ads. You have to enjoy investing, and I promise that reading the same old black-and-white ads each day for a few years can cause brain damage.

The real key with classified ads is (do you know me well enough by now to guess?) *educated persistence.* After three fruitless weeks of reading ads and making calls, you are likely to give up in despair. And then two days later, if you are still trying, you find that one gold nugget that will make more money for you than six months on your old merry-go-round job.

2. ADVERTISING FOR SELLERS

It was a nightmare: Every time the phone rang it was another seller, trying to sell me his or her house, offering me thousands and thousands of working, smart dollars. I couldn't sleep or eat because of the hundreds of deals that I was bombarded with day and night. I finally yanked the phone out of the wall, but it kept ringing and ringing and ringing . . . and then I woke up.

Don't expect your telephone *ever* to ring off the hook with thousands of desperate sellers. But you can get the sellers to call you occasionally (up to five a day) with well-placed, well-worded ads that announce your willingness to buy houses.

Several years ago I saw a small ad in the paper in which a man was advertising that he wanted to buy a home for his family in a certain area for a certain price. The idea hit me like a ton of bricks. Why not advertise that you are interested in buying a home? I created my own ad, which I ran in a local newspaper:

> Young family man seeks to buy single-family home or
> smaller rental unit in need of repair with a low down
> payment. Call Marc 444-5566

It's exciting to come home to your answering machine and have several people each day wanting you to call them about buying their properties, in addition to your regular calls to people who have advertised.

Another method of advertisement is the advertising flier. Why not have an ad hung on every doorknob in a neighborhood? This shotgun approach may only get one response in a thousand, but at the minimal cost, an investment of $100 may return $10,000 with the purchase of just one good property.

Here is a flier that has been successful for me:

WE BUY HOUSES

WE ARE NOT REALTORS · WE ARE NOT ASSOCIATED WITH ANY REAL ESTATE FIRM · WE ARE PRIVATE INVESTORS

Do you need to sell your house? You may have been transferred, or need a bigger or smaller house. You may be having financial difficulties and risk losing your house. Maybe you've experienced a divorce or death that forces you to move. Whatever the case, we'd be more than happy to talk with you about buying your house.

We want to buy houses that we can fix up to resell or houses that would make good rentals. We are specifically looking for houses that need painting, yardwork, new roofs, or major repairs. No job is too large. If you have a problem finding someone to buy your house, look no further—just give us a call.

Marc and DeAnn Garrison
(801) 225-8777

— Save Closing Costs —

As any Madison Avenue ad whiz could tell you, the successful ad is one that first catches the eye and the attention, and then makes its point. Too many amateurs try to make their point without first catching the imagination of the audience. Try wording that you haven't seen. An example, which I've tried with success, is to write an ad that says:

> **I DON'T WANT TO BUY YOUR HOUSE;** I want you to give it to me! But if you insist on selling, give me a call and let's talk terms. Marc 444-5566

Whatever wording you use, make sure it clearly represents you. My most successful flier is a handwritten one that represents me exactly as I am. Ask yourself why you might call this ad, instead of some flashier ones, if you were selling a property:

ARE YOU A SERIOUS SELLER?

I am a family man who is interested in buying your home or smaller rental unit. I am not afraid of some fix-up work.

Please call:
Marc Garrison
(801) 225-8777

Another way to advertise for sellers would be to pass out small cards or half-page fliers in your area that say this:

Property Owners:

I BUY HOUSES AND SMALL RENTAL UNITS

READ AND SAVE THIS CARD

If you desperately need to sell your home or rental unit, please call me. Whatever the reason—closing an estate, being transferred, out-of-state ownership, or management problems—I can help. Whatever your problem may be, I will give you a written offer for your property. Please call me before you list with an agent. I may be able to save you the expense of a commission and the risk involved with tying your property up for months on end waiting for the right buyer to come along. If you aren't thinking of selling right now but know of someone who is, please let me know. If I buy their home I will give you a nice gift to show my appreciation.

Call Marc Garrison (801) 225-8777 24 hours a day

If I am not home, please leave your name and phone number on the answering machine.

We'll talk more about writing effective ads when we discuss selling, where first-class ads are a must. For now, just keep in mind the importance of catching the reader's eye and not coming off too slick. Try to appeal to those truly motivated sellers, with words such as "I will give you a written offer for your property."

If your ad catches their attention and convinces them that you are serious about buying, the calls will come in.

3. REALTORS

Like most real estate investors, I approach the subject of Realtors with some ambivalence. On the one hand, they have access to thousands of sellers through the Multiple Listing Service. Also, they are—or at least should be—experts in the field. Therefore, they can be an excellent source of good deals. On the other hand, they will be expecting a commission—in cash—and although the seller is supposed to pay that commission, they usually do so by raising their asking price by enough to cover the cost. Furthermore, many Realtors aren't very willing to help investors, who as a rule are fussy about what properties they will consider buying. Additionally, if a Realtor does find a good deal, he or she will often buy it rather than pass it on.

I have found that the best way to overcome the negative aspects of using a Realtor's help is through friendship. My real estate agent is also one of my best friends, and is therefore always willing to work with me and give me first shot at the best deals.

I don't think that anyone should feign friendship just to curry favor with a Realtor. But if you find an agent that you seem to be compatible with, the honest effort expended in forming a friendship will pay off many times over.

Take at least one or two days and visit realty offices in your area. Be honest. Tell them that you are a new real estate investor, and that you are looking for a good agent to work with. You are serious about buying real estate, and if you can find the right agent it will mean many sales in the coming years. If an agent seems uninterested or skeptical, keep looking.

Some keys to choosing a good agent:

1. Make sure you and the agent are compatible and have the potential to develop a good friendship.
2. Make sure the agent works full-time. You want an agent who is aware of all the bargains, programs, and deals in your community.

3. Make sure your agent is also an investor. You are looking for someone who is aware of the latest techniques for creative finance and who knows what you're looking for.
4. Make sure your agent has access to the FHA and VA repossession lists, all of the proper forms for buying these properties, and keys to the lockboxes (where house keys of properties for sale are stored).
5. After you have introduced yourself as a new investor, ask the agent a tough question: If you, as an investor, found a good deal that was for sale by owner and you wanted to make an offer, would he or she help you write it up? There would be no commission, of course. Any help given would be in anticipation of a good future relationship. If the agent is unwilling to help you with such a simple task you may have to look elsewhere for someone more cooperative.

If you can find a good agent, this will probably be the least time-consuming and the most effective method for finding the best deals in real estate.

4. WORD-OF-MOUTH ADVERTISING

If you want sellers to call you, there is no better way to keep the telephone ringing than to create a name for yourself as an honest investor. After I had been investing several years, I went over to close a deal with a woman whose husband had died several years earlier. Her husband had dabbled in real estate during most of their marriage and had acquired quite an impressive portfolio. She was interested in selling off some of her properties, since management was getting a little over her head.

I had negotiated the purchase of one of her properties, but when it came time to sell, she seemed as nervous as a cat in a bathhouse. I asked her what was wrong, and she said, "Are you an investor?" I had gotten it into my head at that time that I was pretty hot stuff as an investor. So my reply was, "Sure am, I make a lot of money investing in real estate." Have you ever tried to give a cat a bath? Well, the look in her eye was the same: crazed anger. I asked what was wrong, and she replied simply, "I think all investors are by-products of the world's oldest profession." I asked why. She replied that a friend of hers had sold a home to an investor who really took advantage of her.

This lady said that she just wanted to sell her house to someone who was "normal." Needless to say, that deal died on the vine then and there. It seems that wherever we go and whoever we talk to, we leave some type of reputation. You simply can't please everyone. But you can try your best.

I still haven't recovered fully from that widow's vehemence. As I've traveled around the country teaching real estate investing, I've been surprised by how many people share her opinion. How unnecessary! You can combat that attitude best by being honest and fair in your dealings. Don't worry; even without "I win, you die" tactics, there are still tremendous benefits. And by far the greatest one is that you will establish a reputation as an honest investor.

You can give that reputation and word-of-mouth advertising a real boost by offering an incentive to people you sell houses to. Offer to let them miss a house payment if you buy from or sell to a person referred by them. What homeowner wouldn't be willing to recommend you to a friend who was trying to buy or sell a home, especially if it means skipping one payment. Talk about motivation!

I've added a slight twist to this method, offering a cash bonus to housewives, college students, and neighbors—anybody who doesn't have a steady income—if they help me either sell or rent a home I own. By offering bonuses and incentives—by sharing my own good fortune—I am able to have my reputation as an investor spread faster than a good rumor in a bridge club.

By combining honest investing with offering incentives to helpers, you will find that after only a few months as an investor the deals will come to you. Some people when reading this may say, "Marc, cut the religion and Polyanna pitch; I want to make some money." Let me just end this section by saying that this point isn't just ethics or morals, it's business. If you want to make money in the long run and have people refer other people to you, remember that word of mouth will snowball your investing to a point where you are getting 90 percent of your investment leads off referrals from people who enjoyed doing business with you. Look ahead and work toward that.

5. "FARMING"

Some of the very best real estate investors and agents are farmers. They don't own one pig or horse, they don't raise hay while the sun shines, and they probably don't get up when the cock crows. But they are the most successful farmers in town.

In real estate lingo, a "farm" is a well-defined section of a community, usually several square blocks, in which an individual agent concentrates all of his or her efforts. By knocking on doors and making phone calls, the agent usually manages to become a nuisance to a few select citizens, rather than the community at large. All of this concentrated effort pays off, however, when Karl and Polly Sailler are ready to list their home for sale. The "farmer" is the first real estate agent in town they think of, and it's his phone that is the first to ring.

As an investor, one of the tools that will give you deal after deal is to become a farmer yourself. Get a map of your county and drive through every neighborhood looking for areas in which to invest. (You can purchase a good county map at your local county planning and zoning commission. They are called county plat maps.) The best streets are those with the bread-and-butter houses, the homes of middle-income families, who can afford to take good care of their modest homes but can't afford to live in the fancy manors on the hill. In this area you catch people moving both up and down the economic ladder.

Once you have chosen several promising areas, talk with several Realtors and ask them about those neighborhoods. Find out which neighborhood has experienced the most housing sales and movement in the past couple of years. Then look at an agent's MLS book (multiple listing sales book) and see what homes are selling and renting for in that specific neighborhood. Ask the agent to show you the section in the MLS book that shows recent home sales. Then write down the addresses and sales prices of some homes in the neighborhood that have recently sold. Drive by some of these homes to get a good basic definition of sales and rental values in your farm.

If you want, drop by the local police departments and ask them which areas have the lowest crime rates. People like to live in safe neighborhoods. That knowledge can be a selling and renting point. Color code your map, marking areas as great, good, and stay out. (I use highlighter pens and code great areas green, good areas blue, and bad areas red.) Then start to plant your seeds.

As a real estate farmer, you may want to go from door to door, introducing yourself; or you may want to simply put fliers on doorknobs every two months. You may combine every technique discussed in this book. But you have to stick with an area for a while in order for farming to pay off.

The effective method of farming for an investor is the same as for a Realtor: get to know every house on every block in every neighborhood that you want to farm. Your goal as an investor-

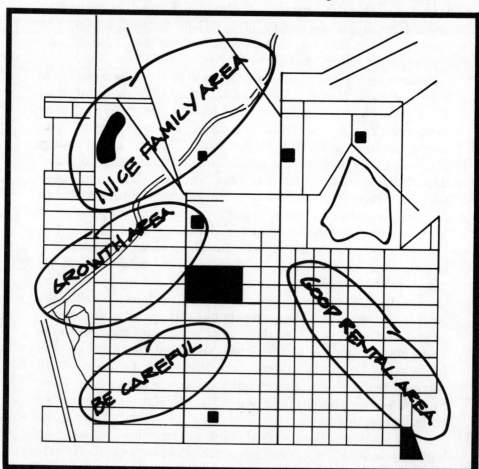

farmer is to have your business card and flier in every home, so that when the owners are ready to sell, they call you first—even before their agent-farmer. Successful farming requires a consistent effort, but don't forget: the dictionary is the only place where success comes before work.

A word of caution: Limit your initial investing to an area of farm that's not more than one-half-hour travel time from where you live. You need to be able to spend time investing, not driving out to properties.

6. EMPTIES

This tool is just what you would expect: empty houses. No doubt you've driven through a neighborhood and seen one house that sticks out like a sore thumb, with an overgrown lawn, no curtains in the windows, and no sign of life anywhere on the property. In the past, you probably passed the house without a thought, but it's time to change that. It's time to stop and ask yourself,"Who owns that house?"

I love empties. In fact, this has become one of my personal favorite tools for finding houses to buy. There are many reasons for these mini–ghost towns. Sometimes the owners have moved out under duress, leaving the bank to foreclose, or the family has been transferred out of the area and has been unsuccessful at selling the old homestead. Perhaps there's been a death in the household, or an out-of-state landlord had his tenants move out and now has a "rental problem." The reason why homes become empty can go on forever.

In just about all cases, *somebody* is making payments on that loan, and that somebody is losing money every month. (Would that make you a motivated seller?)

Researching empties, I have found in talking to owners and bank officers that most owners will continue making payments on a house for about eight months before giving up and allowing foreclosure. That gives me (or you) at least that much time to locate the owner and make an offer. And chances are that the owners have given up actively advertising their home for sale, so there will be little or no competition for your bid.

I recently bought a home in Utah from a man who was transferred to Southern California. His move was extremely sudden, and he left his home for a neighbor to watch over and a friend to sell. The neighbor did the best he could, the friend tried a little bit, and seven months later the man was still paying his monthly mortgage payment on a vacant house. He tried selling long-distance, but he had little control over the situation from 750 miles away. He was having difficulty paying the minimum bills in California, and a new house there was out of the question until his old home was sold. Does this sound like an opportunity for a good deal?

You've noticed how much emphasis I place on establishing a reputation. Well, one of the neighbors, who had bought his house from me, gave me a call and suggested that I look into this deal. The neighbor even gave me the name and telephone number of the homeowner in California.

In this case, success was only a phone call away. I called the owner and established his needs. He only wanted enough out of his house to get into another house. He was willing to take $2,000 cash and let me assume his 11.5 percent VA loan. So I was able to pick up a $63,000 home for only $53,000 with $2,000 down. The owner was ecstatic at having sold his ball and chain; now he could get on with his life. I was ecstatic; with very little effort I had been handed a golden opportunity on a silver platter. And I assume the house itself was ecstatic, if houses ever get ecstatic; it was now cleaned up and rented out.

To locate these empties you need to keep your eyes open when you drive around. Some things to look for are:

1. a house that resembles the haunted shack at the county fair
2. a broken window on a house
3. a house with a lot of papers and trash piled up around the front door, and a mailbox overstuffed with envelopes
4. a house with no cars in the driveway, and a for-rent or for-sale sign in the window
5. an overgrown or dying lawn, and a general appearance of neglect

A combination of two or more of these signs is a good indication of a winner. Then comes the real fun: the detective work. Many people who can figure out for themselves that an empty is a gold mine may still give up quickly. How can they find the owners? Stop for a minute here and think: how would you stalk the missing family? Put the book down and use your brain. What steps would you take?

Good, you're back. What did you come up with? If the best you could do was "knock on the door," you will realize what a good investment the price of this book was. Put on your deerstalker and follow me; here are some effective methods that I have used (and there's been only one owner that I never did find).

Walk around the neighborhood and ask the kids who are playing outside about the owners. They will usually know the names of the owners, how long ago they moved, and where they moved to. They will also offer special insights, such as, "Billy Johnson always cheated at hopscotch."

Knock on the neighbor's doors closest to the empty house until you find someone who's home. Tell the neighbor that you are interested in buying the Johnsons' house and that you need to find out their address and phone number in _____ (insert city the kids give you). Ask them if they know how to get a hold of the Johnsons or someone else who might know.

When doing this, make sure to let them know you are interested in buying the house. Neighbors want nothing more than to have that house occupied. Often they have been left with the charge to "look after the place," or to keep their ears open for word of a buyer. You may be just the person they have been listening for.

I recently found an empty house that looked like a perfect investment. It was just run-down enough to be too shabby for anyone looking for a place to live, but all it really needed was a good manicure. When I went next door to inquire, I was greeted by a housewife with a scowl usually reserved for encyclopedia salesmen, but that changed instantly when I told her I was interested in buying the house next door and needed the forwarding address of the owners. She took to the stairs like an Olympic sprinter in her hurry to help me. Out of breath, she handed me the address and said, "Please buy it. That place has been an eyesore for months!"

If the neighbors can't help, go to the post office and request the address change information on the property located at 1010 Elm

Street (or whatever it was). For a small fee (usually $1.00) the post office can supply you with the change of address. They will have you fill out a simple form (called a Change of Address Information Request Form), and in minutes you'll walk away with the previous occupant's new address.

If you haven't found the owner yet, the next step is to look up the property at the county courthouse and contact the lender that is listed as holding the mortgage. The lender may not even be aware that the house is vacant and will often be happy to assist you in locating the owners. Remember, the bankers know what a vacant house means too, and the last thing they want is to foreclose on a property.

Next, look up the tax rolls and see who is paying the property tax. (Boy, isn't this just a detective thriller?) Just go to your local courthouse, ask where the property assessor's office is, and ask them for a copy of that property's tax assessment. The most current billing name and address will appear on the assessment.

Call all the other Johnsons in the phone book (and wish the last name had been Klinkermann). Relatives often live in the same city, and a relative is sure to know the forwarding address. In fact, a local relative may have been charged with the responsibility of selling the house.

The last thing you could do is tape a note on the door boldly marked ATTENTION OWNER and hope that someone gives you a call pretty soon. This is often more effective than any of the other methods, especially when the owner has only moved a few miles out of town and comes once a week to collect the mail and look after the house. I was contacted recently by a property owner eight weeks after I had left a note for him.

This unusual method of looking for bargain properties has really been a gold mine for me. I enjoy the detective work and the fun in finding out who the owner is. And even better, when you do find the owner, you will find someone who will bless you forever. You came in when hope was lost and took away an alligator that was showing no signs of leaving.

One way to find more of these empties is to use "bird dogs." The idea is to find some people who will tell you about properties that are empty in your area. One perfect bird dog is your local postman. Go to your post office at 7:00 some morning and give each postman your business card; tell them you will pay them a nice reward if they call you about any empty homes they find that you later buy.

The only drawback with this method is that I have had a couple of postmen who saw my success and who suddenly became real estate investors. That won't happen with my other favorite bird dogs, the paperboys. Stop your newspaper carriers and make the same offer you did to the postmen. They are much less likely to become investors in the near future (at least not until they're eighteen), and they expect a smaller bonus.

For people who already own a few rental units, a twist on this technique of finding empties is to enlist your tenants. Simply contact each one and say that you are interested in finding empty homes in the neighborhood. Tell them that if they tell you about any empty home, and if you end up purchasing it, you will allow them to forget about a month's rent on their apartment. You will be on your way to having so many leads you won't know what to do with them all. You will have truly created a wealth-building team.

7. "FOR RENT" ADS

Not all owners who advertise their homes for rent really want to rent; many of them would love to sell but can't seem to find buyers. They either listed the house with a Realtor, whose commission forced them to ask for a too-large down payment, or they advertised the home for sale themselves without knowing how to write an attractive ad and never were able to sell it. Some of them will be the transferees, as discussed above, who simply ran out of time and have decided to rent their old house out "just until they can find a buyer." There are also rental property owners who are just finding out that managing a rental property is not the easy way to wealth they had imagined it would be.

When you pull open your paper to peruse the classifieds, look under the column labeled "Houses for Rent." Call about the homes that look attractive to you and ask the person who responds if she or he is the owner. If not, ask for the owner's telephone number. This is one time when you must talk to the right person; there's no need to carry on an extended conversation with a renter.

Tell the owner that you may be interested in buying a property like the one they have for rent. Ask the owner whether or not he or she ever thought of putting the property up for sale. The worst you will get is a no, and the best response I have had was from an owner who said, "I'm so glad you called; I've been trying to sell that house for months."

When you look through the ads, here are a few key things to look for that may indicate an investing opportunity:

"must rent quick"
a long-distance phone number
"available now"
"lease with option to buy"
"rent to own"

As you call on "for rent" ads, make sure you get the owner's address. Send a follow-up thank-you letter with a business card. Let them know that you might be interested in buying one of their properties in the future. As with farming, it's important to plant your seeds and cultivate regularly so that you will have the rich harvest you deserve.

Well, that's seven tools; three to go. All three are related to the same subject: the foreclosure. All good deals have one thing in common: the sellers are desperate. They—many times through no fault of their own—are in a position where they must sell. They need someone to buy their property immediately; that's why they are willing to give up their equity, and that's why the properties are good deals.

The factors that lead to good deals are the same factors that have given investors a bad name for years. An investor is seen by much of the public as a vulture, waiting for a hapless victim. What the public is generally unaware of, however, is that to the victims an investor is more like a knight on a white steed than a vulture on a dead branch. You are the person they were praying for; without your aid, the house would be foreclosed, and they would lose out entirely.

Whatever the reasons that led to foreclosure proceedings, once the owners have missed a few payments they need your help. You can buy a property during three phases of foreclosure: from the homeowner before foreclosure, from the trustee at foreclosure, or from the bank after foreclosure. And those are the remaining three tools.

Before we discuss each of these tools, let's take a look at the entire foreclosure process. It is a complex process, full of legal pitfalls at every turn. Therefore, it is not always the best place for the novice investor to start, in spite of its high rewards.

As a pilot, I have learned to appreciate the fact that my first solo flight was in a small Cessna instead of a jumbo jet. By comparison, I do not recommend that you try to get an investing career off the ground using foreclosures as your vehicle. They are powerful, but they are also a tricky business. I don't recommend this method to the beginner. I suggest that you start with a classified ad and, after you've bought and sold a couple of houses, only then try your hand at investing in foreclosures. If you've had some experience, read carefully and decide whether you are ready for investing in foreclosures. This caution is not to be taken lightly, as many investors, drawn by the huge rewards, have lost their financial lives investing in foreclosure properties.

In the United States there are two basic ways to foreclose on a mortgage or trust deed secured against a home. They are referred to as judicial and nonjudicial foreclosures. The basic difference between the two is that in a judicial foreclosure the home is foreclosed on through legal action as the result of a court judgment. In a nonjudicial foreclosure, the foreclosure comes as a result of action required in the original trust deed, and is brought about by the trustee because of nonpayment. The basic foreclosure procedure is different in some ways from state to state. (I would strongly suggest that before you invest in any foreclosure property you seek competent legal counsel from an attorney familiar with your state's foreclosure laws.)

In general, though, the time frame for foreclosures goes something like this:

The Foreclosure Process

Month	Action by home owner	Action by lender
1	Misses a payment	A late fee is charged.
2	"	"

3	"	Personal phone calls and a visit from the lender. Notice of default is filed.
4	"	Letters fom attorney.
5	"	"
6	Usually owner is moved out by now. The home is vacant.	A notice of sale is posted and published.
7	"	"
8	"	"
9	"	The sale.

The Cure Date

Between the date when the notice of default is filed and the foreclosure sale takes place, a date is set, according to state law, known as the "cure date." This date is, in most states, the point of no return for the home owner. On or before this cure date the loan must be brought current, either by the home owner or the party to whom the owner sells the home.

Bringing the loan current means paying all the delinquent payments, late fees, and usually the legal fees incurred by the lender for the foreclosure proceedings. You should check with the bank or lending institution holding the loan, but usually a loan brought current before the cure date will not suffer any further penalty. The original owner or the new owner will simply continue making payments to the lending institution as if nothing had ever happened.

Having established the basic mechanics of a foreclosure, we are now ready to look at the last three tools for finding good deals:

8. FORECLOSURE—BEFORE THE AUCTION

Very few home owners, when facing foreclosure, will run an ad in the "for sale by owner" section of the paper. Most people are very optimistic up to the end and would rather give up their home to foreclosure and let the cards fall where they may than give it away to a greedy investor. I have seen people hang on to the very end dozens of times, grasping at straws and every high-rate loan, just to hang on to the bitter end.

Investing in preforeclosure properties requires two steps: 1) finding these properties, and 2) teaching the home owners how it might be advantageous to sell to you rather than losing everything.

Learning about these properties involves more than reading the paper every night. You will have to locate a publication of foreclosure proceedings. The information must be made public, so the trustee must print a public notice of foreclosure. Where this notice is found varies from city to city. In most major urban areas the foreclosure notices appear in a special business, financial, and legal newspaper. In smaller areas, similar to where I live, these notices appear in the regular newspaper near the classified ads. If you're not sure where to find these notices, don't worry. I have developed a two-call method of locating the legal journals and notices in any area.

Three Steps—Two Phone Calls

Step 1 Look in your phone book and find the number for the local bar (legal) association. Usually it will be listed as something like "The Castle County American Bar Association." Call the association during normal business hours.

Step 2 When the receptionist answers at the bar association, you say the following: "Hi, I hope you are someone who can help me. I am trying to find out which publication in your county publishes the foreclosure notices. I am specifically interested in the notices of default and trustee sales. Can you help me?"

I have called hundreds of local bar associations and received the requested information from either the receptionist or someone else within the office in all but two cases (in those cases I had to call back later to talk to someone who wasn't in when I first called).

Step 3 The last step is to call the legal journal or notice publication and verify with them that they do publish the foreclosure information you need. If they do in fact print these notices, request a copy of their publication.

The notices will list the names of the trustees, of the owners, and the address of the property. That will give you enough information to contact the owners. If the owners have moved away, use the methods described above to locate them, and make your offer. Chances are whatever you offer will be better than the best alternative—foreclosure and at least seven years of bad credit ratings.

Buying from the owner is not without risk, of course. Many of the owners, unaware of the seriousness of the situation, will not be willing to consider selling their homes. For some perverse reason, they would rather let the bank take their home away than sell it to an investor. Many consider the matter to be very personal and will be offended at your proposals. Still others will delay selling, hoping for a stroke of good fortune to save them, until it is too late.

Some investors enjoy the direct approach: "Hi! I hear you're losing your house. Well, you might as well sell it to me, right?" (These investors are rarely elected president of the Dale Carnegie fan club.) I prefer a more indirect approach, mailing a letter to every owner. In the letter, I announce myself as a person who is interested in buying a home. I don't think it's necessary to pour salt into a wound, so I don't mention the big F word, *foreclosure.* Instead, I let them know that I buy houses and that if they are considering the sale of their home, or if they know of someone else who is interested in selling a home, they can give me a call.

This shotgun method may only get one return call in twenty, but when you compare the returns with the cost, a few stamps is a small price to pay for a house bought $10,000 under market value.

Sometimes the owners, realizing early that they have little chance of making up the back payments, will list their homes with a real estate agent. If they have, a quick drive-by will establish the fact. Simply call the number on the sign that the Realtor has pounded into their lawn, and you can deal with the owners through the conventional channels.

Buying from the owners is usually easiest, because they will often give up their equity if you will make up the back payments and cover the legal fees. And for your part, the only challenge you will face is convincing them that it is far better to walk away, letting you take over their problem, than to stay and fight a losing battle. If the home owners are not convinced that it is in their best interest to sell, I always suggest that they call the attorney of their choice for advice. Most attorneys will confirm what I have already told them.

While it's true that they are between a rock and a hard place (and you are the hard place), it is also true that you didn't create the rock—they did. And if you weren't there, the rock would surely crush them. All of the people who decry your efforts should consider what would happen if there were no investors available to help these people out. In every case, the bank would take the house back.

If you can't work out a deal with the owner before the cure date, what then? Well, you must then move on to tool number nine:

9. FORECLOSURE—AT THE AUCTION

When a property is foreclosed, a date is set for a foreclosure sale. This sale is generally held in a public place, such as the front steps of the county courthouse. A court-appointed official stands on the steps of the courthouse and reads the legal description of the foreclosure. The official then opens up the sale to bids on the property. The starting bid is the loan amount being foreclosed on plus the legal fees that have been incurred. The trustee or bank that is foreclosing on the loan comes ready to buy the property for the loan amount plus a few more dollars to guarantee that it will not be sold for less than the loan amount due them.

The property then is auctioned to the highest bidder. The successful bidder then usually has only a few hours in which to bring the cash or a certified bank check to pay for the home in full. The large amount of cash involved to buy properties this way limits most small investors. (In 99 percent of today's foreclosure sales, no one bids on the home but the bank.)

I have seen several small investors who are quite successful in buying properties at foreclosure auctions. To get the amounts of cash required at foreclosure auctions, these small investors usually find a wealthy investor with a lot of cash to back them.

Examples of people who might have cash would be your doctor, dentist, lawyer, or plumber. They use this investor's money and credit to buy the properties and to immediately get long-term financing.

To illustrate how this works, let me tell you about a property that was purchased at a foreclosure auction several months ago. This should serve as an excellent example of the profit potential in foreclosure properties. I'll first give you some background information before I list the facts and figures of the purchase.

The foreclosed home was originally purchased new by a young man with the help of a large down payment from his father. His father told him that after he closed the loan he would no longer give him anything financially. Well, the son closed the loan and moved in.

After several months in this new property, the son quit making the payments. In fact, after several months of nonpayment, with the banks and attorneys starting to get on his back, the son just moved out and abandoned the property.

The property sat vacant until the foreclosure sale. During this time the lawn died, weeds choked out the flowers and shrubs, and some kids broke in a back window and tracked mud all over the home. This once-beautiful property was a shambles. It seemed that no one wanted it. The bank held a $43,000 note against the property. Banks are not real estate investors, and they don't like having messy properties on their hands. A sharp investor found this property, saw beyond the mess, and realized that this was a place that had sold for $57,900 as a new home just eighteen months before. The investor looked past the weeds and dead lawn and saw a yard with a custom automatic sprinkler system.

The property was purchased by the investor at the foreclosure sale for $43,100. He put $400 into fixing up the yard, cleaning the inside walls and carpets, and replacing the broken window. He financed the property for $50,000 (the property was now appraised for over $60,000) and sold it to someone else for $58,000 with $5,000 down and the balance of the equity carried on a second mortgage at 12 percent interest for five years.

After the sale the investor immediately pocketed about $12,000 and held a note for $3,000 which with interest was paying him $832.23 a year for five years—not bad for the use of some money for just two weeks.

There are many investors who limit themselves to *only* buying properties at foreclosure auctions, and they generally do very well. But it is a specialty, and it requires research, patience, and a *lot* of cash to buy at auction.

10. FORECLOSURE—AFTER THE AUCTION

After the auction, if the property is not bid on by anyone but the bank, the property ownership goes to the bank. Today, because of the increasing numbers of foreclosures, the banks and loan institutions are flooded with properties that they have been forced to take back. The term used to refer to these properties that the banks have taken back is *real estate owned* (REO).

The bank is now put into the position of having to fix up, advertise, and sell properties to get out from underneath them. To relieve this headache, banks quite often find a real estate agent to do it all for them. Large banks may even have a whole division set up to dispose of these properties. Regardless of how the banks do it, if you are aware of properties that a bank might be receiving, or has received, you can personally meet with the bank officer in charge of the REOs and negotiate some excellent terms.

I have never found an officer in charge of a bank's REO portfolio to be anything but helpful, friendly, and eager to get rid of these properties. They are doing a good job for the bank if they don't have any properties to work with. You as an investor can help them out.

There is an interesting thing I've discovered about bank foreclosure officers: they can't ever really talk to people about their job. When they go to parties, they aren't likely to admit that they are in charge of foreclosing on people. It would be like E. F. Hutton in reverse; they would talk, but nobody would listen. Meet them one-on-one in their own environment—at the bank. Get them to talk about their work. You might be the first person who has shown a positive interest in their job, and you might walk out with a dozen good leads.

Buying REOs through banks and having them finance the transaction can be a great help to a young investor without established credit. The bank is in a position where they will overlook a lot of things in giving you the loan. To succeed in getting the loans, I have found that a professional, honest attitude is essential. They may overlook a lot of things, but they aren't going to go out on a limb with a slick or dangerously uneducated investor. The last thing they want is to have to foreclose on the property again.

FHA and VA Foreclosures

A common misconception most home owners have when they get a Federal Housing Administration (FHA) or Veterans Administration (VA) loan is that the government agency is actually lending them the money. The truth of the matter is that the FHA or VA in almost all situations is only guaranteeing the loan. The way that a typical FHA loan works is that the buyer first applies for the FHA loan through a local bank or savings and loan. The loan institution does all the checks and qualifying, then sends the completed loan application to the regional FHA office for approval. Once the loan is approved, the closing is done through the lending institution.

As for the interest, on loans approved before 1984 one-half point extra interest is charged on the loan to insure it against the possibility that the borrower might default and force the bank to repossess the home, causing the government agency to buy the home from the lender. (This insurance charge is referred to as the loan's MIP or mortgage insurance premium.)

Beginning in 1984, the Federal Housing Administration changed the rules concerning the payment of the insurance premium for new FHA loans. Instead of paying an extra half point of interest, you borrow, on closing, a prepaid insurance fee. This insurance fee varies according to loan amount. On a $43,000 loan this fee is over $1,200. So under the new program you would borrow on your loan $44,200 instead of $43,000. Under this method your interest rate is not raised by one-half point.

Thus the protection offered through these government loans guarantees the private lender that in the event of the necessary foreclosure of a government-issued property, the government agency will buy the property from the lender. The private lender with this type of loan will not be stuck with another property to fix up, advertise, and sell; the government will.

In most major areas there are dozens of government (FHA and VA) foreclosure properties available for sale. It is staggering to see what good deals there are.

These government agencies offer these properties for sale to the general public. Usually every two weeks a list is sent out by mail to investors and Realtors or inserted into a major Sunday paper, listing the homes the government has for sale. Some real diamonds in the rough are hidden in these government repossessions.

Let me explain the major differences between the VA and the FHA programs. In both, the homes are initially put up for sale on a bid basis. These properties are listed for sale with a bid date given. If you are interested in bidding on the property, you fill out one of the government purchase forms (available from the government offices or through your local real estate agents that are listed with the government agencies). Along with this purchase form you must give a refundable earnest money deposit.

On the specified date all offers are opened, and the best offer is the one accepted. If there are no offers made, or if none are acceptable, this process is repeated, or the property is put on a first-come first-served basis, in which case the agency will accept the first acceptable offer.

The big differences between the VA and the FHA loans come in the form of qualification and financing. The Housing and Urban Development (HUD) program, which covers all FHA repossessions, requires that purchasers obtain their own outside financing. This means that you would have to go out and qualify for a standard FHA or conventional loan and put up with the standard qualifying process.

The VA program offers purchasers long-term, thirty-year financing at competitive market rates. These loans, or "contracts," do not contain acceleration or due-on-sale clauses. They are really a very attractive loan instrument. The qualifying is easier than the typical "pound of flesh and quart of blood" that FHA requires on its loan applications.

There are loans available from time to time that offer special financing for investors and even money beyond the purchase amount, which allows the investor the necessary cash to "rehab" a property back into condition so that it may be occupied.

For more information on FHA and VA repossessions in your area, contact your state's FHA or VA housing offices. The addresses for these offices are listed in the reference guide of *The Real Estate Greenbook,* which can be purchased through the National Committee for Real Estate Investment, P.O. Box 796, Provo, Utah 84603, (801) 225-8777. These government offices can provide you with full information on the dates of sales and any special local restrictions.

To restate my warning: Foreclosures are complicated and require much more knowledge than I can provide you with in this section. Each state has its own unique foreclosure laws. Learn the laws for your state.

Don't worry; even though I can't teach you everything in one chapter, I won't leave you hanging. There are several experts in your own city who can give you a thorough education, such as real estate attorneys, bank officers, real estate agents, and other investors who specialize in foreclosures. Also, it doesn't cost anything to attend a foreclosure auction. Find out where notices are published, read the notices carefully, talk to the owners, attend the auctions, and ask the experts. In time you too will be an expert, and you will be ready for this exciting, rewarding method of finding good deals.

Ten tools. I have tried every one of them myself, and they all work. They are the best tools for finding good deals in real estate that exist. Which one are you going to start with? My own personal favorites are buying foreclosure properties from the bank, after the sale; playing Dick Tracy and tracking down owners of empties; and the good old classified ads, where I've found most of my good deals.

If you think that one tool is especially well suited to you, give it a try. You don't have to actually buy any property yet, if you're not ready. But start talking to people. Let them know you are interested in buying properties. Make a few phone calls and personal visits, and in no time at all you'll find yourself feeling comfortable talking to sellers about their homes.

Good deals are all around you, and if you don't take advantage of them, somebody else will. Walk before you run, but start walking *now.*

CHAPTER 6

Buying Right

The man who insists upon seeing with
perfect clearness before he decides,
never decides.
  —HENRI FREDERIC AMIEL

The big school Christmas included a gift exchange. Every guest brought a gift, and the presents were stacked on a table. One stood out easily; larger than the rest, it was magnificently wrapped in gorgeous paper, bedecked with ribbons and bows. Every eye was on the same box as the guests drew numbers. The girl who got number one lost no time in selecting the gaudily wrapped package. Holding her breath in anticipation, she shredded the beautiful paper in her hurry to get at the gift. Inside the box was a single scrap of paper with this note:

"I only had enough money to buy the paper and ribbons. Sorry, no present."

It has taken me several years to reach a point where I know what I'm going to find under the wrapper. Even now I'm sometimes initially deceived by outward appearances. Everything looked great right up until closing, when, suddenly, there were little surprise charges tucked neatly away between the lines of the contract. That didn't mean they weren't great deals, although I have backed out of one or two at closing.

You must know exactly what you are getting into before you buy a property. You have to be able to analyze your investments, and that means knowing every hidden flaw. Part of that, of course, is learning how to recognize the value of a deal without being deceived by outward appearances.

In the last chapter we looked at tools for finding good deals. But when you've found what appears to be good, how can you be

sure? What do you look for, and what do you look out for? How
do you cover yourself legally, and how can you get the best deal
possible? This chapter answers all of these questions and more,
as we investigate some of the dangers in buying; how to write an
offer that covers your assets; and what to expect at the closing.

There are a few dangers to be aware of when you look at a
property for the first time:

> Nonassumable loans
> High mortgage rates/payments
> Negative cash flow
> Adjustable-rate mortgages
> Short-term balloon mortgages
> Large down payments
> Overpriced properties
> Properties needing major repairs
> Properties in bad areas of town

As you can see, there are many factors that could increase the
risks of buying a property far beyond the benefits. However,
there are many ways for an investor to lessen or even entirely
eliminate these risks in the search for a good deal. Most properties that seem to have a great many liabilities may actually turn
into good deals, if you can avoid in advance the problems described below.

Nonassumable Loans

If you are new to real estate, you may not know what the word
assumable means. Quite simply, if an existing loan is assumable,
the buyer can take over the payments from the seller and assume
responsibility for the loan. If it is nonassumable, the buyer is
stuck finding a new loan at current rates. Since interest rates on
older, assumable loans are usually lower, it makes sense to look
for them.

There are legal manuals to help you work around the nonassumable loans that you may come across. But why hassle with
them? All that takes is a lot of time and trouble. Assumable loans
are much easier to find and to use.

For example, loans through the Federal Housing Administration (FHA) or the Veterans Administration (VA) are ideal. The cost for an investor to assume one of these loans is only $45, and the qualifications are easily met. The conditions of these loans were probably best stated by the Rice Brothers when they said, "The only qualification to assume one of these loans is to hold a mirror under your nose and be able to fog it up." Of course, the process may take slightly longer than that, but the point is a good one. Why tangle yourself up in a nonassumable mortgage when there are so many of these other loans available?

About 1978, most banks found themselves in a horrible position: they were forced by the money market to pay higher interest rates on savings accounts than they could collect from their old real estate loans. To put an end to such a catastrophe, they began to include a "due-on-sale clause" in every real estate loan. This clause states that the full amount of the loan may be called due upon sale of the property. Such a loan is automatically nonassumable, and therefore one to avoid. If you are considering a purchase, find out how old the existing loan is. If it is pre-1978, chances are good that it is assumable.

For the bank, calling the loan due is merely an option, but if the interest rates have risen since the loan was written, the bank will probably ask you to qualify for the loan (if it doesn't call for complete repayment) and then adjust the interest rate upward in order to increase the bank's earnings.

High Mortgage Rates/Payments

Is the property that you are interested in able to pay for itself? If the property is a single-family dwelling, is the mortgage payment affordable to people in the middle-income range? If the property is a rental unit, does it have a positive cash flow already? The more attractive the property is, the more likely that it will prove advantageous for you to own it.

With the advent of graduated payment mortgages (GPMs), which start with a very low monthly payment and then increase every year, many people who could not afford to buy a home were suddenly able to make the first- and second-year payments. They tied themselves into a GPM, thinking that in three or four years they would—thanks to raises and cost-of-living increases—

be able to afford the higher payments. But when the expected pay increases didn't materialize and the house payments continued to rise, they ended up in serious trouble, many times in foreclosure.

The temptation for the investor is to think that these distress properties are excellent deals. They can take over the loan and buy the property with nothing down. And the owners are willing to walk away without anything for their equity, so what could be better? The payments are a little high, and due to get higher next year, but the price is right, and it's a nothing-down deal.

Don't be fooled. When time comes to sell, who is going to buy the house from you? If you can't offer low monthly payments, price is meaningless.

Negative Cash Flow

There is only one way to lessen the risk that a negative cash flow can bring to an investment: avoid it like the plague! If you are going to have to take money out of your wallet every month to keep the property afloat until you can sell it, you are *not* finding a good deal. There are too many positive cash flow properties out there to waste your time asking for trouble.

Yes, I've heard the argument that if you can withstand a negative cash flow for a year or so, you'll more than make it up in tax savings and in profits when you sell. But I have never had to invest in negative cash flow properties to make money, and you shouldn't have to either. And you'll sleep better at night if your properties are breaking even or making money each month, rather than costing you precious cash.

Adjustable Rate Mortgages (ARMs)

Use caution in deciding to accept this method of financing. You should be aware that as interest rates in the country go up, your mortgage payment will go up too. Before you commit to an adjustable rate mortgage, be sure that the payments after the increase in interest rates are still reasonable.

Let me give you some guidelines concerning adjustable rate mortgages:

There are hundreds of different types of ARMs. Some are much better than others. The two most important areas to scrutinize are: What protection do you have against large increases in monthly payments, and how will these increases (or decreases) be handled? To find out, ask your lender the following list of questions:

- On what financial index are changes in payments based?
- Can this index be changed during the course of the loan?
- Does the loan have a cap (maximum amount of interest or highest payment that can be charged)?
- If this cap is on the payment, how is the negative amortization handled?
- Is this cap for the life of the loan?
- Is there an annual cap?
- What happens if the index decreases?
- What are the reverse caps?
- How often is the index reviewed and the payment adjusted?
- How much more would this ARM cost than a fixed rate loan under a worst situation scenario?
- Can this loan be assumed?
- Can the loan be refinanced?
- Are there any prepayment penalties?

The things I especially look for in ARMs are assumability, the ability to convert the loan to a level interest loan, low annual and lifetime caps on the interest rate that avoid negative amortization, and a tie to a longer-term index. My best advice concerning ARMs would be the wise adage *caveat emptor*, meaning "let the buyer beware."

Short-term Balloon Mortgages

You should almost always try to avoid balloon loans (loans that come due in a large final lump sum). However, there are occasions when you might consider assuming a balloon. In those situations, you should require that the loan has at least seven years of low payments until the large, balloon payment is due. The reason behind this requirement is simple. If you decide to hold on to the property for two years before selling it, there will remain a five-year period of time before the loan comes due, and to a buyer, five years is much more attractive than three months.

Avoid a short-term balloon (less than five years) for yourself. There is too much of a chance that it will backfire. But there is a way to use a balloon loan to create a good deal. Instead of taking one out yourself, look for someone who has a short-term balloon coming due. Here you will find a distressed and flexible seller.

A word of caution: If you do take on a balloon mortgage, it is never too soon to start examining your options in the event that you do not or cannot sell the property. You may be stuck with the balloon payment after all, and it would be best for you to be prepared. Whatever you do, don't let that balloon pop in your face!

Large Down Payments

Leverage ... what a beautiful word. Use leverage correctly, and you can move yourself into a position of financial freedom faster than you would ever believe possible.

There is no question that large down payments can be a problem. The more you must pay in a down payment, the sooner you will run out of cash. A large down payment will also make it harder for you when it comes time for you to try to sell the property. A good rule of thumb is this: Whenever you sell, always recover the full down payment that you originally invested, plus a little extra.

You should set a standard for what you expect out of a sale. For example, whenever you buy a house, you could set a limit of 6 percent or less of the asking price as the down payment you would be willing to pay. Later, you would be able to sell the house, asking for less than 10 percent of the price down, and still make a healthy profit.

Overpriced Properties

An overpriced property is not a good deal. If you are paying more than the property is worth, you are defeating the purpose of real estate investing. When you buy an overpriced property, you will have to hold on to it for a long time in order to build up the equity that will enable you to make a profit by selling it. As trite and overused as this statement is, it still contains an ageless truth—buy low, *sell* high!

Properties Needing Major Repairs

I'm not saying that these properties can't be profitable. Some may be very beneficial to you, but they will *always* be costly. The price that you could pay to renovate a broken-down property could even exceed the price of building a brand-new one! And this is ignoring the cost of professional labor, if it is needed to bring wiring or plumbing up to local building codes, as well as any inspection fees you may need to pay.

If you are planning on doing the renovation yourself, ask this question: Would it be more profitable for me to spend my time buying and selling homes or renovating homes? Buying a property needing extensive repairs is a very different thing from buying a lower-priced property needing a bit of fixing up. Buy that home in need of a little cosmetic work; forget the one that will require a face-lift. In this area, as in every other, let common sense be your guide. Use caution; above all, be realistic!

If you have trouble recognizing just what you should be looking for when you analyze a property to see if it needs major repairs, please see chapter 11. There you will find a complete description of a property analysis system that includes an on-site physical checklist. If in doubt about a property's physical condition, always seek expert advice. In this case an ounce of prevention is worth a lot more than a pound of cure.

Properties in Bad Areas of Town

Just because a property has a low down payment and small mortgage installments, it is not necessarily a good deal. Any benefit that you may get from buying a property cheap will pale in comparison to the disadvantages of having to sell below market value or being forced to rent at a negative cash flow. If you are in an area that does not rent well, your vacancies will cost you money—a lot of it.

Before you buy, do a property analysis. Remember, there are more factors that define a "bad area" than trashy streets or vagrants. The considerations of safety and cleanliness are, of course, important, but you should also think about the way that you will be using the property. Is the area right for your purposes? If you are planning to sell a property soon after you buy it, look for an area with stable property values in a reasonable price range. An analysis such as this should help you a great deal when you are deciding what and where to buy. Fill out an analysis form on each property that interests you, then evaluate the information to find the best situation for you. If a property fits within the guidelines that you have set, *buy it!*

Avoid these nine problems at all costs, especially when you're just getting started. By doing so you will avoid some of the snares and pitfalls that cut a lot of investors' careers short.

Next are a few things you should look for, ask for, and (whenever possible) insist on when buying real estate:

> Low payments
> Assumable loans
> Instant equity
> Escape clauses

Low Payments

At the bottom line of every mortgage is the monthly payment. If you cannot afford the payments, or if the rent won't make the payments, you are buying an alligator (the buzzword in real estate for a property with a negative cash flow). The name is accurate, because these negative cash flows can be very powerful animals, and they are safe—as long as you can feed them. But the minute you run out of green stuff to keep them sated, they will eat you up. Maybe you can afford to feed a whole alligator zoo, but I would rather pass up what appears to be a great deal if I can see that it is an alligator in disguise.

Structure *every* deal so that your payments are within your budget. Instead of giving a seller $2,000 down and $300 a month for five years, offer the same down payment with $150 a month for ten years. Keep your payments low and all potential alligators under control. If you cannot structure low-enough payments, I would strongly suggest that you look elsewhere; you are only looking for the best deals.

Assumable Loans

I've already mentioned assumable loans. But the fact that a loan is assumable doesn't mean the seller will be willing to let you assume it. And yet your only alternative is to visit your local bank and get a new loan.

Whenever you have to go to the bank to get a conventional loan, just try to get out paying only the charges they told you about when you sat down. By the time they are through with their "origination fees" and "points" and this and that other charge, you will likely walk out feeling as though you have been professionally fleeced. Every time I close a bank loan I want to call the police and report a robbery.

To gently coerce the sellers into letting you assume their loans, you must convince them that you are a good credit risk. One of the best ideas is to put together a biography—just a short history that shows your stability, accompanied by recommendations from respectable people, such as a minister, an attorney, or a local politician.

If the sellers still seem unwilling to cooperate, explain that, with the extra cost of a new loan, you will have to lower your offer substantially if you can't assume their loan. If that doesn't work, you probably aren't working with motivated sellers.

Instant Equity

Go for the instant equity, if there is any. Instant equity is the difference between what you pay for the property and its actual market value. If you find a property worth $100,000, should you buy it for $110,000? Of course not! What about $100,000? No way! You need to buy equity; $80,000 is more like it. The same holds true for any amount of money. If someone wants to sell you a baseball card for 50 cents, should you buy it? Well, if you want to sell it and make money, you need to have some idea of the card's market value, don't you?

I recently got a call from an investor who needed advice. He told me all about the property he was considering—about the new paint, the 13.5 percent VA loan he was to assume, and what a great price he was paying. He said he was getting this home for only $78,000, with $15,000 down. I asked if the property had been appraised, and he assured me that it had: it was worth $90,000.

Then I asked him the question that he should have asked long before calling me. "What kind of appraisal was done?" He wasn't sure, but he thought it was an accurate appraisal. I strongly suggested that he find out more about the appraisal: was it a formal appraisal, prepared by an accredited appraiser, or was it a market appraisal done by a Realtor? In this case it was neither; a neighbor down the street had suggested that the house might be worth "around $90,000."

When he followed my suggestion and insisted on a professional appraisal, it turned out that the property was actually worth $72,500—a far cry from $90,000, and well under the $78,000 price he was prepared to pay. Determine the true market value of a house as part of your analysis, and only buy properties with built-in equity.

Escape Clauses

In every offer you make, include at least a couple of escape clauses. What are they? They're clauses that allow you to back out of the deal without suffering any consequences if something should go wrong between the acceptance of the offer and the closing.

Always include a lifeboat when you set sail. I hate to tell another war story so soon, but this important lesson was driven home only a few days ago, when I got a call from a desperate man in an eastern state. He had retired there, taking his $25,000 savings with him, "to invest in real estate." He had heard how much money could be made with a few shrewd investments, and he could hardly wait to get started.

P. T. Barnum would have said that there is an investor like him born every mintue. In his first deal he was required to turn over $16,000 cash earnest money to the sellers. (This is not a made-up story; it's real life, in Technicolor!) When he went to the bank to apply for a loan on the property, he put "unemployed" in the blank that requested employment information. The application was immediately rejected. When he returned to the sellers to ask for his $16,000 back, what do you think they told him? They said that he was breaking the contract, so he would have to forfeit his earnest money.

I agonized to think of this man's lifetime dreams shattered by a few too many weasels and not enough weasel clauses (another name for escape clauses). I advised him to seek the best legal aid he could afford. Other than that, there is really nothing he can do; he is an adult, capable of entering into a contractual relationship the same as you or I.

Where did he go wrong? Well, first, he gave a cash earnest money to the seller; second, he made that earnest money for more than $100; and third, he failed to include an escape clause.

An escape clause is a clause that every buyer should include in an offer; it allows him or her to wriggle out of a contract should anything unforeseen (such as a loan rejection) come up that will make a deal infeasible or impossible. It is a lifeboat that should be on every investor's ship, so that when the *Titanic* deal hits an iceberg, a safe escape is possible.

Let me give you a few escape clauses. Don't ever make a written offer without including at least one of the following:

1) *"Offer subject to partner's approval."*

If you don't have a partner, find one. You do need a second opinion, and even if your partner is only your best friend or your spouse, you are able to change your mind any time between the time your offer is accepted and the day of the closing. You can simply say, "I'm sorry, but my partner will not approve this deal, so I cannot go through with it."

2) *"Offer subject to satisfactory inspection of loan records and rental records."*

This is another case of not taking anything at face value. Just because you were verbally promised that every unit in the fourplex was rented out at $450 does not mean that you will ever see $1,800 in rents. And when the owners assure you that the payments are only $450 a month, don't be surprised to find out that they made a little mistake and that they meant to say $540. With this escape clause, you are free to cancel your offer if you do not approve of the past records—no matter what was said.

3) *"Offer subject to purchaser being able to obtain 30-year permanent _____ (conventional/FHA/VA) financing at an interest rate less than _____ percent, with no more than $_____ being paid by buyer for total origination fees, points, and closing costs."*

This is a big one. If you are unable—for any reason—to obtain satisfactory financing (the problem our friend faced), you can back out of the deal with your earnest money in hand.

4) *"Seller to provide a complete inspection and written report of all mechanical systems by an appropriate licensed contractor. Inspection to be at the expense of the seller. Offer subject to buyer's approval of the completed written inspections."*

With this clause you are forcing the seller to help you appraise the entire house, and if the inspection does not produce a clean bill of health, you are free to walk away without losing dime one.

You can also make each offer subject to having the home inspected by the local county or city building inspector and certified that it is up to code. The fee for this inspection is usually $10 or less. The inspector will go through and warrant that the property meets the city housing codes. If it doesn't they will note on a rejection card which items need to be brought up to date.

Your offer can state that any deficient items must be brought up to code by the seller before closing. This wording can save you thousands in repairs.

While it is true that there is more aspirin in the world than headaches, think a minute about the man who failed to include the proper clause in his home purchase. I believe that some headaches—when they get into the $16,000 range—would require an aspirin the size of Mount Everest.

You should understand the function of the earnest money itself. In any legally binding contract, consideration must be given for a promise to be binding on the promisor—the one who makes the promise. This consideration must be of some value, and money will do just fine. It does not, however, have to be $16,000, as was offered by the man in Florida. I try never to give more than $50 as earnest money.

You should not give cash if you can avoid it, and if the seller absolutely insists, do not make a check payable to the seller. Instead make it out to the title officer, real estate attorney, real estate sales company, or closing agent to hold in escrow until closing. Once that money is gone, even if you have to back out of the deal and are covered by a good parachute clause, you may have to take the seller to court to recover it. Always make the check payable to the title company that is handling the transaction, or give the seller a promissory note, like the one shown below. Not all sellers will accept a promissory note as sufficient earnest money, but most will, so you should at least try.

MARC GARRISON   PROMISSORY NOTE   No. _____
P.O. Box 1096, Orem, Utah **84057**

The undersigned promises to
PAY TO THE ORDER OF _____ $_____

_____ DOLLARS

Memo: This promissory note is to ~~SAMPLE~~ earnest money for the purchase of the property located

at _____ ,

provided all items and condi... of the Earnest Money Receipt and Offer to Purchase signed and

dated _____ by signer are agreed to be Sellers (copy attached). This promissory note is

due and payable at closing of aforementioned offer.

The National Committee for Real Estate Investment, P.O. Box 796, Provo, Utah 84603

The closing itself will present you with some costs that you need to be aware of when you are analyzing a transaction. Here are a few of the typical expenses that will be involved in a closing:

1. Assumption fees: Usually about $45, but check with your bank; they can vary greatly.
2. Processing fees: This is to pay the title officer or attorney for closing the loan.
3. Recording fee: This is to pay for recording the new deed.
4. Title insurance and abstract examination: While the seller usually pays for this, there is no firm or fast rule other than *make sure it gets done!*
5. Appraisal: You may want to make your purchase offer contingent on having the property's value formally appraised. When you think about it, this is some very inexpensive in-

surance to guarantee that you are getting a good deal when
you first begin.

6. Credit report, loan points, origination fee: All of these are
fees charged by the lending institution when you have to
get new financing to buy. They vary widely in every situation, and you must know exactly what you are going to
have to pay before you go to closing. Check with your
banker about these frightening fees.

Whew! All of this is a lot to think about. It's almost like chewing two wads of gum while drinking a pop, eating a sandwich,
playing the piano, and reading a book. But I sure bet you could
find a way to do all of these things at the same time if you knew
you would make $10,000 for your trouble.

When you are starting out, consider taking on a partner for
your first investment. I have had a lot of good experiences with
partners. I have also heard a lot of war stories about some of the
perils and pitfalls. The best advice I can offer is get to know your
partner well before you get hitched, so to speak. By doing this you
can save yourself a lot of grief.

However, there is one partnership I recommend highly. Find an
experienced investor and work out a one-time partnership. You
can work together, and with your brawn and the other investor's
brains (experience), you can share the work and the profits.

Buying right includes everything you've read so far, and more.
You must use one of the tools for finding a good deal; you must
actively seek problem sellers and yet avoid problem properties;
you must structure your offers so you can enjoy positive cash
flow and instant equity. Next we'll look at negotiating with the
seller and actually making a written offer. That's not really the
hard part, but for first-time investors an attack of sweaty palms at
this stage often holds them back from actually making an offer.

Making Money at the Kitchen Table

Fear nothing, for every renewed effort
raises all former failures into lessons,
all sins into experience.
—KATHERINE TINGLEY

Unless you can talk the owner into seeing things your way, you will always end up paying more than you need to. I have learned—usually the hard way—what works best with home owners who are selling their houses.

First, understand that they are not investors. They are doctors, grocery clerks, housewives, househusbands, and every other stripe of citizen imaginable. They will only be involved in two or three such transactions in their lifetimes, and most of them are afraid when it comes time to talk terms. Their fears are based on a lack of knowledge; most real estate terms are hard to understand, and few people take the time to study even the basics.

Imagine how many times that fear is multiplied when they are trying to sell the home without the help of a real estate agent, and some know-it-all investor starts talking about "negative amortizations" and "escape clauses."

Try a tactful, helpful approach. I always introduce myself as a young family man interested in buying their home as an investment. I don't pull out the HP-12C calculator, and I always discuss terms on their level. If it is apparent that they don't understand what I am talking about, I back up and explain myself carefully. A well-structured deal should satisfy all of their needs and mine as well, and I know that I can structure just such a deal in every case.

111

Whether you know it or not, you begin the negotiating process the moment you meet the seller. You both automatically size each other up, trying to figure just how much to give and take. In many ways this is the most crucial aspect of buying real estate. If you are able to negotiate a good deal with the seller, face to face, it's usually a simple matter of writing up the offer and signing it. After that it's all red tape and formalities. The sale is actually made at the kitchen table, not at the closing.

Here are a few basic negotiating strategies to keep in mind, whether you are buying or selling.

First impressions count. Before you stop by to visit the sellers, take a look at yourself in a full-length mirror. Are you looking at someone you would want to sell your house to? As an investor, you will often want the sellers to take their equity on an interest-bearing note, rather than in cash. Do you *look* like a good credit risk? Their impression of you when they first open the door will often make the difference between a sale and another disappointment.

Establish rapport. Your first task once inside the door is to make the sellers feel at home—which is exactly where they are. Find common ground; talk about your interests, or show an interest in something of theirs, such as a picture on the wall or a piano in the living room. Forget about the house and the price for a minute, and get to know the owners.

Talk price last. Don't jump into a discussion of price and terms just yet. As you walk around the house, talk about features and faults, but leave the price tag out of the picture. Talk about dollars after your cursory inspection is finished, and then get the seller to name a price.

Never give unless you get. Start with the assumption that you will get everything in the house, from the Tupperware to the wedding albums, and work from there. I'm being a little facetious, but if you start there, then every time the owner takes something away from you—such as the kids—you can expect a concession in return. If they want to keep the refrigerator, say, "Fine, but I assumed that was included. Of course that will be reflected in the price."

If they say yes, keep working on it. Both parties to a negotiation establish negotiating ranges. If they accept your first offer instantly, you obviously were near the top end of their range, and you can always ask for more. For example, if they accept your first offer of $50,000 (and they were asking $56,000), continue your offer with, "Of course, that includes the cars out front and your firstborn." Now you're more likely to find yourself somewhere closer to the bottom of their range, and the real negotiating can begin.

Ask open-ended questions. I always lead the conversation with open-ended questions. For example, when a clerk in the drugstore approaches and asks, "Can I help you?" you are perfectly free to say "No, thanks." If, on the other hand, the clerk asks, "How can I help you?" your "No, thanks" isn't a workable answer. The second question is almost the same as the first, but it doesn't allow a simple yes or no answer. Start your questions with *how* and *why*, and avoid questions that can be answered with a simple yes or no.

The second trick of guiding a conversation is to ask questions that begin with a statement and end with a request for agreement. An example is, "This bathroom does need a lot of fixing up, doesn't it?" The question only allows two responses: agreement ("Well, yes, I guess it does.") or defensive disagreement ("No, not too much work . . ."). In either case, you are directing the flow of the conversation. Comment on every room in the house. Not all of your comments should be derogatory; if you like something, say so. But if there is something that you dislike, attach a "Don't you agree?" question to your comments.

Establish your negotiating range before you talk price. You will often know the asking price before you actually sit down and make an offer, and you will be expected to have a specific dollar amount in mind by the time your tour is finished. If you know the sellers are asking $60,000, how much should you offer? And how high will you actually go? That's the basis for your negotiating range.

If you've been doing your homework, you shouldn't have too much trouble estimating a fair market value for the home. As an investor you should not be willing to pay that price, unless a minimum fix-up investment will substantially raise the value of the home.

In the example above, where the owners are asking $60,000,

you have determined that the real value of the home is between $56,000 and $58,000: that's what you could resell it for. Now you must decide how much to offer, and how much you are actually willing to pay. There is no set rule for determining your range, but in this case you might decide that you will offer $52,000 and pay no more than $55,000. If the sellers are unmotivated, your offer will likely be rejected out of hand. If they really want to sell, however, they will probably reject it but show an interest in continuing the negotiation.

Another important factor in setting a range is that by offering less than you actually expect to pay, you are inviting the sellers to negotiate, and they will have the opportunity to save face when you begrudgingly give ground and raise your offer. Many new investors, in an effort to make a fair offer, start the bidding at the top of their negotiating range. Then they're surprised when the sellers don't accept the first offer. They have no more room to give, and they lose the deal.

Let the owners know you are willing to negotiate. An offer made with a "take it or leave it" attitude—especially an offer at the bottom of your negotiating range—will often be left, and the sellers will shut you out mentally. If that happens, you might as well take a walk, because you will have lost the rapport you established at the beginning.

Don't talk price and terms until you are sitting down at the table. As they say, there's a time and a place for everything. While you're walking around the house, that's the time for looking at the features, such as the peeling paint on the outside trim or the broken railing on the stairs. Look at each room carefully, without allowing yourself to be sidetracked by a discussion of price and terms. Wait until you are sitting down with a legal pad, a pen, and a calculator. That's the time and place for money talk.

TALKING TERMS

We all come to that dreadful moment of truth when we must sit down with the seller at the kitchen table and come to terms. And here is where we seem to have the most difficulty. It shouldn't be that much trouble, really.

Sit down with the seller and talk to him or her, face to face, in plain English. Discuss what you like and dislike. If you seem to be faced with an impasse on one subject, such as the price, put off further discussion for later and agree on some of the minor points.

Avoid the confusion of legalese. Talk about monthly payments, the assumption of the existing loans, and the price as though you were haggling over the price of a toaster at a garage sale.

Keep in mind that your best bet is to assume the existing loans (if they are assumable) and give the seller a contract for his equity. As you discuss a contract, remember that the payments are a function of price and interest. You can offer a higher price if they will lower the interest rate, and your payments will stay the same. This will affect their tax consequences, but in a positive way, since more of their profit will be in the form of long-term capital gains and less in the form of interest income. (Check with a real estate attorney or a CPA about current tax laws. At the time of this writing, a bill is due to become law that would require sellers to charge an interest rate competitive with conventional lenders.)

If you don't know how to figure out what your payments will be, buy and learn to use a financial calculator. They can be found for under $30, and they are absolutely indispensable. I use Hewlett-Packard's HP-12C and recommend it highly. It can tell me almost instantly what my monthly payment will be on any kind of loan I can imagine.

As you talk to the seller, write everything down. Take a legal pad with you, and every time either of you makes a suggestion, write it down. As you come to agreement on this point or that, circle it and initial it. Then, when you have agreed on every point, write up your offer on an earnest money and purchase offer form, available in any stationery and office supply store.

If you don't know how to fill out the offer properly, have an expert help you. Your title officer, real estate attorney, or an experienced investor can help you translate the terms you have agreed on into legal mumbo jumbo.

Once you have come to terms with the seller and your written offer has been accepted, you are pretty much done. Your title officer will explain how to close the deal, and all you have to do is show up at the closing, pay the closing costs and down payment, and sign a few papers. That's it; you own your first investment property!

Preparing to Sell or Rent

Frustration is not having anyone to
blame but yourself.
    —*Bits and Pieces*

Have you ever seen a car after it has been detailed by a car dealer? Talk about miracles. A friend of mine traded in his old junker for a new car recently. If all the old, beaten-up cars in the world were laid end to end, his old car would still stand out like a sore thumb. Later that week I drove by the lot where he had traded it in, and I saw a car that resembled his clunker—but this car *couldn't* be the same one; I didn't think anyone could resurrect my friend's dinosaur. Curious, I stopped for a closer look.

There was just enough resemblance to convince me that this was the same car my friend had turned in only a week before. The tires were that glossy black that tires only are for the first fifty miles or so, the chrome shone like new, the stains in the upholstery left by uncounted Pepsis were gone, and the carpet had been ripped out and replaced.

By this time the dealer's C.A.R.S. (Customer Approach Radar System) had alerted him to my presence, and he was on his way out to sell me one of his beauties. I asked what had happened to the bomb that had existed only a week before. He laughed and explained "detailing." It was my turn to laugh; that's exactly what I had been doing to my investment houses for a couple of years.

When you are preparing to sell a property, what is your first consideration? It should be the buyers you will be looking for. What can you do to convince them they should pay top dollar for the property? And what is top dollar? How much fixing up is enough, without being too much?

There is an idea so universal and true that economists have even given it a name: the law of diminishing returns. According to

117

this law, each dollar invested in production will produce a greater return than the previous dollar, up to a certain point. At some point the return is the same as the investment, and thereafter less than the investment.

The law can be applied to almost anything. If you buy one Popsicle and eat it, your enjoyment will be greater than the price invested in the Popsicle, or you wouldn't have bought it. That might hold true for the second and third Popsicle as well, but at some point your enjoyment—the return on your investment—would not exceed the cost, and you would quit eating.

This law can be demonstrated graphically:

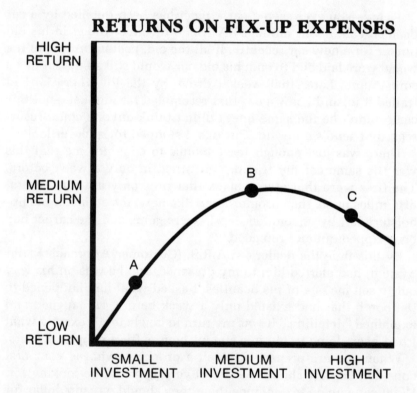

RETURNS ON FIX-UP EXPENSES

At point A, a small investment would mean cleaning up the yard by mowing it, trimming the plants, edging the grass, and pulling the weeds. It would also include going through the home and taking care of minor cleaning. Things to include on this list would be to have the carpets cleaned, wash the windows, wash down the walls, clean the bathroom and kitchens and all appliances.

A moderate investment—somewhere near point B—would mean doing the basic items plus painting some walls, replacing some cracked windows, exchanging the burner trays on the stove and doing some minor home repairs, such as fixing the doorbell.

An extensive investment—point C—would mean fixing the home up so it looks like new. New carpet, new cabinets, a new furnace, water heater, and complete landscaping and sprinklers. You now may have to move in, because no one will be able to afford to buy your property.

From point A to point B, the return is greater than the investment. From B to C, the return is equal to the investment, and at every point after C the return is less than the investment. Too many investors jump zealously into fixing up a property, pouring dollar after dollar into points beyond B. I *never* invest a penny beyond point B, and I usually stop before that point.

Remember that if you put $2,000 down on a property and have $1,000 tied up in closing costs and fix-up expenses, you will have to charge at least $3,000 when you sell it to return your original sunk investment. Every time you buy and sell a property you have to at least get your original investment returned; otherwise, your investment capital keeps going down and down until you are no longer an investor. Ask yourself this question: "How many $3,000 checks do I have lying around the house?"

One of the best investments you can make—especially as a beginning investor—is in "fixer-uppers," those run-down houses you wouldn't consider living in. I consider these homes to be hidden treasures. With a little bit of polishing you can reap great rewards.

The rewards are a result of home-buyer mentality. When people are looking for a place to live, they want a home, not a run-down, secondhand house. They may be fully aware of how little work is really needed, but that's beside the point; they are looking for a place to live.

Most of these houses could be easily sold if someone would take the time to mow the lawn and slap a coat of paint on them. That someone is usually a smart, rich investor. Smart because he looked beyond the overgrown lawn and peeled paint, rich because he bought it at a bargain price, fixed it up for a couple of hundred dollars, and sold it at a $10,000 profit.

I looked into just such a property last month. The long-distance telephone number clued me in to the fact that I might be dealing with a motivated seller, so I called. The woman who answered said that she and her husband had rented out their three-bedroom house for a few months after they were transferred, but the tenants had been hard on the house, and it was simply too difficult for them to manage so many miles away. The house had been appraised at $52,000 (an FHA appraisal) only three months before, and she would consider selling for $45,000 with nothing down: they didn't need any cash at all.

Picking up the key from the neighbor, I took a look inside. She had underestimated the destructive powers of a tenant; the place looked worse than a teenager's bedroom. There were holes in the wall the size of a fist, and in the carpet were globs of gunk the color and texture of overcooked oatmeal. Nobody looking for a place to live would even consider buying this mess. But I could see that with a little of my money and somebody else's work I could easily do enough detailing to turn this clunker into a beautiful home. The carpet could be cleaned, the lawn could be mowed and watered, and the holes in the walls could be easily patched and painted over.

The total fix-up costs would be under $1,000, and I knew I could make $5,000 or more in profit. I didn't take the deal, however, because the payments on the existing loan were too high. I probably could have found buyers willing to make the payments, but I don't buy houses based on "probably," so I passed this one by. Nevertheless, it was a good example of the return possible on a little detail work.

Whenever I buy a property, I know exactly how much fixing up I will do, and I know exactly how long it will take and how much it will cost. In this chapter I'll give you some specific tips on exactly how to make these judgments.

Very rarely will I buy a house with the sole intention of renting it; the real money is made in selling. I do keep the occasional property that offers positive cash flow and tax write-offs, but those are the exceptions to the rule; in today's market, you're usually better off looking for the instant-equity properties that can be bought and sold quickly for a profit.

Forget the old idea of buying a house and renting it out until it appreciates enough to sell. If you keep buying and holding properties, soon you run out of money and turn into a landlord. You will usually be lucky to swing a neutral cash flow. Instead, hold a property for six months—at most—to get the tax advantages of long-term capital gains. Why settle for $100 a month rental income when you could be getting the same $100 a month on a contract sale—with no ownership or management hassles?

I prefer selling properties at a profit to holding them and playing landlord, but some rental properties are necessary to keep the IRS at bay, so we'll talk first about fixing up and selling, and then about hassle-free landlording and property management.

I enjoy working on a house, and if I have the time I will usually do as much of the work as I can. I try to remember, though, that when I am painting the trim on a home I am getting paid as a painter, and when I am out investing I am getting paid as an investor. Keeping that old law of diminishing returns in mind, I estimate the cost and return of alternatives and then I get to work.

FIXING UP

The Exterior

The first place to concentrate your efforts is in the front yard. If the house isn't selling because of its poor "curb appeal" (how it looks as a prospective buyer drives up), you must start there. When judging curb appeal, pay particular attention to the following:

1) *Yard condition*. If Tarzan would be comfortable in the front yard, few home buyers will. Start with the lawn; does it need water, or a mower, or both? If it needs a good cutting, rent a mower and put it to good use. I always rent, and I always pay extra for the insurance waiver; no sense in chewing up old bones with my own mower. Second, pull the weeds and trim the shrubs. Third, if the front looks really lifeless, buy a few instant flowers (bedding plants); they will return a hundred times their cost.

The yard doesn't have to be manicured down to the last blade of grass, but the front should be attractive, not repulsive, if you want to sell to Mr. and Mrs. Home Buyer.

2) *Paint and trim.* Look closely at the exterior paint and trim. If it is peeling and chipped here and there, you can usually scrape it down and touch it up with matching paint. One or two gallons should be enough for a nice detail job. If the entire house needs to be repainted, beware; an average two-bedroom house will cost a lot more to paint than you think, and the law of diminishing returns begins to set in.

I suggest that you go out and buy your paint in five-gallon cans. You should choose one basic trim, exterior, and wall color. By buying paint in the large cans and staying with the same colors, you will save a lot of money in the long run. You will never get to that point of having a dozen half-filled cans of paint around your home.

3) *The roof.* Take a close look at the roof from the outside, and look at the ceiling carefully on the inside. It's surprising how many home buyers notice the condition of the roof, and if there is a leak, you will have to fix it before selling. It's also surprising how much a little roof repair will cost, so beware here as well.

The Interior

Let's walk inside and take a look at a few simple, inexpensive repairs. Replacing the entire carpet is rarely feasible, but there are a few things to look for:

1) *Holes in the wall.* Toothpaste (the regular white kind) can be used to fill in the little nail holes. Just put a dab on your finger and wipe it over the hole, then clean the excess off with a wet rag. The bigger holes may need some plaster or other repairs.

2) *Dirty walls.* Many home owners, especially those in a "must sell" situation, will walk away from minor cleanup jobs. They are sick and tired of the house, or time is pressing and they can't take the time to scrub the walls. Few of them realize that it is the splotches of peanut butter on the kitchen wall that are preventing the sale of their homes.

If paint is needed, match the paint and touch up the worst parts. You don't have to repaint every wall in the house, and if a touch-up will do the trick, why invest beyond the point of diminishing return?

3) *The bathroom.* This is one of two rooms that will be the deciding factor in a sale. I'm not crazy about scrubbing a toilet bowl any more than the next person, but the slightest stain in the toilet, bathtub, or sink will scare off most buyers. Remember, they are considering the purchase of a *home,* not an investment property.

4) *The kitchen.* This is the other room. Extensive studies done by real estate sales researchers indicate that it is the wife who ultimately makes the buying decision. This fact may be losing credibility every year, as we move away from traditional sex roles, but for now it is still the norm. For hundreds of thousands of home buyers, the home will be the domain primarily of the wife and mother.

As a result, you as an investor must pay special attention to the one room that will sell the house for you—the kitchen. A dark, forbidding kitchen with peeling linoleum and burnt Formica will never sell. Here is where you can afford to invest a little money and expect big returns.

There are a few tricks of the trade that every Realtor knows, and one of the best is to bake a loaf of bread in the oven just before showing the house. That smell will linger for hours, and the pleasant feelings evoked by the aroma of fresh bread will do more for the sale than all the sales talk in the world. And, of course, you get to eat the bread afterward.

Another little trick for those who can't bake bread: In a small saucepan, boil about a cup of water with cloves and cinnamon sticks in it. By the time the water boils away, the entire house is filled with a clean sweet-spicy smell.

Make sure the kitchen is well lit. Replace any bulbs that have burned out, and use 75- or 100-watt bulbs wherever it is safe. That rule holds true for every room in the house; a dollar invested in a couple of light bulbs may increase the sales price and decrease the selling time substantially.

Another hint for the lighting fixtures: Take down all of the glass covers on the ceiling lights and wash away the accumulated dirt in warm, soapy water. Rinse and dry the covers and replace them. Five minutes' work will do wonders for the overall appearance.

5) *The carpets.* Clean the carpets and sanitize them. A carpet

will hold a lot of odors that detract from the sale or rental of a home. Few people will pay top dollar for a house filled with the odor of Fido and Fifi and Mr. Cigarette. The price you pay to have a thorough carpet cleaning done is well worth the cost.

Getting the Work Done

You know how much fixing up is needed, and you know how much you will spend for materials. Now you have to face a tough decision: Who will do the work? You really only have three choices: You can do the work yourself, hire cheap labor, or hire experts. A word or two on each is in order here.

My first suggestion is to do as much as possible yourself when you first start investing. I, for one, enjoy working with my family—scrubbing, painting, mowing, etc. A few weeks ago my wife and children helped me fix up a condominium we had purchased. We had fun pitching in, putting our shoulders to the wheel and working together. I think the lessons my children learn about the value of work are invaluable, and my wife appreciates the profits all the more for her efforts.

The day will come when you just don't have the time to do the work yourself (I know; you can't wait for that day), but when you are starting your career, your labor will be well rewarded. I think the greatest advantage is in learning exactly how much time and effort is required to do a good job. You will have to judge someone else's work at some future date, and wielding a paintbrush all day Saturday should give you a little perspective.

When you have done enough of the work yourself, or when the task requires an expert (roofer, carpenter, etc.), you will have to decide whether to use a high-priced, experienced person or an "inexpensive" teenage helper. Be careful here; a high school student is great for mowing and weeding, but when it comes to more skilled labor, such as painting the trim, the expert is usually the best deal.

You no doubt saw the ad for the dishwashing liquid that cost a few pennies more. Then, on hidden camera, Mrs. Housewife was shocked to find out that the bargain brand could only wash a fraction of the dishes that the name brand could when compared penny for penny. The same holds true when it comes time to have the roof repaired or the trim painted. I mention the trim twice for a reason: I learned my own lesson on a trim paint job. I hired a young man to paint the exterior of a house I wanted to sell. His prices were very reasonable, and he assured me that he could do a good job. (I was a little naive at the time.)

During the next week, as he slopped paint here and there (occasionally getting some on the trim itself), the owners of the house next door hired professional painters to do a similar job. By the end of the week, when the pros had packed up and left, and the house next door looked like new, my own painter had managed to mess up three sides of my house and was ready to tackle the fourth.

During the next three weeks I ended up going over there dozens of times to teach my "painter" how to paint. I could have done it myself in half the time. When the job was finally done to my satisfaction I felt like I was the one who should have been paid. Live and learn!

Believe me, I've weighed the pros and cons, and when it comes to value for your labor dollars, one pro weighs at least three times as much as a con. Don't get conned into paying twice as much for half the work.

Whenever I think about fixing up a property to sell it, I run through a checklist that helps me see it through the eyes of the buyers. First, before you put a property up for sale, drive up to it and do a little role-playing. Imagine in your mind that you are a buyer and are considering purchasing the property yourself as a home. Try and see the home as your prospective buyers might. Here's a checklist for you to use in considering what repairs to make on your real estate investments:

Seller's Checklist to Maximize Sales Price

Outside

1) Yard

   Look at lawn, curb, and shrubbery.

   To maximize your sales price:

   Mow lawn, fertilize and reseed if necessary.

   Weed and hoe flower beds.

   Trim hedges and prune trees.

2) Exterior walls

Look at masonry walls for cracks, and siding and exterior surfaces for weathered paint.

To maximize your sales price:

Renail and caulk loose siding.

Paint siding and trim (especially in the front).

3) Roof and gutters

Look at the condition of shingles. Inspect flashings around roof stacks, vents, and chimneys.

To maximize your sales price:

Clean gutters and downspouts.

Repair or replace loose or damaged shingles.

Repair any loose mortar or bricks on chimney.

4) Driveway

Look at the condition of the asphalt or concrete.

To maximize your sales price:

Repair the driveway surface. (Most asphalt driveways can be easily repaired and improved with an inexpensive new blacktop finish.)

5) Foundation

Look at walls, retaining walls, walks, and patios for cracking, disintegration, or buckling.

To maximize your sales price:

Replaster foundation wall. Repair any major cracks.

6) Garage

Look at the condition of the exterior paint.

Test electrical circuits.

To maximize your sales price:

Lubricate garage door hinges and hardware.

7) Windows and doors

Look at windows; check for smooth operation.

Check the fit of the doors.

Test doorbell, chimes.

To maximize your sales price:

Replace broken or cracked panes.

Repair glazing.

Wash the windows.

Inside

8) Floors

Look at floors for squeaky boards.

Check for loose or missing tiles and for worn linoleum.

To maximize your sales price:
    Nail down any loose floorboards or stair treads.
    Glue down any loose tiles.
9) Bathrooms
Look at the operation of toilet and plumbing fixtures.
Check condition of painted or papered walls.
To maximize your sales price:
    Remove mildew.
    Put a "blue" toilet bowl freshener in your water tank.
    Repair dripping plumbing fixtures.
10) Kitchen
Look at and test all appliances.
Check range hood for proper ventilation.
Look underneath sinks for plumbing leaks.
To maximize your sales price:
    Wash all appliances.
    Clean exhaust fan and filter.
    Remove any grease or dust from walls, floors, and from
      under appliances.
11) Basement
Check pipes for leaks.
Inspect supporting beams.
Check for signs of cracked or crumbling walls.
To maximize your sales price:
    Remove clutter.
    Organize basement storage into neatly stacked
      boxes.
12) Electrical system
Look at and test each plug and light switch.
Inspect all exposed wiring for proper insulation.
To maximize your sales price:
    Label each circuit in the breaker box.
    Repair any loose or broken switches and cover plates.
13) Plumbing system
Look at system for any leaks.
Turn each faucet rapidly on and off to detect any loose,
    banging pipes.
Check each drain to make sure it isn't clogged or slow.
To maximize your sales price:
    Clear any clogged sinks.
    Repair any leaky sinks.
14) Heating and cooling system

> Look at system, turning on and checking for proper opera-
> tion.
> Check filters.
> To maximize your sales price:
>   Change or clean filters if necessary.
>   Clean area around equipment.

Not everything on this list will need to be repaired, but a thorough review will aid you in selling your house for the best possible price. Make a copy of this checklist and show it to your prospective buyers. Not only will they be impressed with your diligence, but you will take away most of their possible reasons for not buying your property.

PROPERTY MANAGEMENT

Okay, you've got the place fixed up; now what? Well, of course you want to sell—at a handsome profit—as soon as possible, and we'll talk about the tricks of advertising and selling in more depth presently. But for now, let's admit a nasty fact: for a while, at least, you just might have to rent the house out. And that means asking for trouble—a renter. Oh, I'm not that strongly set against renters: didn't we all rent at one time? But I haven't met an investor yet who didn't have at least a few horror stories to tell about those few renters who really went out of their way to destroy a house or apartment.

I've had my share of experiences. I've made mistakes; I've been swindled, been driven nuts, and made a few good friends. To make your own landlording as painless as possible, I've come up with a list of suggestions culled from experts across the country—as well as a few tricks I've come up with myself to handle this necessary evil.

There are three main things to worry about with tenants; take care of all three and you may even enjoy the experience. The first is making sure you select the best possible tenants; the second is knowing what could go wrong and preventing it before it does; and the third is getting the tenants to take care of the property themselves.

Selecting Tenants

There are a few things to look for when shopping for good tenants. (Yes, you must do a little comparison shopping: there are a million species of renters.) The following factors will help you in your search:

1) *Occupancy period.* You should attempt to find tenants who want to rent as long as you own the property. This not only adds value to your property, but it also makes your job a lot easier. If you get a last month's rental deposit and security deposit, these long-term tenants can be worth their weight in gold. I met a lady who had lived in an apartment for eighteen years. Wasn't she a great tenant? Think how many "for rent" signs weren't sold to the owner of that property.

2) *Compatibility.* A close friend is ready to throw in his landlording towel. He is no longer in control of one complex he owns; he's a referee. And the problem could have been so easily avoided by choosing tenants who were compatible.

A warning is due here: Be very careful when you reject a prospective tenant. More than one landlord has been given a forced lesson in discrimination law. Such laws vary from state to state, so you should check with a local attorney or apartment owners' association for applicable laws.

Despite legal restrictions, you do have quite a bit of latitude in rejecting tenants, so be careful about tenant compatibility. Renting one half of a duplex to a family with small children and the other half to a motorcycle gang is not an example of perfect compatibility.

3) *Housekeeping ability.* If you have renters moving from a nearby area, try this: Have them fill out a rental application and promise to get back to them soon. Then drop in at their current home to talk to them. Take a look at what your own property will look like in a few weeks with them as tenants. The effort spent performing this little private eye routine may save you hundreds of dollars and thousands of headaches.

Use the same tactic when screening home buyers. Stop by and talk to them about their offer. If you don't like what you see, think twice before accepting them as buyers; if they default someday, you will be the inheritor of their domicile—and their problems.

4) *Credit rating and employment history.* This is common knowledge, and every landlord should have enough sense to at least verify the creditworthiness of a prospective tenant. And yet I hear time and time again, "But she (or he) looked so honest . . ." Every rental application will have a place for credit rating and employment information, as well as permission for you to investigate the validity of all claims. Make the calls and do the necessary checking before making a final decision. Don't forget to call previous landlords. Call the landlord before the current one; if they are lousy tenants, the current one may claim that they are excellent, just to get rid of them.

Avoiding Problems

Problems with tenants are like summer colds: they aren't fatal, but they are extremely irritating, and they are inevitable. Sooner or later you'll have one. There is one all-important preventative medicine, which will stop about 99 percent of the problems before they exist, and there are some measures that can be taken to solve the problems that do occasionally crop up.

First and foremost: *Do not rely on the tenants to read the contract.* Rental contracts are weighted to the advantage of the owner (as far as the law allows), but don't take too much comfort in that fact. Far too many landlords have rested on their contracts, only to find them unenforceable or worthless: how can you sue someone for $5,000 who doesn't have $50 to his or her name?

Time for a quiz, to wake up those in the back row. Quick, now: How many contracts have you read from beginning to end? And how many of them have you understood? Take that number and multiply it by your age. If the product is greater than zero, go to the head of the class. I'm not sure that even lawyers fully understand the meaning of every contract. I think there must be professional contract writers holed up in dark little attics, whose only pleasure in life is making up words like heretointhereinafterthereforeasabovementionedbelow. Never assume that tenants will read the contract, and *never*, ever assume that they will understand the contract.

Explain the terms of the contract, and have them agree verbally with you on every point. On the real biggies, such as remodeling and late charges, have them explain the terms in their own words so there is no misunderstanding. This whole process may seem like too much trouble, but think of the satisfaction you'll have when your tenants don't tear out a wall to install a 500-gallon fish tank.

The following are the rules of the game that are most often broken by tenants, and they should be guarded especially well:

1) *Tenant remodeling.* Called "creative interior decorating" by some of the more imaginative of tenants, this can range from simple epithets spray-painted on the walls to the super fish tank cited above. Explain carefully and clearly before renting that any changes made in the apartment must be approved by you, in writing.

2) *Apartment maintenance.* You must establish minimum standards of upkeep, and you must expect those standards to be maintained at all times. Of course, your minimum standards should not be on the order of an operating room, but neither should small fungoids be allowed to thrive in the living room carpet. Again, spell out the conditions clearly in advance, and make sure the tenants understand your right to enter and inspect the premises or show it to prospective buyers.

3) *Late rents and nonpayment of rents.* I have a hard time with this one, because I really am too softhearted. The only way to avoid this problem is to lay down the law and then enforce it. If your tenants are allowed to be "just a few days late, just this one time," I guarantee it won't be the last. They may not intentionally delay paying, but once you have shown them that you are willing to forgive and forget, somehow the rent doesn't have the same priority it used to.

This is a business and you are a businessperson. You must enforce late payment penalties.

The second—nonpayment of rent—must be dealt with swiftly and surely. Eviction proceedings usually take weeks, and you cannot afford to delay a necessary eviction. It's true: you are throwing people out of their only house and home, and it may be no fault of theirs that they can't pay the rent. But your alternative is to subsidize them for who knows how long, so what choice do you have?

The best way to prevent this from becoming an even bigger problem, involving a lawsuit, is to ensure that you get a last month's rent and a hefty security deposit before renting an apartment or house. Then if the tenant can't afford to pay, at least you will not lose the last month's rent. Find out all of the laws regarding security deposits and eviction of tenants; they vary widely from state to state.

Nick Koon, a real estate investor and a good friend, always includes in the rental agreement a provision whereby he can charge the rent to his tenant's MasterCard or Visa in the case of default. As long as the account is good for that amount, he can use the account number to ensure payment.

I have MasterCard, Visa, and American Express merchant accounts for this purpose. If the payments are late, I want to have some immediate recourse.

4) *Bounced checks.* If you've never bounced a check, you're in a class of people as rare as honest politicians. Most bounced checks are the result of an honest mistake—a number transposed in the checkbook, or a deposited check bouncing. But here again, you must not allow a tenant's problems to become your own.

Insist in the rental agreement—and discuss this verbally as well—that there be a charge of at least $30 on returned checks. That may be steep compared with the grocery store, but the store can afford to sustain a lot more bounced checks at $30 or $40 apiece. You cannot afford to have too many $400 or $500 checks returned; you need that money to run your business.

Occasionally you may have a tenant move out, paying the last month's rent with a bad check. The best way to prevent a problem there is to not release the last month's deposit (that you collected when the tenant moved in) until the rent check clears.

I recently heard of an ingenious solution to a prickly problem. A tenant paid his last month's rent with a bad check. By the time it was returned to the landlord, the tenant had skipped town. The investor was left holding a worthless $600 check, and the bank refused to clear it.

Going into the ex-tenant's bank, the landlord asked the teller to find out for him exactly how much the tenant would have to deposit to make the check good. It turned out that the account contained $575—just $25 short. So the investor made a deposit to the man's account of $26 cash and then cashed the $600 check. When the tenant found out, he was enraged. He called the investor to chew him out, and he was politely informed that he could repay the $26 loan at his convenience.

5) *Utility payments.* If you haven't enjoyed a good ulcer for years, here's a recipe: Take two or three tenants and pour into rental units. Add utilities as needed, and make sure they are in your name. When bills are prepared and ready to be served, try to get tenants to pay. Watch them cook up excuses and complaints. Tempers will heat up quickly and juices should begin to flow. Toss in a few choice words and voilà! Guaranteed to get you burned every time.

If, on the other hand, you would like to avoid one of the worst problems in landlording, *always* have the utilities turned on in the name of the tenants only (except water and sewer services) and stay out of the picture entirely.

In addition to the above suggestions, I recommend that these general rules and conditions be added to your resident rental agreements. Each may save you everything from minor headaches to major lawsuits:

> No pets.
> No waterbeds.
> Children are not allowed to play in the common hallways of building.
> Tenants must park in their assigned parking spaces.
> Tenants will refrain from playing loud TVs, radios, stereos, or in any other way disturbing the peace of other tenants between 10 P.M. and 8 A.M.
> All rent must be paid on or before the fifth of every month, to the landlord in person.

Getting the Tenants to Take Care of the Property

I am proud of this last section. It has taken years of experience for me to develop what I think is a foolproof system of managing rental properties. By implementing everything mentioned above I have been able to avoid most of the hassles of managing, but there is still one bug in the system: nobody likes to take care of the yard, or the trash, or the snow shoveling. That's the job for the landlord.

So I created a goose that has been laying golden eggs ever since. Whenever I run an ad in the "apartments for rent" section of the paper, I include the phrase, "discount rent for management responsibilities." To every caller (and the phone rings constantly) I explain that if the tenants pay before the fifth of every month, and if they don't call me unless the place is burning down, *and* if they maintain the property—yard, carpet and wall cleaning, minor repairs up to $25, etc.—then I will rebate a portion of the previous month's rent. The rebate is contingent upon an on-site inspection at least once a month (usually on the fifteenth). It is a check for up to $25 that is made out to the lady of the household (or whichever tenant takes care of the house) and personally delivered to her on the mid-month inspection date. (Do you think she might make sure the rent gets in on time and the place stays clean? It sure works like dynamite.)

This concept of rewarding people for good behavior has never failed, and the small fraction of the total rent that I give up to have the tenant take care of the property more than pays for itself. When I reward people instead of punishing them, I find they react positively. The rent is in on time, and the places are kept up. Also, by advertising "discount for management responsibilities," I am advertising to rent my properties to people who are willing to work. I have noticed that a large segment of society today get ill when they see the word *responsibility*. They wouldn't think of calling an ad that mentioned such profanity. And I probably wouldn't want to rent my property to them.

I really despise this business of renting. Too many people have problems that I can't solve, and I feel like an ogre when I have to enforce a rental agreement to protect myself. Landlords have had a bad name since . . . well, since the first landlord evicted the first tenant (probably from a cave). But for a real estate investor, these difficulties are a fact of life; management is a necessary evil and a price that you must be willing to pay for success.

The tax and appreciation benefits of owning real estate are worth having, as long as you can manage your properties without a lot of headaches. My system of management has fulfilled that need for me, and it will do the same for you if you put it to work.

CHAPTER 9

Selling Right

The first and greatest commandment is,
"Don't let them scare you!"
—ELMER DAVIS

Don't you have a love-hate relationship with Baskin Robbins? You love the ice cream, but you hate having to make up your mind; after all, thirty-one different flavors of the world's best ice cream is a little overwhelming.

I've given you ten tools for buying, hints for fixing up and renting, and now I'm going to inundate you with information on selling. Don't get overwhelmed! You only need to pick up one or two tools as we go along. Just make sure that the tools you choose fit your personality like a surgical glove, and you shouldn't need more than one or two for success.

I love selling properties. I love it because that is where you make money. If you look around in the world you'll soon realize that the people who make money are those who are involved in selling something.

Selling is a lot of fun too. I remember well paying for scout trips with the proceeds of candy sales or Christmas card sales. I can't remember a time when I didn't enjoy the challenge of making a sale.

When you are ready to sell a property, the first choice is whether to sell it by yourself or enlist the help of a real estate agent. You may have guessed by now that I sell most of my properties by myself, but I'll try to be fair in showing you the pros and cons of each alternative.

Before we continue, let's set the stage. At this point, you've mastered the ten tools for finding good deals in real estate, and you've used one or more of them to locate an ideal property.

You've made a careful analysis, including fix-up and selling cost estimates, and you've made an offer (with escape clauses) bound with a promissory note, which was accepted. You've bought the house, getting title insurance, and now you have fixed it up and ready to sell. Or you may have it rented temporarily, and now you're ready to sell.

As a seller, you must decide a few things in advance. First there are the selling terms: How much do you want to sell for? Do you want the cash up front, or will you take your equity in payments? What interest rate should you charge if you decide to sell on contract? You must also take into account all selling costs, which we will discuss one by one. Failure to add up all of these miscellaneous costs will give you a nasty surprise at closing. Last—but certainly not least—you must decide whether to sell with the help of an agent or by yourself. We will take a close look at each method.

We can really get into a heavy, advanced course on calculating internal rates of return, or returns on investment, when we discuss the terms of a sale. But to be honest, there is nothing more complicated about structuring the terms of a sale than just simply making sure that you make money instead of lose it.

I love a simple, direct approach to investing, and when it comes time to sell, I love simple, direct terms that are easy to understand. It reminds me of the story of two M.B.A.'s who ran into each other two years after they graduated. One of them had graduated at the top of his class—he could perform complex analysis in his head—and was now working for a large accounting firm, counting widgets in factories forty hours a week. The other M.B.A. had barely made it through school, and he had never been noted for his academic abilities. Somehow though, he was now a multimillionaire, the owner of a large importing firm.

The brilliant widget-counter asked the other man what the secret of his success was. "In all honesty," he answered, "I have never figured it out. All I know is that I can buy something for $3.00 and sell it for $6.00. I never realized you could make so much money with just a 3 percent profit!"

All you have to know in real estate is that if you buy a house for $40,000, with 5 percent down, on a thirty-year, 10 percent loan, and then sell it for $50,000, with 10 percent down, on a thirty-year, 12 percent loan, you will make money. Let's take a look at those figures:

Purchase price	$40,000
Down payment (5%)	−2,000
Amount to be financed	$38,000
Interest rate	10%
Length of loan	30 yrs.
Monthly payments	$333.48
Selling price	$50,000
Down payment (10%)	−5,000
Amount to be financed	$45,000
Interest rate	12%
Length of loan	30 yrs.
Monthly payments	$462.88
Monthly net income	$129.40

What else do you need to know about investing? You invested $2,000, plus some fix-up and closing costs, and you received $5,000 cash when you sold it. Estimating $1,000 for those extra costs, you made $2,000 on a $3,000 investment immediately, and $129.40 every month for the next thirty years—a total of $46,584. Is that making money or not?

Of course a finance major would never settle for such a simple explanation, nor would an economist. After all, we do need to discount all of those future payments to come up with a real rate of return. But so what? While they are plugging numbers into their calculators, I am plugging profits into my bank account.

The simplistic—and admittedly ideal—situation described above is the perfect example of how a *wrap-around mortgage* works. This is one of two ways to sell real estate that I think are so superior to all others that I use them exclusively. There is almost an infinite variety of terms and techniques for selling, but after looking at most of them, I am perfectly happy with these two, and they are the ones I teach.

THE WRAP-AROUND MORTGAGE (AITD)

This is the best idea, and the one I use most. When I buy a house, I always try to assume the existing loans. The reason is simple: they usually have lower interest rates and therefore lower payments. The only alternative is to come up with new money, and that means going to the bank and paying not only the higher rate for my money but all of the origination fees and points they can come up with.

Having assumed the existing loans, I can then pay the seller's equity on a contract. Now comes the real trick to the program: when I sell the property, I do so on an *all-inclusive trust deed* (also called a wrap-around mortgage). This is an all-new contract for the full selling price. The new owner does not assume the underlying loans; I keep them in my name and continue to make the payments.

Each month I collect a payment ($462.88 in the example), make a payment ($333.48), and put the difference in my bank account. Not only that, but I can get a local title trust company to do the collecting and paying for me. They will send me a check for the difference, less about $5.00 for their service.

With this system one of three things will happen: the new owner will decide to pay off the contract early, in which case I will be forced to pay off the old loans and put the $5,000 or so cash difference into another property; the buyer will continue making payments and I will continue receiving that monthly cash flow without any management or ownership problems; or the new owner will default on the payments and I will have to take it back for free and resell it, making even more money.

It's a no-lose situation. If you can average $100 a month on every deal, and if you can buy and sell two houses every month for the next five years, that would build up a monthly income of $12,000. How much do you need to retire?

I really love those commercials for the Ginsu knives and other culinary delights that slice, chop, grate, cut, pare, shred and do everything else imaginable to your vegetables. The real genius is in the final tag line, after they give you the price. They always say, "But wait! There's more!"

Look at what I've given you above, for the price of a book. You can go out and get a return on your money immediately *and* get a monthly income for thirty years. How much would you pay for information like that? But wait! There's more!

That's right; not only do you get the immediate return *and* $129.40 every month, but with this offer you also get the entire

$462.88 every month after the first twenty years or so. Why? Because the underlying loans that you assumed were probably in existence for five or ten years before you bought the property. That means that when they run out you will continue to collect payments of $462.88, but you will not have to pay more payments on the old loans. Now that's retirement in style!

Again, don't let the numbers scare you off. If it still seems complicated, ask your title officer or another investor to help you with the details. Any competent title officer can help you through this process, and if your title officer doesn't understand AITDs, find a new one.

Understand me well: *buying and selling a house is no different from buying and selling a can of beans.* If you can buy a can of beans wholesale for 52 cents and sell it retail for 59 cents, you will make money. Don't let anyone convince you that it is a complicated business.

TAKING A SECOND MORTGAGE

The second of my two favorite techniques is to accept a second mortgage for my equity. That means, simply, that I will let my buyer assume all of the underlying mortgages (instead of keeping them in my name, as in the wrap-around above), and I will accept a note—a second mortgage—for the balance.

Using the same figures as the example above, the buyer would take over the payments on the $38,000 loan that I assumed (making payments of $333.48), and I will take the remaining $7,000 owed me on a note for, say, ten years.

A note for $7,000 over a ten-year period, at 12 percent, will pay $100.43 per month. You can see the primary advantage of the wrap-around mortgage, which pays much more over the long run. The wrap-around has another advantage as well: since you are holding the only trust deed, you will know the minute your buyer defaults. In the case of a second, you will have to file a "request for notice of default," and even then it may take two or three months after the buyer stops making payments before you hear about it.

Using second mortgages, however, offers its own advantages.

First, such a mortgage is much easier to sell to another investor or a mortgage broker; second, it is easier to sell a property when you offer to let the buyer assume the low-interest loans with the lower monthly payments.

Of the two methods, I prefer selling on a wrap-around. However, both work very well and allow you to remain in control of the terms, rather than having to turn the reins over to a banker. It's just you and the buyer; only the two of you are calling the shots. The choice is similar to deciding whether you will use Phillips- or regular-head screws when you put up your for-sale signs. Either one will get the job done and move you one step closer to retirement.

Whatever terms you arrange with the buyer for the sale, you will still have to face a few closing costs. Since you will be arranging your own terms, it is best to get the buyer to pay as many of those costs as possible. Let's quickly look at each of the typical seller's costs:

Abstract and title insurance. These expenses cover research into the past ownership of a property and insurance against the cost of any liens or ownership disputes that are not discovered before the closing. The seller is usually the one charged for these costs; however, there is no set rule. I always (yes, always) just write in the contract that the buyer is to pay for one half (or even try all—they can only say no) of all closing costs including title insurance. I have always been successful in getting the buyer to help me out with this cost.

Other typical seller's costs may include:

> new deed
> termite inspection/bond
> survey
> agent's commission
> loan points
> new mortgage fees
> closing fees

Do not take unfair advantage of buyers who don't understand each of the costs mentioned above. But once they do understand, then you can negotiate for each point and come to an equitable agreement. I have never had a deal yet in which I felt either side had an advantage at the expense of the other side.

You have one more decision to make before selling. You must weigh the advantages—and disadvantages—of selling by yourself or through a Realtor. I think you know which I prefer. If a Realtor receives the standard 6 percent cash commission on a sale, that's 6 percent that won't end up in my pocket. On the sale of a $50,000 home, I am giving up $3,000, enough for a week-long trip to Hawaii for my wife and myself. On a $100,000 house, it's 6,000 big ones.

Nevertheless, there are some serious drawbacks to selling by owner, and I have to earn every penny of that commission when I sell the home myself. Let's look at each:

SELLING THROUGH AN AGENT

I have a close friend who is a real estate agent. That means he has been licensed by the state to advertise and market real properties, find and qualify potential buyers, negotiate a sales contract, arrange financing, and arrange a closing. He complains occasionally about the misinformation that a lot of sellers have about real estate commissions. Too many people, he feels, think that the agent who sells their property collects the entire 6 percent commission. Actually, that agent is likely to collect only 1.5 percent—and sometimes even less.

The reason for this is that there are usually two agencies involved: the listing agency and the selling agency. An agent works for an agency, which is managed by a broker. When home owners agree to allow an agent to sell their homes, they are actually (in most cases) allowing the agent's agency to advertise and list that home for sale.

If a second agent—from another agency—finds a buyer for the home, then the commission must be split between the listing agency and the selling agency (each receiving half, or 3 percent of the total sale price). Then the agent for the seller must split his or her commission with the broker of the agency. That leaves only one quarter of the total commission for the agent who did the actual selling.

Using a $50,000 sale as an example, the total commission would be $3,000. One quarter of that is only $750, and there are many struggling agents who count themselves lucky if they can sell even one house each month.

When you sell a property through an agent, keep in mind that many agents are willing to list your house and then sit back, waiting for another agent to make the sale through the Multiple Listing Service book.

Finding the rare agent who will work hard to both list and sell your property may be difficult. Ask other investors for recommendations: your time is too precious to waste it waiting for a poor agent to get in gear.

There is more than one type of listing contract. Each has advantages and disadvantages, and it is up to you, as the seller, to decide which kind of listing agreement to sign with your agent.

Exclusive Right-to-Sell Contract

This contract is exactly what its name implies: it is an agreement that gives the agent the exclusive right to sell the property. That means that if the property is sold during the period of the listing agreement (usually ninety days)—by *anyone*—the agent will receive the full commission.

This is great for the agent, obviously. It is also advantageous for the seller, because the agent will be highly motivated to sell the property. However, if Ima Buyer makes an offer to you personally, without any help from the agent whatsoever, you are still obligated to pay that agent the full commission.

Exclusive Right-to-Sell Multiple Listing Contract

The added feature of this contract is that the seller requires the agent to not only market the property through contacts but also through the local Multiple Listing Service. This Multiple Listing Service is an organization that puts out weekly or monthly books to every agent in the area who is an MLS member. The idea is that the MLS will greatly increase the seller's chances of meeting the right buyer.

If an agent from another agency finds a buyer, the agencies will split the commission. However, it is the listing agent who represents the seller.

Net Listing Contract

A net listing means that the seller is able to stipulate a net amount that he or she requires from the sale. For example, in the $50,000 house we are using in this chapter, the seller insists that he or she must receive at least $50,000—after the agent's commission. That means that the agent can try to sell the house for, say, $55,000, collecting $5,000 as a commission.

This is an interesting incentive program for the agent, because the lower the selling price, the lower the commission, and yet the higher the selling price, the less chance that the property will sell at all. It is up to the agent to hit a jolly fortune-teller . . . I mean, a happy medium. (Just checking to see if you're awake.)

This isn't a bad listing arrangement, if you have found an agent with a lot of initiative and drive.

Open Listing Contract

An open listing is practically no listing at all. It gives the agent the right to sell the property and collect the commission, but since the right is not exclusive, the seller is free to sign the same kind of listing with every agent in town. With that kind of first-come-first-served competition, there is little incentive for the agent to work hard for the sale.

This listing is really only good if the agent already has some interested buyers who fit the property exactly. Otherwise, it is just a waste of time and effort, and you might as well sell by owner.

Exclusive Agency Listing Contract

This listing is my favorite. It really combines the best of all the listing contracts. The agency is guaranteed that it is the only firm that has the listing on the property, but the owners, under this contract, have the right to sell the property on their own and pay no commission, unless the agency can prove that it was the source of the lead.

The agency has some incentive to work for you, since they are guaranteed the listing commission if they can find a buyer for you, but if you find one yourself they have no claim. The real advantage should be obvious: you are able to sell by agent and by owner at the same time.

When you are beginning your career as an investor, consider using the exclusive agency listing to sell all of your properties. That way you can get experience with both methods of selling.

It's really easy to list a house with an agent. If you have asked around town (other investors, people who have recently bought or sold a home in the area), just call one of the agents that was recommended. Tell him or her that you would like to sell your property, and that you would like to do so on an exclusive agency listing. Everything after that point will be handled by the agent.

My hesitancy about selling through an agent was reinforced last week when I called on a house for sale by owner. The lady who answered was very discouraged; her husband had been transferred 300 miles away, leaving her behind to sell the house. They had known about the transfer for nearly a year, but had trusted a real estate agent to sell their home. The agent had given his "expert" opinion that the house was worth $85,000—about $10,000 more than its actual market value—and had listed it at that price. The agent had nothing to lose: if another agent sold the house, he would get a commission; if the house didn't sell, he had only wasted a few hours' effort.

Needless to say, the house didn't sell, and a frustrated couple are now in the unenviable position of having to practically give away their home. If you want to sell through an agent, beware. Find a real go-getter who will do more than list it and wait for an easy commission.

SELLING BY OWNER

If you decide to do the selling yourself, you must realize what this entails. You will have to figure out the financing terms and negotiate with the buyer; you will have to advertise well enough to attract buyers; you will have to qualify prospective buyers (if you don't have them go to the bank and get money to cash you out); you will have to show off the home; and you will have to arrange for the closing.

Taking care of that many *yous* can be a time-consuming, frustrating experience if you don't know what you are getting into, so I'll go through each of these steps one by one.

Your first step will be to decide on terms. You need to establish not only how the property is sold, as discussed earlier in this chapter, but for how much. You will have to balance the selling price with selling time. The higher the price, the longer it will usually take to sell.

After deciding on price and terms, you must advertise. The key to effective advertising is to sell the *benefits*, not the *features*. Write ads that offer people what they are looking for. Bedrooms and bathrooms are vital information, but what terms are you offering? How much are you expecting as a down payment? Are you willing to be flexible on the price or the interest rate? What kind of monthly payments are you asking for?

The secret to a successful ad is to stress a few of these key ingredients:

Low monthly payments
Low down payment
Owner will finance, with no qualifying or credit checks
Low-interest financing
Nice/beautiful/clean, etc.

Here's a couple of ads; you decide which one would catch your eye if you were looking for a house to buy:

MUST SELL. Owner desperate, will sell for only $49,900, with only $3,000 down. Very flexible. Payments of only $475 for this beautiful 3 bdrm home in Rockville. No bank qualifying. 555-4899 or 555-3423

FOR SALE by owner. Nice 3 bdrm, 2 bth house in Rockville. Close to school and shopping center. Only $49,900. Call evenings 555-4899.

The first owner sounds willing to negotiate. Here is someone who is ready to sell; notice the two phone numbers, indicating that you can call any time. Also, as buyers look through the classified ads, which one catches them where they really live—in their pocketbooks?

The first one is specific about the low down payment and the low monthly payments. The second one offers proximity to schools and stores—so what? Those things may be important, but they can be added to the sales pitch when the calls start coming in.

Which leads to the next point: answering the phone calls. If your ad is attractive to enough people, you will be flooded with curious callers. The best thing you can do is anticipate every call. You should know:

- How close is it to the elementary school?
- Where is the closest park?
- What are the terms of sale? (How much will you need as a down payment?)
- What special features can you offer that you didn't mention in your ad?

In short, you must go through a whole list of questions you would ask as a prospective buyer, and have your answers prepared before the questions are asked. Many buyers will be turned off if you stumble around too much with a lot of unsure I-don't-knows. You should also leave an information sheet by each phone in your house. It really helps the other people who might answer the phone when you're not there to have something to tell the people who call on the ad.

Don't rely totally on the effectiveness of your newspaper advertising. Utilize all of these sources of buyers as well:

Neighbors

Residents within a few blocks of your property may know of someone who is interested in moving into the area. A simple personal phone call or a talk with each might reveal the names of dozens of possible buyers.

A flier distributed throughout the area is even easier, if somewhat less personal. The flier should announce to local residents that you will be selling the house at 810 Elm Street and that you would appreciate being recommended to anyone who they knew was interested in moving into the area. Offer a $50 finder's fee and everyone in town will be calling friends to find a buyer for you; most people will probably have a friend or two that they would love to have move into the neighborhood. (Check applicable state laws in your area to make sure this method is legal.)

Your Farm

You already have learned what a farm is; now you can develop a selling farm. Get to know investors, attorneys, and other professionals who would be interested in buying properties. Find out what their specifications are and sell accordingly.

I have a friend who has compiled quite an impressive farm of lawyers. Whenever he gets wind of a good deal that he knows he can sell to one of them he buys it immediately. Then he turns around and sells it with one telephone call. He may not sell it at a retail price, but he deals in a different market: He buys sub-wholesale and sells wholesale.

Satisfied Customers

You might want to go back through your list of past sales and contact the buyers to see if they might be interested in buying another investment property themselves, or if they know of someone else who might be interested. You could even offer them a cash bonus for providing you with a lead, or let them miss a payment to you in exchange for a lead.

Multiple Listing Service

Try to get a copy of the Multiple Listing Service book in your area and look up what properties have sold recently. You might want to contact the sellers to see if they are interested in buying another property. A lot of people who have sold an investment property will need to get into another one as soon as they can to help their tax situations.

New People in the Area

People who are new in an area are particularly good prospects for selling a home to, because many banks require at least one year of continuous employment for qualifying for a new loan, and if the new job is with a different company than the one left behind, newcomers may find themselves renting for a while. You are offering them an opportunity to buy a home that they would not otherwise have.

You don't know how to find out about these people? Join your neighborhood welcome wagon organization and volunteer to make them feel at home. Your local chamber of commerce can also help you meet your city's new residents.

Creative Advertising

A strange lesson I have learned is that if you really want to be successful, you sometimes have to do things backwards. I have developed a shotgun approach to finding buyers. The gist of the program is to advertise for buyers at the same time you advertise to buy properties yourself. I have developed an "I sell houses" flier that has given me a backlog of interested buyers. My investment program then turns into a matchmaking service where I find homes for sale to match people who are interested in buying. I tie up these homes with escape clauses and promissory notes (so I have no cash on the line) and then present them to my buyers. It works like a charm.

Consider putting out a few hundred of these "I sell houses" fliers every month in apartment complexes or trailer parks where young couples live. Before you know it you will have a stack of qualified buyers waiting for you to find them a home.

Negotiating the Sale

Negotiating with a buyer can be a tricky business, like a tightrope act. When you are selling, rather than buying, you must be careful to remember some points that are unique to this situation. First, be especially careful about establishing rapport. Buyers tend to be more wary than sellers.

On the one hand, if you sound as though you know everything there is to know about real estate and you've been through this a hundred times, they will be scared off, afraid that you will take advantage of them. On the other hand, if you don't appear to be competent enough to handle every aspect of the sale, they are

WE SELL HOUSES

Tired of paying out rent? Tired of landlord hassles? If so you might be in the market for a house—either now or in the future. We are not real estate agents, and we're not associated with any brokerage. We do, however, have houses for sale that, for the most part, require small down payments and no qualifying. If you would like to be put on our list for houses, please fill out the following questionnaire and mail it back. You'll hear from us soon!

Marc and DeAnn Garrison, P.O. Box 1096, Orem, Utah 84057, (801) 225-8777

Name _____

Address _____

City _____

Phone _____

I am looking for:
- ☐ 1 Bedroom
- ☐ 2 Bedrooms
- ☐ rooms

- ☐ 1 Bath
- ☐ 2 Baths
- ☐ Under 1,000 sq. ft.
- ☐ 1,000 to 1,200 sq. ft.
- ☐ 1,200 sq. ft. and over

- ☐ Garage
- ☐ Carport

I have for a down payment:
- ☐ $1,000
- ☐ $2,000
- ☐ $3,000
- ☐ $4,000
- ☐ $5,000
- ☐ $ _____

I can afford monthly payments of:
- ☐ $400
- ☐ $500
- ☐ $600

- ☐ $700
- ☐ $800
- ☐ $ _____

Other things I could use for a down payment:
- ☐ Car
- ☐ Boat
- ☐ Building lot
- ☐ Airplane

- ☐ Mobile Home
- ☐ Camper
- ☐ Trade _____
- ☐ _____

My gross monthly income is $ _____

I am employed at _____

Yes, I can qualify for new financing. ☐

No, I'd rather not or can't qualify for new financing. ☐

Preference for where I would like to live:
- ☐ Salt Lake
- ☐ South Salt Lake Valley
- ☐ Northern Utah County

- ☐ Orem
- ☐ Provo
- ☐ Springville

- ☐ Spanish Fork
- ☐ South Utah County
- ☐ _____

equally likely to be scared off by your apparent ineptitude and the deal will still be blown.

Walking that hair-thin rope is a skill that you will develop as you work with buyers and sellers, but I can give you a few tips that may help.

1) *Establishing rapport.* In selling a house just as in buying, you must be standing on common ground before you can see eye to eye. The first step in establishing rapport is to understand the buyer's level of sophistication. The idea of an "all-inclusive trust deed" may be totally foreign and more than a little intimidating. And if you casually state that you want to sell the house on a wrap-around, they may think you intend to throw a roll of Saran Wrap into the deal.

You don't have to tell buyers that you are an investor unless they ask. Many buyers may feel that an investor is a con artist who will be trying to sell them oceanfront property in Kansas. Test the water a little before you jump in.

Find common ground at first, walking through the house and discussing the architecture or carpeting. Find out if they have ever owned a house before, and if so, what kind of financing was arranged on that sale. Broach the subject of creative financing gently, assuring the buyer that "We will be able to work everything out."

Don't profess to know more about real estate than you really do, and if a question comes up that you're not sure of, don't try to bluff your way through it. Smile and say, "I'm glad you asked that question. I have an excellent (attorney, title officer, etc.) who has offered to help us out if we have any questions, and I'm sure this won't be any problem."

My own approach is simple, direct honesty without volunteering any unnecessary information. It's like a game of Go Fish; you don't have to give away any cards unless the other player asks for them, and then you give only the cards asked for.

As you talk, try to find out exactly what the buyer needs. Don't go into a half-hour spiel bragging about how close the home is to every church in town, only to find out that your buyer is an atheist. Again, it's a matter of selling benefits, not features. Find out what the buyer wants and needs and then show how this particular house will suit those needs perfectly.

2) *Determine the buyer's motivation.* As soon as possible, before you put a lot of time in with the buyers, determine whether they are serious or not. Do they really want to buy the home or are they just looking around? Find out if they have been or will be transferred into the area. Do they own a home locally? Why are they thinking about buying a new home? These questions can be asked quite candidly once the ice has been broken, and if they are a "looky-loo" you won't have to waste your time.

3) *Obtain the buyer's confidence.* As you talk with the buyers, tell them about other homes you have sold in the past and suggest that they make a call or pay a visit to people with whom you've done business. (Get permission first.) If you haven't sold other houses yet, tell them about yourself. If you just got out of Alcatraz you may want to avoid that fact. But you must find a way to get the buyer's confidence and loyalty.

4) *Determine the buyer's financial strength.* After I had been involved in buying and selling properties for about two years, I sold a home to someone who owned a small business in town. He seemed prosperous, and I was sure he was good for his debts, so I took back a $12,000 second mortgage, which would net me about $3,000 annually for several years.

The first annual payment was on time, and I was delighted with my profitable deal ... until the second payment came due. The buyer informed me that he couldn't meet his obligation. Further, he said, he was filing for bankruptcy, and he had not been paying his bills for some time.

What a terrible experience for a beginning investor! I was forced to take the property back, and it made me feel somewhat like the bad guy in a melodrama, foreclosing on the mortgage and driving Penelope and her grandmother into the snow. (Actually, it was summer, and he owned a rental property that he could move into.) The fact that I knew I was doing nothing wrong eased the pain a little, but it was a nasty, troublesome situation, and I felt as though I had been burned.

I was determined to continue investing, so I learned everything I could about prequalifying buyers. How would a banker, for example, have found out that my buyer was a poor risk? I learned a few keys that I think will help you avoid the same mistake:

First, never assume that the buyer is a good credit risk just because he or she is well dressed and drives a nice car. Appearances can always be deceiving. Here's the most important thing that you can do to protect your interests (pay attention): *Make your contract contingent upon your receiving from them—and approving—a complete credit history.* Insist on a personal balance sheet and a report from a credit bureau. The following points are the most important to consider:

- Source of down payment.
- Monthly payment the buyer could carry.
- Employment information for each wage earner.
      Position
      Name and address of each employer
      Length of employment with previous employers
      Outlook for future employment
      If they are presently a two-income family, is that likely to continue, or will the wife quit work soon to have a baby?
- Monthly and annual income figures for the past several years (including any outside income).

If the buyers will be using the property as a personal residence, the total debt service (principal, interest, taxes, and insurance) should not be more than 30 percent of their monthly income. If they are buying the property as an investment, they should have sufficient income to handle any balloon payments or negative cash flows from vacancies or unexpected emergency repairs.

Lastly, the buyer's credit history should have no record of delinquency or default against a previous mortgage loan.

One of the difficulties that we all have as sellers is discussing the finances of the buyer. The subject seems rather personal, and it's one of the things that the bank usually takes care of. I've found that the simplest thing to do is bring up the subject when you are talking on the phone, before they ever come to see the property. Remind them that you are asking $3,000 cash and that the payments will be over $450 a month. Ask if that will be a problem. Most unqualified buyers will let themselves out of the deal at that point, since very few people will lie when they know the lie will be discovered later.

5) *Explain the benefits of purchasing the property with owner*

financing. It is exciting to show buyers just how much money they can save by not going the traditional route of financing by a bank loan. Not only will they save the time and trouble of the bank's red tape, but they will save loan origination fees and the higher market rates. Few buyers need to be convinced that the seller can offer a better deal than the bank, and those few can be turned around with a little honest education.

6) *Commit to the buyer.* This may sound strange, but I commit myself to the buyer's satisfaction before I commit myself to making the sale. I make no attempt to squeeze a buyer into the house if he or she doesn't naturally fit. With the hundreds of buyers out there, if a prospective buyer is an obvious mismatch, I offer to try to find him or her another house. Because I have made contacts in real estate agencies, banks, title offices, and with other investors, I can usually find a house that will fit the buyer, and I collect a finder's fee for my troubles.

If I don't know of a contact with just the perfect house, I will look for one that I can buy, fix up, and sell to this buyer. There is always a way to make people happy and make a dollar or two as well.

The bottom line when negotiating with potential buyers is getting them to say yes. To do this I use a type of question similar to the reflexive statements mentioned in the chapter on negotiation. The trick to these questions is to get the buyer to start saying yes. I will walk around the home and start pointing out important features of the home that I don't feel the buyer has noticed. I use statements similar to these:

> The closet space in here sure is roomy, isn't it?
> The living room is well decorated, isn't it?
> Hasn't the yard been well cared for?
> Doesn't the mechanical system look like it's in great shape?
> The kitchen sure is cheery, isn't it?

This isn't just a gimmick. Think about your experiences last time you bought something at a store because of a good salesman. Think about what he did that encouraged you to buy something and what he did that really bugged you. Then simply try to put into action the good things you have noticed in other sales situations, and avoid doing the things that really bug you. That is exactly what I have done to make the selling of my investment properties the fun experience it has been.

Well, are you excited about selling? I remember the very first time I tried to sell a home. I called up an agent (at the time I thought that that was what I was supposed to do) and listed the property. I don't want to go into too much detail, but the whole experience was one big disappointment. I was really upset; after all, wasn't the agent supposed to sell the property?

I took the property off the listing, started to study everything I could about the selling process, and made several visits to title companies to ask about making up an offer. A few days later I had my buyer, and before I knew what had happened we had closed. Afterward I felt like I had just gotten off one of those roller coasters in an amusement park. My head was spinning, not because of the hassle, or setting everything up, but because it was so easy.

When the dust had settled on that first deal and somebody else owned the property, I went back and did a little calculation. I had cleared $3,660 with just under twenty-two hours' work. Breaking that down with a calculator, I realized that I had made over $166 an hour—not bad for a few hours' work.

I don't think you will really enjoy the process of investing until you close your first sale. It won't be until you have that cash in hand and a steady income stream for years that you will get really enthused. The first deal is the hardest, but if you can make it all the way through to that first sale, your investing career will take off like a rocket.

PART III

Special Tips for the Beginning Investor

CHAPTER 10

Looking Back . . . A Review

Success is a journey,
not a destination.
    —BEN SWEETLAND

Where do you go when you want to be alone to think? I love to jump in my car and drive down one of those long and lonesome roads the West is famous for. I was on such a road yesterday, thinking about the last twenty-four years. It was twenty-four years ago, give or take a month, when my mother bundled a little boy up in a big coat and sent him off to school for the first time. I've spent twenty-one of those twenty-four years attending some type of formal education. Imagine that.

Now, looking back over the thousands of hours that were spent in hundreds of classes, I am unable to remember one lesson on achieving personal success. I memorized centuries of history and juggled jillions of numbers, but I was never taught how to set a goal and see it through.

Amazing.

All of these thoughts swarmed in my brain as I chewed up a hundred mountain miles. I asked the same question that has puzzled successful people for years: what is wrong with our system of education, that we turn out generations of graduates capable of building skyscrapers and saving lives, but unable to save enough money to retire in comfort? I know that the American Dream is not dead. People can do anything they want with their lives, but so many don't. Why? What is wrong with the people?

157

The real question is, what is missing in our system of education and training? And the answer: There is no course in school that teaches individual responsibility, that teaches entrepreneurial skills. There is no Success 101.

Let's look at the idea a little further. Why is success not taught? Is it because of a lack of knowledge, a lack of teachers, or a lack of interest? The answer, I think, is none of the above. We know what is necessary for success. It is quantifiable and teachable. A course could certainly be offered that would allow students to identify their needs, establish their own definition of success, and set goals accordingly.

Maybe it is a lack of qualified teachers. After all, if you want to teach piano, you must know how to play. If you want to teach ballet, you must know how to dance. An instructor can't just teach students these skills by reading them out of a book. It stands to reason that if you want to teach success, you must be successful. And few teachers are truly successful as entrepreneurs. Few of them can do what they want to do, when they want to do it. They have docked their boats in the safe harbor of educating, which frees them from the risk-taking demands of carving their own financial freedom in the "real world."

Well, where are the people who could teach others this missing course, Success 101? They probably are so busy making money for themselves that they don't have time to help others, right?

I think I can lay that argument to rest. Of the many successful people I know or have read about, I cannot think of one who would not love to teach such a course. I'm sure Robert Allen would teach it. So would Og Mandino, Charles Givens, and Art Linkletter. In fact I think that these people are already teaching it, in their own way. Every one of these people has devoted years to teaching success. How are they doing it, you ask? They have written and published countless books, have been recorded on TV and audiocassette giving lectures at national conventions and investment forums. If the establishment of public education would elevate success to its rightful place—at the top of the curriculum—these would be the teachers, and their books, tapes, and videos would be brought into the classroom. No, I don't think that there is a shortage of teachers.

Why don't our schools teach our children how to take control of their lives and shape their own destinies? Why isn't Success 101 being taught in schools? I'll hazard a guess: it would destroy our establishment. It would literally destroy hundreds of years of so-called progress if suddenly everybody learned—and was forced to apply—the keys to success.

Where would the factories find assembly line workers? People would all insist on working for themselves. If grade school children were taught how to budget their pennies instead of just how to make change for a dollar, they would have enough in high school to start their own enterprises. And then who would serve you your Double Whopper?

If every college freshman had to set specific, success-oriented goals, and then had to achieve those goals before the end of the semester to pass the class, what would the result be when he or she graduated? Everybody would insist on setting goals and then working toward achieving those goals. Nobody would be satisfied with a weekly hand-to-mouth existence.

Chaos would reign. There would be no human robots left to perform the menial tasks that need to be done. We would finally be confronted by true capitalism at its best.

So I suppose we should be grateful that success isn't taught. But still, it's kind of a shame that millions of Americans go to bed every night feeling frustrated and worthless. Maybe that's the price for progress. Just think what would happen if everybody knew how to buy houses at wholesale prices. Both the wholesale and the retail markets would adjust, and we, as investors, would be confronted with competition from every citizen.

Of course I'm being facetious. I would rather that everybody would learn the keys to success. The alternatives for any person are virtually limitless, once they learn how to apply their energy toward achieving a goal. Armed with that knowledge and confidence, they could achieve success in anything they chose, be it real estate investing or starting up a company for making coat hangers.

Let's take everything we've looked at so far and put it all together in one picture:

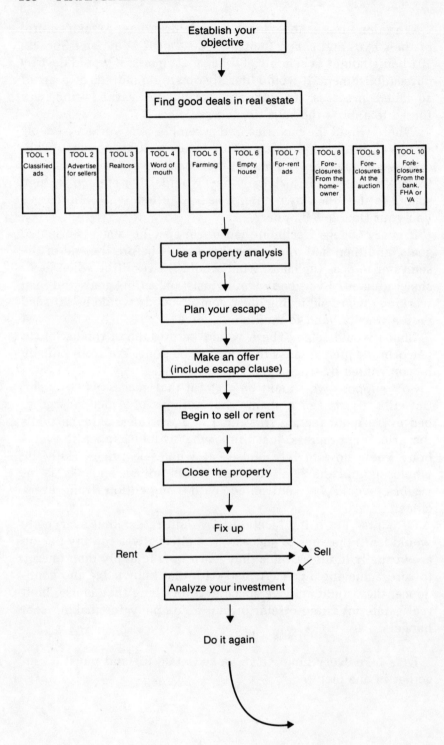

If, as you look over this diagram, you see a few weak links, backtrack and review those chapters. Every step is important and you cannot afford to ignore even one.

So far a book like this is the only type of success course offered for investing other than some seminars and workshops . . . oh yes, and life itself. Unfortunately, life waits about seventy or eighty years before giving the final, and when you finally realize why you failed it's usually too late to retake the course.

This book is meant to be a success book, and it has a very clear-cut message about how to reach that degree of success you desire. I firmly believe that, through study and experience, you can find in real estate the monetary base you will need for true wealth—wealth that cannot be measured in dollars and cents.

I believe strongly that if you will apply every one of the tools to your life, every day, you cannot help but succeed. To me it is as obvious as saying that if you jump in front of a speeding train it will run you down. It's true; once you jump onto the track of success, there is no escape unless you jump off again. It's not just a principle of success; it's a law.

What I have shared with you is a proven plan for achieving financial freedom through real estate investing. I know that real estate investing is the surest, safest road to financial freedom. But you could take real estate out of my plan. Use any other vehicle for your success; if you work with educated persistence toward a clear goal, the result will eventually be the same. If you need to choose something other than real estate, then great. I just believe that real estate investing will get you there faster.

What I have tried to do is teach that class you didn't get in school. If you take this class seriously, I don't think you will be willing to climb someone else's ladder; you will build and climb a ladder of your own.

America is the land of opportunity. In no other country can people take their lives in their own hands and determine their future as in America. It's the reason why so many people look to this country as a beacon of hope, a chance to succeed. Hundreds of thousands of people have come to this country with no more than a pocket full of dreams and a suitcase full of hopes and have reached their financial goals. These people weren't conditioned to believe that "it can't be done . . . the economy is depressed . . . the country is falling apart."

I hope that I have helped strip away the years of negative conditioning that have stopped you from achieving your dreams. The economy is on track, the opportunities of yesterday live on. Today is a time when anyone willing to put forth effort can achieve any dream they have.

— CHAPTER 11 —

Investing Profitably in Your Spare Time

I am a great believer in luck, and
I find the harder I work the more I
have of it.
    —STEPHEN LEACOCK

While the chapter title suggests something akin to "licking stamps in your spare time for fun and profit," the truth is that you can invest—successfully—in real estate, using no more than five to ten hours a week. For the person who is content with his or her job, who has no desire to retire early and escape from working-class drudgery, this is the easy way to invest.

There is no reason that an investor must do everything himself. Friends, relatives, college students, part-time help, Realtors, bankers, and countless others are all available as assistants. By borrowing money from other people and paying them back later, you are leveraging your money; by using other people's time and efforts and paying them back later in the form of real estate commissions or increased business, you are leveraging your time.

Real Estate's Two Main Keys to Success

Two items have proved to be necessary keys to success in real estate investing. Those keys are *educated persistence* and *the ability to find good deals.* This book has been written to serve you as a source of education, motivation, and reference, to help you develop that educated persistence. Learning this lesson is essential preparation for your journey to financial freedom.

No matter how well this or other books have been prepared,

163

they cannot and will not ever change your financial life unless they turn your dreams and desires into a concrete plan of action. With that plan you must then dare to succeed, conscientiously working to turn your goals into reality. How does that happen? There is no other way than through your own hard, smart work and guts.

The other necessary key is the ability to find good deals. You might know how to be the perfect manager, how to structure a hundred and one creative contracts, but if you can't consistently find and recognize good deals in real estate, you will never make a dime. You will be like a painter without paints—lots of talent but no product. To find good deals, people often spend countless hours driving around looking at homes for sale by owner or listed through a realty agent. They begin to realize through the frustration of these wasted hours that there must be a better way. Many people stop investing at this point because they feel confused. They know of the potential in real estate investing, but they can't seem to make it work in their lives. So they give up.

Those who don't give up, force success on themselves by putting more and more time into real estate investing. They spend even more hours looking for deals, as if they were building a home without power tools. After I had been investing for a while I found myself spending fifty or more hours a week trying to find those good deals. I was on my road to success, but my wife, children, and mental health were in jeopardy. I was making money but losing or missing out on the things that I really consider to be important.

Necessity is the mother of invention, and this necessity drove me to find another way that would fit the life of someone who wanted to be human, enjoy his family, and still make it in real estate.

THE PROPERTY ANALYSIS SYSTEM

When I started to think about putting together a system for finding good deals in real estate, I realized that the normal methods of finding them are analogous to hammering in a nail with a teaspoon. It can be done, but it takes about three months of full-time work. I knew there must be a better way—a hammer, so to speak, that could pound the nail in in seconds instead of weeks. There must, I thought, be a better system for finding good deals.

I went through every problem I had faced—lack of organization, wasting time visiting properties I didn't want to buy, etc.— and developed one of the greatest investing tools in existence.

How the Property Analysis System Can Help You Find Bargain Properties

Before I explain the system, let me explain three of its main attributes.

1. You as an individual investor can, through the use of the property analysis sytem, vastly improve the focus of the time and effort you spend in finding bargain properties. What the property analysis system can do to your investing portfolio is no different from what a magnifying glass does to the rays of the sun. It can concentrate your efforts into a powerful force.
2. It will organize your efforts to the point where you can buy several good properties a month with less than ten hours of your time each week.
3. It will remove most of the risk associated with investing in real estate. It will help you know exactly how much each property is worth before you buy it, how much repairs will cost, what the property can be resold for, and how much it can be rented for. With these figures in an organized system, success will be assured.

That's an awfully big claim, but it's true. You will find that by using this system you will no longer be wasting your time burning up your gas trying to find that golden property. You will only visit properties that you already know you want to buy. You will visit the properties to verify some facts and to do a physical inspection. You won't be guessing all the way up to closing if you are buying a good deal.

Let's look a minute at "normal investing." Most investors find that about two out of one hundred people they contact are what they can really call motivated sellers. Of those two people who want practically to give away their homes, only about three out of ten cases really have something to offer that is worth buying. In the other seven cases, something makes the deal unprofitable, such as the property's financing or state of disrepair, and the investor wouldn't want to touch it. The danger here is that some investors may not recognize that many of the deals which look good on the outside contain a hidden flaw. How can they get to the point where they can recognize these hidden flaws? Have patience, we'll get to that.

In other words, most investors have to kiss about 166 toads to find a good deal using the conventional Realtor/newspaper ads/waste-your-gasoline/drive-yourself-around-town-and-drive-yourself-nuts method.

To illustrate the use of my analysis system let's begin with step one.

Step 1: Locate some prospects.

You should have already started using several tools for finding good deals in real estate. In other words, you should now have several lines baited and cast out into the water. For explanation purposes, let's choose the most basic tool for finding real estate bargains there is, newspaper ads, though you could substitute any of the other real estate tools in its place. Let's not scoff at using ads, though. I know someone who has purchased 251 rental units in four months using "just real estate ads."

The first thing I do when I find out about a potential good deal is to prepare a property analysis worksheet. See the following pages for a sample of the form I have developed.

When you read the paper and find ads that you would like to call on, simply cut them out and place them in the large square in the upper right-hand corner of the worksheet. Do this with all of the ads that catch your eye. If you are using a tool other than ads, such as advertising for sellers, just write this information in the space provided.

If you can't call right then, place the analysis sheet in the first section of a property organizer. (I have developed a binder for organizing these sheets, which includes seven laminated dividers and a complete supply of property analysis worksheets. The first

Property Analysis Worksheet

Ad date _____

Phone date _____

Inspection date _____

Ad or Picture

1   GENERAL INFORMATION

Property address _____

Owner's name _____

Owner's address and phone _____

Tenant's name and phone _____

Type of dwelling _____
(single-family, duplex, etc.)

2   Zoning _____

Selling price _____

Total amt. of current loans $ _____

Total equity $ _____

3   LOAN INFORMATION

Loan amount	Payment	% Rate	Assumable	Type	Held by

P. & I. _____

Taxes _____ ÷ 12

Insurance _____ ÷ 12

Total _____ P.I.T.I.

SAMPLE

4   TERMS:

5   RENTAL INFORMATION

	Rental income	Comparable rents	Square footage	# Bedrooms	Baths
Unit 1					
Unit 2					
Unit 3					
Unit 4					
Total Rents					

6   Utilities paid by:

	Owner	Tenant	Separate meters	Estimated cost
Gas				
Electric				
Water				
Sewer				
Trash				
Other				

(continued on next page)

divided section is titled "properties to call on." These property analysis systems are sold through The National Committee for Real Estate Investment, P.O. Box 796, Provo, Utah 84603. Feel free to contact them for ordering information.) Then, as soon as you can, call on the properties you have filed.

168 FINANCIALLY FREE

(continued from page 167)

7 NEGOTIATION PREPARATION QUESTIONS

1) Owner's reason for selling _____
2) How was price determined? _____
3) How long has it been for sale? _____
4) Owner's need for down payment _____
5) Brick or frame _____
6) Age of dwelling _____
7) Current condition of property (owner's stated!) _____

Actual Physical Inspection Checklist (Good, Fair, Poor)

Interior

Paint _____
Door knobs _____
Sinks _____
Carpets _____
Doors _____
Toilets (flush) _____
Insulation _____
Linoleum _____
Light fix. _____
Shower _____
Insects/Termites _____

Appliances (turn on and check each)

Refrigerator _____
Stove _____
Dishwasher _____
Air conditioner _____

Garbage disposal _____
Heater _____
type _____
type _____

Exterior

Lawn _____
Drive _____
_____
_____
Porch _____
Windows _____
Foundation _____
Shrubs _____
Sidewalk _____
Roof _____
Garage _____

Location Consideration

Proximity to parks _____
Proximity to schools _____
Public transportation _____
Shopping centers _____
Grocery stores _____
Flooding problems _____

Type and Condition of Neighborhood

Single-family residences _____
Rental area _____
Commercial area _____
Condition of neighborhood _____
Other _____
Business area _____

SAMPLE

NOTES

OFFER MADE _____
(Date)

© The National Committee for Real Estate Investment, P.O. Box 796, Provo, Utah 84603

Step 2: Make the initial call.

An ad that all us have heard is one put out by Ma Bell that says, "Let your fingers do the walking." This is exactly what you are doing in making the initial phone call. Instead of driving out to a property only to find out that it is something that won't fit your investment portfolio, you make that decision in three to four minutes on the phone. By asking the right questions when you call, you will save yourself time and gas money. How much time? If you were to look at five properties a day, my experience has shown you would be spending seven or more hours. The average time to look at a property is a half hour, with a total of another hour spent driving out to it and back home again. Using the analysis system, you can cut that down to five minutes, with the same results.

The questions that the worksheet prompts you to ask are the product of eight years of investing. I had to develop a system that would allow me to get the most out of my time while I was working and going to school full-time. I think it works extremely well, and I know it works better than any system I have tried that someone else developed.

With the worksheet in front of you, an ad taped to the top corner, and a pen in your hand, you are ready for action. Now all you need to do is call the phone number in the ad and start talking.

I've found that the best way to start the conversation is with, "Are you a serious seller?" The usual response is, "Of course."

"Great," you say, "because I am a serious buyer. I have a few questions that I'd like you to answer so I can determine if your property is what I am looking for."

By starting this way, you are putting yourself squarely in the driver's seat. The seller is expecting you to ask questions and is prepared to answer them. This opening, combined with the property analysis sheet's clear-cut format, eliminates a fumbling, confused inquiry.

It never takes more than four minutes to run through the information sheet. Just ask for the information listed, such as "Are you the owner?" "What is your (or the owner's) name?" If the person at the other end of the phone doesn't know the answers, find out when someone will be available that can answer your questions. You will need loan information, which the sellers may not be sure about, but they can find out easily for you.

To me some of the most crucial questions are those about what the sellers are asking for the property, and how they expect to be paid. Will they take their equity on a contract? Are they willing to be flexible on price or terms?

The next section goes into more specific information about the rental income of the property, comparable rents, square footage, and number of bedrooms and baths. You also need to know about the utilities. Who pays them, and how much will they cost? Are the meters separate?

The last section is a series of seven very probing—and very essential—questions—the most important questions, since the answers give away the owner's motivation and can help you negotiate more effectively. You should learn the owner's reason for selling, how was the price determined, etc. The last question is the icing on the cake. It asks the seller to explain what is wrong with the property. Tell the seller that you are very busy and refuse to waste your time driving out to the property to find out that the roof blew off last week.

Step 3: Look at the property.

If the price, terms, and flexibility of the seller are all promising, you have found a property to visit. If not, throw the sheet in the trashcan and go on to the next. Congratulations, you have just eliminated countless wasted hours that you would otherwise have spent driving from house to house, checking on unmotivated sellers.

If the property looks really great, don't wait; drive out there right away. If it looks okay, but not spectacular, save it, together with three or four other homes, and visit them all on a Saturday afternoon.

When you visit the house itself, check every room carefully. Follow every step on the "Physical Inspection Checklist" section of the worksheet. (You may want to leave the worksheet in the car, as many sellers will be frightened off if they see how professional you are in your real estate investing.) Actually flush the toilets. Check the ceilings indoors; a discolored spot may indicate a leak in the roof.

Look for out-of-season problems. It may be sunny and hot outside, and the air conditioning may work beautifully, but what about the heater? Six months from now you may find yourself wishing you had tried the heater in the middle of summer.

When you visit the property, please write down in the note

sections exactly what type of appliances are included in the sale. I have felt too many times the disastrous effects of writing down "fridge" instead of "17 cu. ft. Amana almond refrigerator." It's amazing how a 17-cubic-foot, brand-new refrigerator can shrink to a 9-cubic-foot clunker by the closing date.

On page 172 is an actual completed property analysis worksheet. It should give you a good idea how filling in the blanks will help you eliminate visiting every property you are interested in. With a careful property analysis, you will be able to investigate only the few properties that really are good deals.

If while visiting the property I find I like everything, I will immediately tie the property up with an earnest money agreement—using what? That's right, a promissory note as consideration to bind the agreement, and at least several good escape clauses. If I am not quite sure, I thank the sellers for their time and tell them that I will think about it for a while. Regardless of which step I take, I always do a careful property analysis.

Step 4. Do a financial analysis.

When I decide to do a financial analysis I stick the property into the next section of my organizer, called "properties to do a financial analysis on." Let me tell you the key points of any financial analysis.

1) *Determine the market value of the property.* Find at least three houses in the area that are similar to the house you are considering buying. Try to find houses that are as identical as possible in size, general condition, and amenities. (You can find these comparable homes from your farm records, or by looking up some recent sales of similar homes in your agent's M.L.S. book.) Find out the selling price, and then adjust that price by estimating the value of the differences between those houses and the one you are analyzing.

Set up a grid of comparables like the one on page 174. The average adjusted sales price will give you an idea as to the real market value of the house. That is the value of the system. If a seller is asking $72,000 for a house, how do you know whether or not that is a fair price? With this system you have done your homework and you know that the market value for the house is

Property Analysis Worksheet

Ad date ___6/21/86___
Phone date ___6/21/86___
Inspection date ___6/22/86___

<table>
<tr><td colspan="2">**Ad or Picture**</td></tr>
</table>

1   GENERAL INFORMATION
Property address _1917 Fir Avenue_
Owner's name _J.B. Mikelson_
Owner's address and phone _1917 Fir Avenue_
Tenant's name and phone ___—___
Type of dwelling _single family_
(single-family, duplex, etc.)

2   Zoning _residential_
Selling price _78,500_
Total amt. of current loans $ _58,000_
Total equity $ _20,500_

3   LOAN INFORMATION

Loan amount	Payment	% Rate	Assumable	Type	Held by
58,000	$672	11½	yes	FHA 203	Central Bank

P. & I.	included in
Taxes	+ 12	the
Insurance	+ 12	payment
Total	P.I.T.I.	

4   TERMS: $5,000 (wants) down / needs the
assume first – $15,500 on second mortgage / $5000 – but will
at 11% due in 3 years / deal on the
second!

5   RENTAL INFORMATION

	Rental income	Comparable rents	Square footage	# Bedrooms	Baths
Unit 1	single family	$700	1450	3	2
Unit 2					
Unit 3					
Unit 4					
Total Rents	$700				

6   Utilities paid by:

	Owner	Tenant	Separate meters	Estimated cost
Gas	✓			70 winter 25 summer
Electric	✓			50 " 50 "
Water	✓			16.50 city util
Sewer	✓			
Trash	✓			
Other	✓			

$65,000. Obviously the owner is way off base, and you shouldn't consider offering any more than $60,000, and hopefully a lot less; you have to buy equity.

Add the adjusted sales prices together and divide by the number of comparable homes you found. That amount is the adjusted sales price for the property you are considering. If the property is

7   NEGOTIATION PREPARATION QUESTIONS

1) Owner's reason for selling _Divorce_
2) How was price determined? _From what neighbors sold their home for last year_
3) How long has it been for sale? _6 months w/ agent_
4) Owner's need for down payment _Divorce costs / etc._
5) Brick or frame _Brick w/ al. soffits_
6) Age of dwelling _8 years old_
7) Current condition of property (owner's stated!) _a little dirty / needs repair_

Actual Physical Inspection Checklist (Good, Fair, Poor)

Interior

Paint	_good_
Door knobs	_"_
Sinks	_"_
Carpets	_"_
Doors	_"_
Toilets (flush)	_good_
Insulation	_good_
Linoleum	_fair_
Light fix.	_good_
Shower	_poor (dirty)_
Insects/Termites	_good_

Appliances (turn on and check each)

Refrigerator	✓
Stove	✓
Dishwasher	✓
Air conditioner	✓ (electric)

Garbage disposal	✓
Heater	✓
type	_gas_
type	

Exterior

Lawn	_poor_
Driveway	_good_
Paint	_poor_
Fence	_good_
Trees	_good_
Porch	_"_
Windows	_"_
Foundation	_"_
Shrubs	_"_
Sidewalk	_"_
Roof	_"_
Garage	_"_

Location Consideration

Proximity to parks	_close_
Proximity to schools	_close_
Public transportation	_(no bus)_
Shopping centers	_poor_
Grocery stores	_poor_
Flooding problems	_none —_

Type and Condition of Neighborhood

Single-family residences	✓
Rental area	_no_
Commercial area	_no_
Condition of neighborhood	_good – family's_
Other	_—_
Business area	_none close_

NOTES   _Offer to include 19 cu. ft. Amana fridge_

OFFER MADE   _6/24/86_
(Date)

to be fixed up, find at least three houses in the area that are similar to what the house will be like when you are through with your repairs. Do exactly the same as you did with the current condition estimate and you will have a good idea what the market will bear when you are finished working on the property.

COMPARATIVE ANALYSIS GRID

ITEM	SUBJECT PROPERTY	COMPARABLE #1	ADJUST-MENT	COMPARABLE #2	ADJUST-MENT	COMPARABLE #3	ADJUST-MENT
PRICE	?	$63,500		$67,000		$62,300	
SIZE	100'x200'	100'x250'	–500	100'x200'	0	100'x200'	0
LANDSCAPE	GOOD	POOR	+500	GOOD	0	POOR	+500
SQ. FEET	1200	1100	+1,000	1150	+500	1200	0
AGE	5 YRS.	10 YRS.	+1,000	2 YRS.	–2,000	10 YRS.	+1,000
EXT. FEATURES	PATIO	PATIO	0	NO PATIO	+500	PATIO	0
EXT. FEATURES	SPRINKLERS	NONE	+500.	YES	0	NONE	+500
LOCATION	GOOD	POOR	–1,000	POOR	–1,000	GOOD	0
TIME OF SALE	CURRENT	3 MONTHS	+500	3 WEEKS	0	LAST MONTH	0
FINANCING	11.5 ASSUM.	12.5 ASSUM.	+1,000	9.5 ASSUM.	–2,000	NON-ASSUM.	+2,000
EXTRAS	APPLIANCES	NONE	–1,000	MOWER/STOVE	+1,000	NONE	–1,000
TOTAL ADJUSTMENTS			+2,000		–3,000		+3,000
ADJUSTED SALES PRICE		$65,500		$64,000		$65,300	

AVERAGE SALES PRICE = $65,500
64,000
65,300
$194,800 ÷ 3 = $64,933 ADJUSTED AVERAGE SALES PRICE

If this is a rental property, find other rental properties that are similar and get comparable rents—for both the present condition and the proposed condition.

2) *Estimate the proposed costs of purchase.* Find out how much the closing and other costs will be. Don't just assume these. For free estimates of those costs, call an expert. Find out from a title company what closing costs would be involved and go through these expenses.

3) *Estimate the costs of repairs.* If repairs are needed you may want to call in a contractor to give you estimates. Most contractors will not charge a dime for this estimate. You could also first have the city inspector come in and point out any major repairs that are needed, then call up a contractor and get a quick verbal bid on these anticipated fix-up expenses. As you get more experienced you will find that you will be able to give your own ballpark estimates of the fix-up expenses.

4) *Estimate your total out-of-pocket expenses.* Your out-of-pocket expenses will include the down payment (unless you are going to borrow that or bring in a partner); the fix-up costs; the closing costs; the monthly payments that you will have to make before you sell the property; the advertising costs when the time comes to sell; any attorney fees for closing or handling the legalities; and the closing costs that you will have to pay when you sell the property to someone else.

If you cannot estimate these costs, call an expert to help you. I recommend that you compile a list of local experts: an attorney who understands real estate; a title officer who is willing and able to help you; other investors who are willing to offer advice; a professional appraiser; and electricians, carpenters, and other contractors who will give you bids on work that needs to be done.

5) *Make your decision.* Write down the estimated resale price (using the adjusted sales price as the actual market value). Subtract the total estimated buying costs, including all financing and closing costs. That will give you an estimate for your gross profit. Next, write the down payment that you think you will receive when you sell. Remember, your property will move quickly if you are willing to accept a small down payment—maybe just enough to cover your out-of-pocket expenses with a little left over for the next deal.

Then subtract the estimated down payment to be received from the estimated selling price. That will give you an idea as to how much equity you will have after selling. You may be tempted to ask for all of that equity in cash, but if you are willing to take it on an interest-bearing note you will have a monthly income for many years, and you will find the property easy to sell.

6) *Flip it or hold it.* To make this decision follow these simple steps: First estimate the monthly cash flow on the property if it were rented. This is done by subtracting your monthly payments from the estimated amounts of net operating income you are generating. If you are in a high tax bracket you might also want to grab a tax schedule and throw in the proposed tax benefits. I then suggest that you estimate the amount of money you have available for reinvesting if you choose to hold the property as a rental.

If this property totally drains your investment fund, I suggest that you consider immediately reselling the property. This would instantly give you a 100 percent return on your investment capital, but also hopefully some instant cash profit besides the equity you may have taken back in an AITD or a second trust deed.

Step 5: Make the offer.

If the financial analysis indicates that the deal is profitable, you should be ready to make a written offer. This is the point where many would-be investors drop out of the pack. If you have in-

spected the property and estimated your profits, nothing should
hold you back at this point. You can obtain an earnest money and
purchase offer form at any local office supply store. *Only use a*
purchase offer form made for your state. You should customize
the forms with some of the clauses we have talked about, such as
escape clauses. If you need help writing up the offer, call a professional—a title officer, real estate attorney, or real estate agent.
You will find that a good real estate professional will be happy to
help you for free if you indicate that you will conduct the closing
at his or her office, or do some business with him or her in the future.

When making an offer, keep in mind that your original offer
may only be a springboard for negotiations. Allow yourself some
room. A rule of thumb is to make your initial offer at least 15 percent below market value and negotiate from there. If you think
the property is worth $56,000, and you know that you might be
able to buy it for $53,000, but you would love to get it for $50,000,
offer $48,000. You are $8,000 away from the actual value of the
property, but that is a good place to start, and you will be amazed
at how many times your offer is immediately accepted.

Take the offer to the owner. What else do you need to do?

Step 6: Buy it, save it, or give it away.

If your offer is accepted, you own a new property. If the owner is
willing to negotiate, all you have to do is iron out your differences
and you own a new property. If the owner rejects your offer and
won't negotiate, file the offer away in an organizer, in a section
entitled either "properties to refer to others" or "properties to
check on later." If you know someone who is looking for the same
type of property, why not turn it over to him or her? You can establish a reputation as a professional investor, and people whose
backs you have scratched will usually be happy to return the
favor.

If you feel that the deal is a good one and the seller is close to
negotiating, file it away to be checked on later. Three weeks can
do a lot for a seller's motivation, and two months can positively
work miracles.

What I do is date stamp each refused offer and call back two weeks later. I ask the seller if he or she is still serious about selling. If he says he is, I then identify myself and say that I would like to make him the same offer again to purchase his property. As crazy as this may seem, at least 25 percent of the people say yes to my offers the second time through. Why? I think it's because they haven't received any better offers, and they are now more aware of the true market value of their property. They are tired of keeping it in the paper. But most importantly, when you say that you are calling back two weeks after they refused your offer to make the same offer again, they are impressed with your organization and persistence. They recognize you as a competent person. In fact, you are someone who they probably now believe would make payments on time. They want to sell to you.

By keeping the entire system up to date, you can literally have an entire book of good deals at your fingertips. So many people

---

Earnest Money Receipt and Offer to Purchase

"This is a legally-binding contract; if not understood, seek competent advice."

1. **Date and Place of Offer:** 6/24 1986 Smithville (city) Conn. (state)

2. **Principals:** The undersigned Buyer Marc Stephen Garrison agrees to buy and Seller agrees to sell, according to the indicated terms and conditions, the property described as follows:

3. **Property:** located at 1917 Fir Avenue, Smithville, (city) Conn. (state) (street address)

with the following legal description: n/a
including any of the following items if at present attached to the premises: plumbing, heating, and cooling equipment, including stoker and oil tanks, burners, water heaters, electric light fixtures, bathroom fixtures, roller shades, curtain rods and fixtures, draperies, venetian blinds, window and door screens, towel racks, linoleum and other attached floor coverings, including carpeting, attached television antennas, mailboxes, all trees and shrubs, and any other fixtures, EXCEPT no exceptions

The following personal property shall also be included as part of the purchase: 19 cu. ft. Amana almond colored refrigerator. At the close of the transaction, the Seller, at his expense, shall provide the Buyer with a Bill Of Sale containing a detailed inventory of the personal property included.

4. **Earnest Money Deposit:** Agent (or Seller) acknowledges receipt from Buyer of five hundred and 0/100 dollars $ 500.00 in the form of ( ) cash; ( ) personal check; ( ) cashier's check; (X) promissory note at 0 interest per annum due on closing 19____
or other n/a
as earnest money deposit to secure and apply on this purchase. Upon acceptance of this agreement in writing and delivery of same to Buyer, the earnest money deposit shall be assigned to and deposited in the listing Realtor's trust account or n/a to apply on the purchase price at the time of closing.

5. **Purchase Price:** The total purchase price of the property shall be Seventy thousand and 0/100 dollars $ 70,000.

6. **Payment:** Purchase price is to be paid by Buyer as follows: Aforedescribed earnest money deposit. . . . . . $ 500.00
Additional payment due upon accept. . . . $ 0
Additional payment due at cl. . . . . $ 4,500.00
Balance to be paid as follows: Seller to take back second mortgage for $7,000. This second mortgage is to be paid as follows: 120 equal monthly payments at 11% interest. There will be no pre-payment penalty changed if buyer decides to pay this off early.

SAMPLE

7. **Title:** Seller agrees to furnish good and marketable title free of all encumbrances and defects, except mortgage liens and encumbrances as set forth in this agreement, and to make conveyance by Warranty Deed or n/a Seller shall furnish in due course to the Buyer a title insurance policy insuring the Buyer of a good and marketable title in keeping with the terms and conditions of this agreement. Prior to the closing of this transaction, the Seller, upon request, will furnish to the Buyer a preliminary title report made by a title insurance company showing the condition of the title to said property. If the Seller cannot furnish marketable title within thirty days after receipt of the notice to the Buyer containing a written statement of the defects, the earnest money deposit herein receipted shall be refunded to the Buyer and this agreement shall be null and void. The following shall not be deemed encumbrances or defects: building and use restrictions general to the area; utility easements; other easements not inconsistent with Buyer's intended use; zoning or subdivision laws, covenants, conditions, restrictions, or reservations of record; tenancies of record. In the event of sale of other than real property relating to this transaction, Seller will provide evidence of title or right to sell or lease such personal property.

8. **Special Representations:** Seller warrants and represents to Buyer (1) that the subject property is connected to ( ) public sewer system, ( ) cesspool or septic tank, ( ) sewer system available but not connected, ( ) city water system, ( ) private water system, and that the following special improvements are included in the sale: ( ) sidewalk, ( ) curb and gutter, ( ) special street paving, ( ) special street lighting, ( ) that the Seller knows of no material structural defects; (3) that all electrical wiring, heating, cooling, and plumbing systems are free of material defects and will be in good working order at the time the Buyer is entitled to possession; (4) that the Seller has no notice from any government agency or knowledge of probable violations of the law relating to the subject property; (5) that the Seller has no notice or knowledge of planned or commenced public improvements which may result in special assessments or otherwise directly and materially affect the property; and (6) that the Seller has no notice or knowledge of any liens to be assessed against the property, EXCEPT n/a

9. **Escrow Instructions:** This sale shall be closed on or before 7/16 1985 by Action Title Company or such other closing agent as mutually agreed upon by Buyer and Seller. Buyer and Seller will, immediately upon demand, deposit with closing agent all instruments and monies required to complete the purchase in accordance with the provisions of this agreement. Contract of Sale or Instrument of Conveyance to be made in the name of Marc S. Garrison and/or assigns.

10. **Closing Costs and Pro-Ration:** Seller agrees to pay for title insurance policy, preliminary title report (if requested), termite inspection as set forth below, real estate commission, cost of preparing and recording any corrective instruments, and one-half of the escrow fees. Buyer agrees to pay for recording fees for mortgages and deeds of conveyance, all costs or expenses in securing new financing or assuming existing financing, and one-half of the escrow fees. Taxes for the current year, insurance acceptable to the Buyer, rents, interest, mortgage reserves, maintenance fees, and water and other utilities constituting liens, shall be pro-rated as of closing. Renters' security deposits shall accrue to Buyer at closing. Seller to provide Buyer with current rental or lease agreements prior to closing.

11. **Termite Inspection:** Seller agrees, at his expense, to provide written certification by a reputable licenced pest control firm that the property is free of termite infestation. In the event termites are found, the Seller shall have the property treated at his expense and provide acceptable certification that treatment has been rendered. If any structural repairs are required by reason of termite damage as established by acceptable certification, Seller agrees to make necessary repairs not to exceed $500. If repairs exceed $500, Buyer shall first have the right to accept the property "as is" with a credit of $500 to the Buyer at closing, or the Buyer may terminate this agreement with the earnest money deposit being promptly returned to the Buyer if the Seller does not agree to pay all costs of treatment and repair.

12. **Conditions of Sale:** The following conditions shall also apply, and shall, if conflicting with the printed portions of this agreement, prevail and control:

Offer subject to partners approval. Offer subject to satisfactory inspection of the property by a building contractor and a termite inspector.

13. **Liability and Maintenance:** Seller shall maintain subject property, including landscaping, in good condition until the date of transfer of title or possession by Buyer, whichever occurs first. All risk of loss and destruction of property, and all expenses of insurance, shall be borne by the Seller until the date of possession. If the improvements on the property are destroyed or materially damaged prior to closing, then the Buyer shall have the right to declare this agreement null and void, and the earnest money deposit and all other sums paid by Buyer toward the purchase price shall be returned to the Buyer forthwith.

14. **Possession:** The Buyer shall be entitled to possession of property upon closing or _n/a_

15. **Default:** In the event the Buyer fails to complete the purchase as herein provided, the earnest money deposit shall be ret~ ~the Seller as the total and entire liquidated damages. In the event the Seller fails to perform any condition of the sale as herein provided, then the Buyer, may, at his option, treat the contract as termina~ ~ments made by the Buyer hereunder shall be returned to the Buyer forth-with, provided the Buyer may, at his option, treat this agreement as being in full force and effect with the right to actio~ ~ance and damages. In the event that either Buyer, Seller, or Agent shall institute suit to enforce any rights hereunder, the prevailing party shall be entitled to court costs and a reason~

16. **Time Limit of Offer:** The Seller shall have until _5:00 pm_ _6/25_ _19 86_
   (hour) _(date)_

to accept this offer by delivering a signed copy hereof to the Buyer. If this offer is not acce~ ~Agent (or Seller) shall refund the earnest money deposit to the Buyer forthwith.

17. **General Agreements:** (1) Both parties to this purchase reserve their rights to assign ~ ~o cooperate in effecting an Internal Revenue Code 1031 exchange or similar tax-related arrangement prior to close of escrow, upon either party's written notice of intention to d~ ~offer by the Seller, this agreement shall become a contract between Buyer and Seller and shall inure to the benefit of the heirs, administrators, executors, successors, personal r~ ~of said parties. (3) Time is of the essence and an essential part of this agreement. (4) This contract constitutes the sole and entire agreement between the parties hereto and n~ ~shall be binding unless attached hereto and signed by all parties to the contract. No representations, promises, or inducements not included in this contract shall be binding~

18. **Buyer's Statement and Receipt:** "I/we hereby acknow~ ~rdance with the terms and conditions above stated and acknowledge receipt of a completed copy of this agree-

ment, which I/we have fully read and understand. Dated _6_ _24_ _19 85_ _8:00 am_
   (hour)

Address _P.O. Box 1096_ _Marc Stephen Garrison_ _____ Buyer
   Orem, Utah _84057_ _____ Buyer

Phone No: Home (_801_) _225-8777_ Business ( ) _(same)_

19. **Seller's Statement and Response:** "I/we approve and accept the above offer, which I/we have fully read and understand, and agree to the above terms and conditions this day of

_____ 19___
   (hour)

Address _____ Seller
   _____ Seller

Phone No: Home (_____) _____ Business (_____)

20. **Commission Agreement:** Seller agrees to pay a commission of_____ % of the gross sales price to

for services in this transaction, and agrees that, in the event of forfeiture of the earnest money deposit by the Buyer, said deposit shall be divided between the Seller's broker and the Seller (one half to each party), the Broker's part not to exceed the amount of the commission.

21. **Buyer's Receipt for Signed Offer:** The Buyer hereby acknowledges receipt of a copy of the above agreement bearing the Seller's signature in acceptance of this offer.

Dated _____ 19___ _____ Buyer
   _____ Buyer

©1983 The Allen Group, Inc. Form B82GL

have said, "I've looked, but I haven't been able to find any good deals." But when they are asked, "How many ads did you call on, how many houses did you look at, how many offers did you make?" the answer is invariably the same: "Well, I . . ." If you call on several properties each night, it won't be long till you have found several properties to look at each Saturday.

Soon you'll be writing one or two offers a week. Soon you'll be getting one to two accepted per month. Soon you'll have enough money to do what you want, when you want. I think you can see how successful you can be if you put just one or two hours a day into this. You'll be getting bites on all your fishing lines and only spending time on the ones that are worth it.

This analysis system works, but only if you do.

Step 7: Do it again.

Here is the real key to success. It really needs no further explanation, does it?

You *can* invest in real estate in your spare time, but you will have to spare at least ten hours a week, every week. (That's just two hours a day, five days a week.) If you can commit that much time, there really is no way you can fail. Once you have educated yourself thoroughly and availed yourself of the many experts in your area, it's just a matter of putting a good property analysis system to work for you.

The good deals are out there waiting for you. What are you waiting for?

— CHAPTER 12————————————

Three Realistic Plans for Financial Freedom

You can't turn back the clock.
But you can wind it up again.
  —BONNIE PRUDDEN

There are only a few common goals that link people together. Every individual has a unique place in life, a past, present, and future that compels him to march to his own drummer. However, everybody desires security and comfort, freedom from worry, choice.

Seeking to satisfy those needs, we embark on careers, making the transition into the mainstream of society as smoothly as possible. A few of us are lucky; we are satisfied with the lots we have cast, thoroughly enjoying our careers. The majority, however, find their dreams shattered by reality and their futures shaped by circumstance.

Even for those who are satisfied—or happy—with the choices they have made, the future is far from certain. The statistics quoted earlier are horrifying, if we are willing to even consider them. A full 20 percent of all Americans have *no* net worth by the age of sixty-five. That magical age sixty-five is when we all hope to be enjoying a leisurely retirement. But think about it: only 15 percent of us will have more than $250 cash at that point! And that means you and me, not just the guy next door. The vast majority will be dependent on the government or their families for even a meager living.

Somehow, retirement poverty is like cancer. Nobody wants to even think about it, let alone talk about it. It's something that happens to someone else, not us—until we wake up in a cramped and dirty one-bedroom apartment, hobbling from the bedroom to

180

the living room to waste another day, and realizing that it's far too late for anything but despair.

The alternatives are clear: accept things as they are, find a new career, or find a plan to save and invest for the future (and the present). I have shown you a basic plan for investing in real estate. it sounds easy, right? But I'm worried. In spite of my best efforts, and in spite of the fact that most readers will be convinced, only a small fraction of them will actually do anything. It's a common reaction when investment experts try to teach, stimulate, motivate, and generally goad the public into action. Most people say, "That was a great book (or lecture), and it should work ... but I still don't feel like I know what to do Monday morning to get this thing off the ground." For lack of a concrete plan of action, they fail to take even the first step.

I read the following article in a Southern California newspaper.

> A bank robbery suspect in Oxnard was arrested Monday after police found him desperately searching for a bill small enough to make change for a pay toilet at a laundry.
>
> A Security Pacific National Bank branch was robbed Monday by a man who handed the teller a note claiming he had a gun and demanding money.
>
> The man escaped with $13,492 in cash and checks. No change, no small bills.
>
> A bank employee followed the man to the nearby laundry and pointed him out to the officer.
>
> A witness inside the laundry said he saw the man pull a large wad of bills from under his shirt and flip through them in search of a denomination small enough to operate an automated change-maker.
>
> The officer arrested the man and described him as "very excited" after the robbery and in need of the bathroom. The suspect was booked on suspicion of bank robbery at Ventura County Jail after being allowed to use the restroom.
> **—as reported Nov. 28, 1984, in the *Orange County Register***

What does that have to do with investing? Well, it's about the best example I've ever heard of someone who failed for lack of planning. You *must* plan now for your future. When I first read this article I doubled over with laughter at how ridiculous this story was. Think, a man had gone into the bank to commit a robbery, had gotten over $13,000 in cash (that is almost as good as Amway), and had lost it all because of a simple lack of planning.

It is sad that millions of Americans are on a downhill slide, and yet, even though they must be aware of its final destination, they refuse to get off. We're no longer satisfied with trying to keep up with the Joneses; we want to *be* the Joneses. We all live within our means, even if we have to borrow to do it.

Do you need help establishing a specific plan? Well, I have three ready-made plans that you can put to work. Find the one that fits you best and get started *now*.

The first plan, designed to take only a few hours a week, will give you the extra cash to afford a trip to Mazatlán in Mexico for sportfishing every spring, or just to pay the bills. This plan will give you the extra cash to allow you to live comfortably and escape the problems of being stuck in a job you like, but which may not pay enough.

The second plan is designed to give you not only cash today, but also to provide the equity buildup to help you have the kind of retirement you deserve. This is the plan that I would like you to use until you get itchy for more money.

The last is a step-by-step plan to accomplish not only cash flow and equity buildup but a net worth in excess of one million dollars in as little as five years. One word of warning: this last plan is for those who are willing to live, sleep, and breathe investing. It is not for the weak-kneed and definitely not achievable by everyone. The first two plans can be achieved by anyone. But this last plan is only for the eagles who are willing to soar alone.

One bit of advice before we get into these plans. A lot of books have been written on "how to be a millionaire." I would propose to you that no one on earth can show you how. I believe instead that someone can lay the groundwork. You have to do the rest.

PLAN 1: INVESTING FOR CASH FLOW

Objective: Extra income

Strategy: Moderately invest in single-family, bread-and-butter homes.

STEP 1: Master classified ads, empties, and advertising for sellers. You should develop at least one good real estate farm. In essence you will have four fishing lines in the water, all trying to catch good deals in real estate. You should set aside one to two hours each weekday to look for real estate bargains.

STEP 2: Develop a real estate investing team. Seek out and work with a good real estate agent, mortgage officer, building contractor, and title officer. Have these people available to help you write up your offers and close your properties. Have them help you understand what you need to do. Tell them how they can help you.

STEP 3: Establish a firm goal to purchase one property every six months.

STEP 4: Achieve that goal by following a weekly investing program that includes further education (books, seminars, workshops, etc.), telephoning, and visiting sellers in person only after filling out property analysis sheets on each property on the phone.

Weekly schedule:

Monday: Call on each possibility that you pulled out of the Sunday paper or got on your answering machine while you were at work.

Tuesday: Drive through your real estate farm and note any "for sale by owner" ads in the windows or on the lawns. Knock on the doors or call the sellers immediately when you get home. Call on any messages you received on your answering machine.

Wednesday: Follow up on any leads you got Monday or Tuesday. Bring some earnest money agreements and promissory notes with you when you inspect the properties.

Thursday: Review your local paper for any motivated sellers. Cut out these ads and place them in your property analysis system. Call on these ads and decide if they are worth investing time in.

Friday: Visit any properties you are interested in buying. Place ads at the stores in your farm area to let the public know you are interested in buying and selling real estate. Go to your analysis organizer and call on every offer that was refused. See if the sellers are interested in accepting your offer. (Think positively! All they can do is say no one more time, and it only takes a couple of minutes.)

Saturday and Sunday: Do something fun with your family. If you absolutely must, spend some time Saturday looking at some properties or fixing up something you have bought.

Every month:

- Pass out ads in your farm.
- Check with your local postal workers and newspaper carriers who deliver to your farm and see if they know of any empty homes or rentals.
- Read at least one new book on investing each month. If possible, attend one real estate seminar or convention. For a catalog of investment study materials or information on upcoming investment seminars and conventions, call or write the NCREI at P.O. Box 796, Provo, Utah 84603, (801) 225-8777.

Buying strategies:

- Assume existing FHA/VA and pre-1978 conventional loans that don't have due-on-sale clauses.
- Only buy positive cash-flow properties. Always structure low payments.
- Determine the maximum amount that you could receive for a down payment if you were selling the property. Then subtract from that down payment figure your estimated repairs plus what profit you would like. Then offer that amount as your maximum down payment. (For example, if you were to estimate that the maximum down payment you could get when you resold a property was $5,000, you would subtract your estimated fix-up costs of, say, $500, leaving you with $4,500. You would then subtract your required instant profit of $2,000—you're greedy—and be left with $2,500 as the maximum down

payment you can offer the seller. Offer $500 and leave yourself a lot of negotiating room.)

Selling strategies:

- Use, on a limited basis, the "I sell houses" flier technique.
- Let your buyers assume your mortgages, and offer to take back a second trust deed on your equity with either a monthly, an annual, or a large balloon payment.
- Maintain control over your loans by using the wrap-around or all-inclusive trust deed technique.
- If you have trouble selling your properties, cut your required down payment and send out fliers with a picture of your property to local rental units.

Profit points:

- Immediate profit from selling your properties.
- Immediate profit from selling your notes at a discount to private investors or loan institutions. (If you take back a second mortgage on the sale of a property, you can sell this "paper" at a reduced percentage of its face value to an investor.)
- Long-term profit from AITDs (wraps) or seconds.

Five-year potential:

One home every six months
   Year 1: 2 homes bought and sold
   Year 2: 2 homes bought and sold
   Year 3: 2 homes bought and sold
   Year 4: 2 homes bought and sold
   Year 5: 2 homes bought and sold

Five-year summary:

Ten homes bought and sold
Conservative five-year projection: $50,000 total profit ($5,000 profit per transaction)

Realistic projection: $100,000 ($10,000 per transaction—my own average)

This kind of profit (an extra $10,000 to $20,000 a year) sure beats working overtime at the old job. It also buys a lot of time to do what you really want to do.

PLAN 2: AFFORDING TODAY *AND* TOMORROW

Objective: Immediate cash and long-term income

Strategy: The basic steps of this investing plan are the same as plan 1 but with important additions.

ADDITION 1: Increase your number of fishing lines by four. Find a good real estate agent and develop a close working relationship. Actively promote yourself as a real estate investor to friends and relatives. Call the "for rent" ads each Tuesday and Thursday, and investigate foreclosure properties after the auction—from the bank, the FHA, and the VA.

ADDITION 2: Increase your investing to a solid two hours or more each day. Also set aside at least four hours a day each Saturday to check on your rentals and tie up any loose ends you need to check on.

ADDITION 3: Start your career as a part-time landlord by keeping the best properties (in terms of cash flow, future appreciation, and low maintenance) you find instead of reselling them immediately.

ADDITION 4: Get a phone answering machine and designate part of your home as your office for tax and mental health purposes. Get a file cabinet, a business phone, and develop a filing system to keep track of your real estate.

ADDITION 5: Buy at least one property every two months.

ADDITION 6: Involve your spouse (if you are married) in your investing. You will need the full support of your marital partner, or your marriage will feel the strain of your new part-time career.

ADDITION 7: Keep at least one property a year as a rental property. Keep the very best one in terms of condition, cash flow, lowest vacancy potential, etc. You should take care to establish from the first a professioal attitude toward property management. Don't become an uncle or aunt to your tenants.

ADDITION 8: Develop a second, third, and fourth investment farm.

ADDITION 9: Have some nice-looking stationery and business cards made up for your investments.

Weekly schedule:

The weekly schedule is the same as in the first plan, only you must increase your time by two hours a day as need demands. You will also be working at least four hours on Saturdays, following up on the leads that you got during the week.

Every month:

- Get involved in your local real estate investment groups. Robert Allen's American Congress on Real Estate sponsors small investment groups throughout the nation. For information on your local investment group, call The Allen Group at (801) 373-8000.
- Visit several real estate offices and leave your cards with the agents you see there. Tell them to call you if they ever come across any good deals.
- Visit several REO (real estate owned) officers at local banks. Leave your business card with them. Ask them to call you if they ever have something they want to sell fast.

Buying strategies:

- Write to your local government repossession agencies and get on FHA/HUD or VA mailing lists, or contact your real estate agent and have him supply you with a copy of the list.
- Advertise for partners. Don't let your lack of funds keep you

out of good deals. It's better to get a piece of the pie than no pie at all.
- Develop a signature line of credit at a local bank.

Selling strategies:

- Become a matchmaker: use, on a regular basis, the "I sell houses" flier technique.
- Develop a list of professionals (doctors, lawyers, and dentists) who might be interested in investing in real estate. Present your properties to them before you buy. (Fill out some analysis sheets with your resale price and figures, and include a good Polaroid-type picture of the property.)

Profit points:

- Immediate profit from selling your properties.
- Profit from buying properties and renting them out with a positive cash flow.
- Depreciation and tax savings. (As you begin to realize some tax benefits from owning real estate you can immediately increase the number of dependents you claim on your W-4 tax form. Check with your CPA or accountant regarding your own situation.)
- Profit from selling (assigning) your contracts to other investors before you close. You can make a profit merely by selling your right to purchase a property to someone else. (Include a clause in each contract that states, "Title to be vested in the name of (your name) and/or assigns.") Consult a local attorney concerning the laws in your state.

Five-year profit potential:

One home every two months
Year 1: 6 homes purchased
         5 sold at a fair profit
         1 kept as a rental

Year 2: 6 homes purchased
         5 sold at a fair profit
         1 kept as a rental

Year 3: 6 homes purchased
   5 sold at a fair profit
   1 kept as a rental

Year 4: 6 homes purchased
   5 sold at a profit
   1 kept as a rental

Year 5: 6 homes purchased
   5 sold at a fair profit
   1 kept as a rental

Five-year summary:

   30 homes purchased
   25 sold at a profit
   5 homes kept as rental units

Conservative five-year net profit from buying and selling: $125,000 ($5,000 profit per real estate transaction)
Realistic five-year net profit from buying and selling: $250,000

Not bad, huh? But what about the five rentals you now own? Don't worry, I didn't forget about them. They are actually the best part. If each unit was purchased for $85,000 at the end of the year, you would be looking at a $63,812.82 increase in values with a mild, 7 percent inflation rate. The total value of your properties at the end of the fifth year would be $488,812.82.

This doesn't take into account the fact that these loans have been paying off (and you have built up a couple more thousand dollars worth of equity as a result), or that you might have been enjoying some nice positive cash flow, or, even better yet, by your fifth year well over $10,000 a year in tax writeoffs.

You now are making as much money by going to sleep at night and having your property appreciate as you would if you had a moonlighting job. (Your property during the sixth year would have appreciated $34,216.90 in value to $523,029.72.) And you are sleeping better, aren't you?

PLAN 3: FULL-TIME REAL ESTATE INVESTING

We each have had dreams of untold riches, of being one of those people who can afford the yachts, trips, and all the little fun toys like Lear jets that most people can't afford. I hope you now realize that there is a realistic approach to investing that every living American can achieve—no matter what level of involvement he or she might choose.

If you only want to supplement your regular income, so you can enjoy the summer in Europe instead of the backyard, use plan 1. If you want to build up some equity for the future, and have enough for more than one nice trip each year, and a new car when you need one—plan 2. Either plan is excellent for anyone who wants to keep the current job and invest. And all they require is five to fifteen hours each week.

Now for plan 3: A cool million in five to ten years. It can be done in five years—as many investors, including myself, can attest—but you will have to commit yourself full-time to your goals. If you want to make it a little easier, allowing yourself ten years might be more realistic. However long you end up taking, ask yourself this: Where will you be ten years from now if you don't do anything? You will have to organize your time, money, and effort, making the most of leverage. But the rewards are somewhere between phenomenal and staggering.

Objective:

$1,000,000 in five to ten years

Strategy:

Begin with plans 1 and 2 and slowly work yourself up to four to eight properties during your first year of investing. If things look good, and if you enjoy investing, then move into plan 3.

Million dollar principle 1: Hire a secretary to do your phone calling for you. Prepare your analysis sheets each night. Have your secretary (perhaps a local housewife who could use some extra money) pick them up from you each morning, call on them during the day, and return them to you in the evening for your review. Pay your secretary on a per-completed-analysis-sheet basis with a bonus each month for every property you end up buying (as an encouragement to be very nice and businesslike when calling).

Million dollar principle 2: Find several partners with a lot of investment capital. With several successful deals under your belt, you will have developed a good track record. Find partners who are willing to put up at least $50,000 on a real estate transaction. To find such a partner, make a list not just of professionals, but of every relative, businessperson, or investor you know who might have access to that much cash. Go visit them all, show them pictures of your real estate investing transactions (make sure you have completed several good deals before you do this), and go through the numbers on your analysis sheets (which you've kept as a record of the properties you have bought and sold).

Tell potential partners that on occasion you are able to purchase properties for as little as 50 cents on the dollar. Offer them a 50 percent position in the property and all the tax benefits if they put up the money. (The property can be owned in their name with your interest being secured by an option to purchase a 50 percent position for $1.) You might go through a dozen people before you find your investor.

Million dollar principle 3: Use the more advanced real estate investing tools, such as foreclosures before the auction and at the auction. Use your investing partner's cash to purchase properties at a substantial discount in these forced-sale situations. You can buy a $60,000 property for as little as $30,000, then refinance the property with an 80 percent, non-owner-occupied loan.

This loan would give you $48,000 cash. The $30,000 would be returned to your investor partner, plus 50 percent of the $18,000 profit. You could then rent out the property or sell it. In the meantime both you and your partner would be enjoying approximately $9,000 tax-free cash. (You don't have to pay taxes on money you borrow against property you own.) As word spreads, you will soon have investors calling you up, offering you access to their cash. Always be aboveboard and honest with your investors.

Million dollar principle 4: Don't go out and hire a full-time staff to maintain or fix up your properties. The overhead and headaches will kill you. Subcontract out every job on a competitive bid basis. Call your local college employment agency and place an ad for a handyman to work part-time. Get a list of experienced painters, carpenters, etc., who are willing to work part-time on a bid basis.

Million dollar principle 5: Buy at least two properties a month. That may seem like a lot, but if you will devote forty hours a week to investing, it will be an easy task. Treat your investing career like a regular job with set hours, and don't deviate from your schedule. Actually keep a written record of how much time you spent each day on real estate and what you did during each hour.

Million dollar principle 6: Keep at least one property for every six you buy and resell. This will allow you to zero out every year on your income taxes. I have never met anyone who was against that!

Million dollar principle 7: Get a separate outside line for your real estate investments. Never use your own personal home line for investing. You will need to have the peace that a separate phone line and an answering machine or service provide.

Million dollar principle 8: Contact your local county and city housing authorities. Find out which federal programs are available in your area. Today I called both agencies and found out more details on a government program that my tenants can sign up for to get new storm doors, windows, insulation in the ceilings and walls, and weather stripping installed for free. I also found out about a federal low-income rehab program that will loan me money to rehab (fix up) units in an area near where I live. The program will loan me one half of any rehab costs at 8 percent interest on a ten-year, interest-only note, provided I follow three of their rules:

I must not convert to condos.
I must not discriminate in renting.
I must advertise any rentals according to a plan worked out with the housing agency.

If I follow these three rules I won't ever have to pay back the principal on the loan. At the end of paying interest only on the note, the principal amount will be waived.

Use these government programs. Be aware, these programs are constantly changing. To keep up on them, stay in contact with the local housing authorities that administer them.

Buying strategies:

Use every technique we have talked about so far. In addition:

- Use options to tie up properties. An option is the right to buy or sell something such as a piece of real estate during a specified period at a specified price.
- Buy discounted paper (notes on real estate) and resell it at a profit. We mentioned in plan 1 how you could take your "paper" (financing that you are carrying on properties you have sold) and sell it at a discount to investors. This discount may be as much as 50 percent of face value. Consider investing yourself in discounted paper. You can resell this paper at a profit, or trade it for full face value on a property you are buying.
- Negotiate deferred-payment notes (owner financing where the payments won't start for a year).
- Negotiate the right to extend any balloon payments you might assume.
- Run an ad in the "real estate wanted" section of your local paper. A sample ad would say something like, "Family man seeks to buy home with assumable loan or seller financing. Call Marc 222-8888."

Selling strategies:

- Sell half interest in a property to a partner to cover any negative cash flow.
- Put out some "I sell houses" fliers every week. Make sure that every laundry in town has one.
- Run an ad in your local paper under "homes for rent." A sample ad would say something like, "Are you sick and tired of throwing away your money in rent each month? I have some

homes for sale. No qualifying and low down payments. Call Marc 222-8888.''
- Exercise your escape clauses before you close if it looks like you're going to have trouble selling or renting a property.
- If you have purchased something with the intention of flipping it (buying and selling immediately), but are having trouble selling it, stop your losses immediately. Rent it out as soon as possible, then try to sell it as an occupied rental.

Profit points:

- From buying and selling contracts (and/or assigns).
- From optioning a property and subleasing it to someone else or exercising your option and buying it for rental or resale.
- From buying and selling properties (flipping).
- From buying and selling discounted paper.
- From trading discounted paper for full value when you buy a property (for example, trading a $10,000 note you purchased for $5,000 for a full $10,000 of equity in a property).
- From the positive cash flow on rentals.
- From refinancing properties.
- From getting low-interest government loans and rental subsidies.
- From bringing in partners.
- From appreciation.
- From good property management (increasing the rents and lowering expenses).
- From changing a property's use. (A friend of mine just bought an older home with some attached land. He's now putting up an office building on the vacant land.)
- From developing part of a property purchase into a building lot which can be sold separately.

Five-year profit potential:

Two homes every month
YEAR 1 (starting phase): 8 homes purchased

6 sold at a fair profit
2 kept as rentals
YEAR 2: 24 homes purchased
20 sold at a fair profit
4 kept as rentals
YEAR 3: 24 homes purchased
20 sold at a fair profit
4 kept as rentals
YEAR 4: 24 homes purchased
20 sold at a fair profit
4 kept as rentals
YEAR 5: 24 homes purchased
20 sold at a fair profit
4 kept as rentals

Five-year summary:

104 homes purchased
86 sold at a profit
18 kept as rental units

Conservative five-year net profit: $430,000 ($5,000 profit per real estate transaction)

Realistic five-year net profit: $860,000

So where is the million dollars? Remember the rentals? With just a 7 percent inflation rate, the appreciation on your rental units has pulled your five-year profit over the $1,000,000 mark. If you had purchased each unit for $85,000, you would have earned in excess of $202,000 in appreciation on your units during those five years. The next year's appreciation alone on the units would be over $300,000. (Are you getting a feeling for how this snowballs?) This again doesn't take into account one dime of increased cash flow from the tax advantages of your properties' depreciation or your ability to write off a great part of your new income as a business expense. You may also have carried back your excess tax benefits to previous tax years and recaptured a great portion of the tax you paid in the past three years. It's legal, if you have a net operating loss. (If your tax write-offs exceed your income, you can recapture—get a refund on—the tax you paid during the past several years or apply the amount to future taxes.) If you do that, please don't invest it. You deserve to blow it on yourself. You have earned it.

Do you feel a little bit scared? Is this a bit overwhelming? If you didn't feel apprehensive I would worry about you. Please read on. I have saved for the last a special section to give you that final direction and push you may need.

---CHAPTER 13————————————

Welcome to Success

Failure is the opportunity to
begin again more intelligently.
—HENRY FORD

Several years ago I became a certified scuba diver. I spent hours in a dry, often boring class, learning the basics of successful diving before the instructor ever allowed me to jump into the water.

I know what your motivation was when you cracked the covers of this book: you wanted to be given specific tools for buying and selling houses. You wanted me to hand over the equipment that you will need to dive in and get started. And that's all you wanted.

Well, I've given you those tools, but I don't want to turn you loose just yet. Instead, I am going to ask you to sit in class for a few more chapters and learn the basis of true success in real estate investing. You need to learn the keys to success before I turn you loose on the investing world. Otherwise, your chances for success are *very* slim. It takes more than the right tools to do the job; you have to know how to use them properly.

If you don't want to "waste" your time learning how to avoid the dangers that catch most investors, and if you want to jump in, go ahead and do so—at your own risk.

If I had taken a tank and a wetsuit and simply dived headfirst into the waves without first learning how to dive safely, I would have surely lost my life or been seriously injured and afraid to ever go out again. The same thing happens all the time to new investors who fail to prepare thoroughly.

Before you begin investing, you have a few choices to make. How many hours will you work each week? Is this going to be a full-time venture, or just a few minutes a day? Do you have the drive and determination to succeed that will see you through the tough spots? Should you give up your job tomorrow?

The remainder of this book will give you what you need to separate yourself from the pack. I want to give you the winning edge. At least nine out of every ten would-be investors never reach their goals, and I believe strongly that they fail because they are unaware of the basic principles of success.

The next two chapters include my ten keys to success. I've reviewed them carefully, and I can't find one of them that is really a lot of fun; they all require time and concentrated effort. But it's effort that every successful person has applied in his or her life, and if you want the same thing in your life, there is no shortcut.

Realistically, I think you should start out slowly. Keep your job and spend only ten hours a week or so for the first few months. Call on ad after ad; visit seller after seller. When you have found the perfect deal, buy it. When you've fixed it up, sell it. Take your time and do it right. Please, learn to walk before you run. I have been teaching the principles of real estate investing around the country, and it has been very gratifying to hear of my students' successes. However, I recently received a letter from a hopeful investor who had quit his job to begin investing in real estate. It was a frightening revelation for me that someone had taken part of what I was teaching—how to find good deals and invest profitably—without heeding my advice to start slowly. The student was now faced with a lack of cash flow and was very concerned. My response was to strongly urge him to go back to work and build his investing career carefully, not blindly. I worked full-time and invested for a couple of years before I quit my job. If you want to reach a point where you can quit working for the boss and start working for yourself, that's great. Set a goal, make plans, and reach that point. But *please* don't put down this book and pick up the phone right now to let the boss know what he can do with that job!

Take as much time as you need, especially with the first deal. Be fussy. And then, when you have finished your first real estate deal, sit down with a blank piece of paper and a pen and review. Draw a line down the middle of the page. On the left side of the line, write everything that went right. What were you especially pleased with? On the other side of the line, explain to yourself exactly why those things went so well. Commit yourself to the same success on every deal.

Now turn the page over and do the same thing, except this time write down what went wrong and why. Analyze your mistakes and figure out how you can improve. How can you keep from making those mistakes again? The first few times you fill out these analysis sheets, you may have a couple of pages of mistakes and only half a page of good points, but that will change after two or three successful investments.

After you've tasted success, and can afford to quit, will you give up your job and become a full-time investor? It's up to you, of course, but here are a few guidelines:

1) *Do you like your job?* A lot of Americans love their jobs. The problem is they can't seem to make enough money. If you fall into this group, then you should continue to invest, but only as a way of supporting the work you love. If you don't like your job, then perhaps your investments could support you through an educational program so that you can eventually do what you really want. (Makes sense, right?) Real estate investing should be the means by which you are able to do what you want, when you want.

2) *Are you a self-starter?* Are you driven? I think few people have the drive to stick to a concentrated program of investing long enough to make the millions that are possible in real estate. I've noticed that most people make a little money and immediately reward themselves by spending their profits. They just don't have the self-control necessary to reinvest.

Those who do succeed in real estate seem to listen to a different drummer. They reinvest most of their profits, keeping the ball rolling *and* growing. They balance their lives so that they make money but still have time left over to be with their families and friends. They associate with other investors. An old saying is that if you want to be an alcoholic, you should hang around in a bar or at a local AA chapter. I would say that if you are thinking about being an investor, you should start hanging around with investors. You should find people with interests that are similar to yours and associate with them. Your investor associates will keep you motivated and on the road to success.

Successful full-time investors realize that there are no time clocks to punch, and therefore they must find other incentives for sticking to investing full-time. Many investors seek areas of real estate investing that they thoroughly enjoy. Some concentrate on single-family dwellings, smaller rental units, or large projects. Others enjoy investing in foreclosures, calling newspaper ads, or advertising for sellers. They find their real estate investing niche.

3) *Are you making as much money with your investments as you were working?* This isn't a hard-and-fast rule, but few people can step down on the economic ladder comfortably. When your investment profits are outpacing your paychecks *consistently,* then you should consider investing full-time.

I love investing full-time, mostly because I have mastered the ten keys to success and now have the freedom to enjoy my time, my family, and my future.

—PART IV————————————

Ten Keys to Success— Points and Pitfalls

CHAPTER 14

Points

He who hesitates is interrupted.
—FRANKLIN P. JONES

There is a land that you've dreamed of, and it's not somewhere over the rainbow; in fact, it's right around the corner. You probably know a few people who live there. When you look through the bars that separate you from this land, you wonder how anyone could get inside. The people look happy; in fact, they are obviously enjoying their lifestyle.

What you don't realize is that the bars are not there to keep you from getting in; they are the bars on your own cell, keeping you from getting out. There are several doors in your cell that would let you out. Most of the doors have thousands of bars and chains that are almost impenetrable. But one of them, marked "real estate," has only ten keyholes. If someone were to give you those ten keys you would be able to escape into the land of success.

Well, I have those ten keys dangling on a key chain that I carry with me wherever I go. And I've made copies of those keys, which I've embedded into the pages of this chapter and the next. Take the keys and insert them into the locks, and I guarantee you freedom. Beware; the keys are good, but the locks won't turn easily. Each key will require work—lots of it. But the alternative is to continue to look through your bars.

The first five keys are the *dos* of real estate, and the second five are the *don'ts*. Once you have mastered all ten, you will be ready to break free. Got your key chain ready? Okay, here's key number one:

Key 1: <u>DO SET ASIDE TIME EACH DAY FOR SUCCESS.</u>

> *Mis-spending a man's time is a kind
> of self-homicide.*
> —GEORGE SAVILLE, Marquess of Halifax

"It was the best of times, it was the worst of times." These words, from Dickens's *A Tale of Two Cities,* seem to sum up a common feeling in today's real estate market. For some, it is the worst of times. When interest rates are high, money is tight, and inflation is running away with housing prices, they are afraid of the market. When the opposite is true—and we're starting to see a swing in that direction—they are afraid of competition and stagnant prices. Their financial growth comes to a virtual halt, and they sit on the bank watching the tides of fortune and wondering when to jump in.

For others, it is the best of times. They recognize that *now* is the time to act. They don't wait to see what will happen; they make it happen. The successful real estate investors know the benefits of investing now, and regularly set aside time to accomplish their financial dreams.

The time is never right for someone who is unwilling to seize opportunities, and it is always right for the rest of us. I have to laugh every time someone tells me that all the money in real estate was made in the '70s. Nothing could be further from the truth. But it takes the right attitude and a willingness to set aside time if you want to succeed. You must learn to set aside time *every day* to study, research, and invest in real estate.

You may be wondering how you should be spending that time right now. The answer is easy: education before anything else. That's the only way to approach any new situation. I'm reminded of the city cousin who went to visit his country cousins out on the farm. He was so eager to be a real farmer that he insisted on taking the bucket down to the milking shed and taking care of that chore himself.

He dragged Bossie into the shed, took the milking stool off the hook, carefully placed the pail under her udder, and waited. And waited. And waited . . .

He's probably still waiting for Bossie to do her stuff. The fact is, too many novice investors trudge out to the milking shed with an empty bucket and a hazy knowledge of how the process works, and then find themselves waiting and wondering when they will reap the tremendous rewards they have heard about.

The second question is, how much time and effort? Start with two hours a day. Don't tell me you don't have the time; *make the time.* Set your alarm a little earlier, give up "I Love Lucy" reruns for a month, or abandon the wasted midnight hours of beauty rest. Which would you rather be, wealthy or beautiful?

How would you like to have an account opened for you at the local bank, with an opening balance of $864? There is one catch to this particular account: at the end of the day your account is cleared—reset to zero—and you start the next day with another $864. You may withdraw any or all of your money and invest it; but if you fail to withdraw any of the money, you lose it. What would you do?

The answer is almost too obvious to write: you would withdraw every penny, every day. And, I'm sure, you would invest your money wisely, so you could be wealthy in no time at all. Well, the bank is open and your account is active. It's the First National Bank of Time, and every second is worth one penny. You start with 86,400 of those litle hummers at 12:00 sharp, and twenty-four hours later every one of them is gone. How many did you invest, and how many did you squander on meaningless trivialities?

Why do you lock your doors at night? Because you fear being robbed. And yet we rob ourselves of treasures infinitely more valuable than Grandma's silver service for eight; we take away the opportunities for accomplishment and success.

Enough sermonizing. I hope I have convinced you that setting aside time for success is a crucial part of the process, and I trust that you are ready to put aside at least two hours a day—every day—for success.

If you can set aside at least two hours a day, five days a week (less than half the time most serious investors spend learning and earning), in a year you will have spent 520 hours working toward the goals you have set. You will also have spent 2,000 hours at work, earning enough to get by from one day to the next. Which hours will pay the biggest dividends? You figure it out.

Those two hours are sacrosanct. They are the hard labor that will be required if you don't want to serve a life sentence in a padded cell. If something does come up, and you absolutely have to give up that time, make it up on Saturday or Sunday, but don't allow one week to go by without spending at least ten hours investing in your future.

Actually scheduling your time will be an extremely difficult task if you're used to living by the credo "I'll get to it someday." I suggest getting used to the idea of budgeting your time, and I further suggest that you use a daily planner, like the Freedom Planner I use. It allows you the freedom of a flexible schedule and yet acts as a constant time organizer and work planner. Write to me and I'll send you some information on it. What can you do about unexpected delays and emergencies? Plan for them and reschedule when necessary. After a while a whole lost weekend will barely cause you to break your stride.

It may at first seem like too much work, but the rewards for organizing your time are unbelievable, and the alternative is to continue wasting your life, wondering how the hours escape you so easily.

As I write this, it is a cold and rainy Wednesday night. The last thing I will do before giving in to the temptation of a warm bed is to consult my planner and prepare for tomorrow. After filling in the "must do" hours—tomorrow there's school and an afternoon appointment—I am free to arrange my priorities and schedule accordingly. I prioritize the assignments I have given myself, so that if I need to reschedule my plans everything that has to be done will still get done.

No, I'm not an automaton; I'm just organized. How much difference does that make? Well, think about it. If you sleep eight hours a night, work eight hours a day (and add another two hours for driving and getting ready for work), and eat for one hour, that only uses up nineteen hours. Out of twenty-four I'll even take off another hour for the minutes between this and that—the going to and coming from time. You still have four hours to account for—and that's on weekdays. You may have plans for the weekend;

you may even think that weekends really were made for Michelob. But the only one ever to achieve wealth with that guideline is the Michelob company.

I'm feeling generous, so I'll allow you one wasted, who-knows-what-happened-to-the-time hour, and one solid hour for your family. That *still* leaves you with two hours!

"But I need my fun time too, don't I?" Sure you do; we all need to have fun. All work and no play not only makes Jack and Jill dull kids, but it warps their spirit and destroys their emotional health. But concentrate your energies on what you are doing. When it's time to play, have a ball. When it's time to work, buckle down and work hard. Too many people lead bland, colorless, marshmallow lives, like an old black-and-white movie with no plot. Just living from day to day in a miasma, never enjoying life's peaks.

Don't let anyone or anything keep you from success. You are the master of your own destiny, and you are the only person standing between your current situation and getting everything you want.

Do set aside time for success. That's the first key. And the second is:

Key 2: DO LEARN BEFORE YOU LEAP.

*The greatest artist was once
a beginner.*
—*Farmer's Digest*

Your first key still shines like the day it was made. Perhaps you've even tried putting it in the lock. Maybe you actually set aside the two hours and committed yourself to reaching your goals. The second key is to use that time to learn how to invest. Read everything you can get your hands on; talk to the experts.

Forget real estate for a minute. Instead, set your sights on becoming a produce manager. You really want to excel; you want to be the produce manager that all the other produce managers are talking about. What would be your first step?

You might attend a produce managers' class. Don't laugh—

there really is such a thing. You would want to know everything there was to know about fruits and vegetables. You would need to know market values: how much is a good watermelon worth in the middle of September, as opposed to the first of July? What is the resale value of avocados after they have been on the shelf three days?

If you don't know all of this and much, much more, you won't last two days on the job. The key to success in the produce manager's world is a good education in fruits and vegetables.

You want to buy and sell houses instead of bananas? Fine, but the same rules for success are valid. If the investor does not gain the necessary knowledge of real estate principles and market values, he or she will have one of the shortest careers on record.

This does not mean that you have to know everything about real estate to buy a property. But you must at least know the basics, and you must have developed the ability to accurately estimate market values so you can buy wholesale and sell retail. How do you acquire this knowledge?

1) *Books and seminars.* When I first became interested in real estate investing, I was stunned by the gibberish that fell trippingly off the tongues of other investors. Every other word was incomprehensible. When I tried to look up definitions I found that there was no reliable investor's encyclopedia, so I wrote one myself. It took a couple of years to get all the information together, but I think that *The Real Estate Greenbook* is the most authoritative encyclopedia and reference guide to real estate available.

2) *Talking to experts.* There is no better way to obtain a free education than by talking to the right people. Is there an investors' group in your area? If so, attend the meetings. Count that as your two hours for that day. Take a successful investor out to lunch, and while the cook is grilling your hamburger you can be grilling the investor.

In this book we met several experts who can help you. The amazing thing is that the education they can give you is often free, if you know how to ask the right questions.

3) *Talking to sellers.* As you continue to learn, start cutting out "for sale by owner" ads in the classified and calling the owners. We've already discussed this as a method for finding good deals, but how do you organize your time?

A simple schedule for following for-sale-by-owners is to read the paper and clip ads as soon as you get home from work, and then call the owners in the evening, right after dinner. If any of them have a house that sounds interesting, make an appointment to see the owner and talk to him or her.

You can spend a whole day at the mall without buying anything, can't you? Why not spend a whole Saturday looking at houses without any intention of buying? Leave your wallet and earnest money agreements at home. (What do you mean, you don't have any earnest money agreements? Get over to the office supply store and buy a dozen.) Talk to owners and walk through houses; what have you got to lose?

4) *The MLS book.* Another source of homes for sale is the Multiple Listing Service book, published and distributed by and for Realtors. If you don't know a real estate agent, get to know one well enough to ask for a copy of his or her MLS book. If that fails, check the garbage behind the local real estate office. A new one is published every month, and the old ones are tossed out. That may seem like tacky advice, but hey, it's free.

The MLS book can be an incredibly rich source of real estate knowledge. When a property is included in the book, it will be described in more detail than you could possibly get by simply driving by and looking. The book will usually have a picture of the property, the asking price, the down payment, the loan information, as well as a complete physical description (bedrooms, baths, amenities). Take a couple of days this month and do nothing but drive around with an old MLS book, comparing features, neighborhoods, and prices.

After just a few weeks of driving around, talking to owners and comparing prices, you should begin to get a good feel for prices in your area.

What's the difference between you and me? Knowledge and experience, and nothing more. You can gain both, if you are willing to apply yourself.

I have already done the necessary studying. I know how to recognize a good deal; I know how to buy and sell a property quickly; I know what I need to know to succeed as an investor. That's the only real difference. Everything else follows from education. It's what allows a surgeon to charge an arm and a leg (to use an expression).

I haven't stopped learning. I study every day, learning new words, and new financing devices and making new contacts. In time I may reach the forefront of real estate knowledge in one narrow segment of the business, but I will never know everything there is to know about real estate. I do, however, know everything there is to know about watching TV, so why should I spend any more time studying the fine art? Why should you?

Here, take this key. It's called education, and it will be the largest key on your chain. When it is inserted into its lock, along with the time management key, all the other locks should turn more easily.

Learn before you leap.

Key 3: <u>DO ORGANIZE YOUR PERSONAL FINANCES.</u>

> *The taller the building, the deeper*
> *the foundation must be.*
> —ROBERT G. ALLEN

I had a dream. From the time I was a little kid, running and playing on the dusty sidewalks of Long Beach, California, I wanted to get away—in an airplane. I suppose all kids want to fly a plane when they are little, but I wanted it so bad I thought I would die if I couldn't be a pilot.

Last week I took a Grumman up and tried a series of accelerated stalls and spins. I love flying; it's everything I dreamed it would be, and more.

The dream has become a reality, and I have real estate investments to thank for that. Coupled with real estate knowledge and experience, the third key allowed me to afford the fulfillment of a dream. If you have dreams that you haven't experienced because they cost money, you need the third key. And you need it even if you never buy a stick of property; you need it to fulfill *any* financial dreams.

This key is an old, rusty skeleton key. It's so old that your grandparents may have passed it down to you from their grandparents. It's such an ugly old key that you are inclined to ignore it completely, eager to get to the good stuff. And ignoring it, you will live like many investors I know, who have a million in real estate and have trouble scraping together ten bucks in cash.

Ready? Okay, the third key is personal financial planning. I know, I know: "Oh brother, not *budgeting!*"

Let me tell you a little more about flying. During the months of study and preparation for getting my pilot's license, I was continually impressed with the importance of checking my plane thoroughly before each flight.

I would literally check each nut and bolt on the plane to make sure it was tight, intact, and ready for the rigors of flying. I would crawl under the plane and check the tires to make sure they would support the loading caused by the stress of takeoff and landing. The engine, gas, and oil reserves, the prop, radios, antenna, carburetor heat, and magnetos would all be thoroughly and methodically checked. Why all this worry?

Because I didn't want to crash!

Your financial foundation must be established now, not after you are wealthy. *Now.* It's time to begin budgeting your money, putting a little aside—not for a rainy day, but for a bright future. It's time—today—to establish a spotless credit record.

One of the best and worst things about real estate is that money is not a prerequisite for success. You can find excellent nothing-down deals everywhere. But you can't eat equity; you need money to live on while you're achieving your goals.

I know an investor who was doing very well—on paper. He had amassed enviable real estate holdings, and he justified his lack of cash by saying that all he needed was enough to get by on while he built up his equity. His sophism finally fell apart one day when he was on his way to buy a house.

There he was, clipping along the highway, contemplating the great deal ahead, when suddenly, *whap-whap-whap-whap-whap*—a flat tire. Not just any flat tire; it was the spare, which he had used to replace another flat only one week before.

Well, he bought the needed tires and watched someone else buy the house and make $8,000 on the resale because he didn't have enough money to close on the deal. He ruined the deal because he bought two tires, so that works out to about $4,000 a tire. (And they were only retreads!) Had he developed his ability to plan for his own finances first, he could have bought the tires *and* the house, and maybe a nice dinner to celebrate. Instead, he is still broke, chasing the few deals that he can afford and passing those that he can't afford to me. Who do you think is getting the better deals, and building a higher building?

Who do you pay first when you receive that paycheck? The bank for the credit charges, or the rent, or a little gas and groceries to get you through until next payday? And who do you pay last, if at all? Yourself. That's what happens whenever you fail to drop a few dollars in the savings account: you are cheating yourself out of a share of your income. Everyone makes money from your labors, and you fall into another week of the same routine.

You may be tempted to say, "But Marc, I'm just barely getting by as it is! I can't possibly save any more." Have you ever tracked your expenditures? You might be surprised how the pennies and nickels slip through the cracks. Try it for a week or two. Record *every* expenditure of cash, check, or charge, noting whether it was an absolutely necessary expense. Don't forget to write down every nickel, dime, and quarter; that's where much of your wasted money goes.

When you have tracked your total spending for two weeks, add up all the unnecessary expenditures and multiply by twenty-six. That will give you a rough idea of how much you could be saving every year. The more accurate you want the system to be, the longer you will have to track your expenses.

You may be surprised to find you could be saving literally thousands of dollars every year. That makes for a pretty poor foundation, doesn't it?

As a practicing member of the Church of Jesus Christ of Latter Day Saints, I believe in the law of tithing; that is, I pay 10 percent of my earnings to the Church. That money comes right off the top; I pay the Lord the first tenth of my income, and myself the second tenth. That leaves me with 80 percent for the butcher, the baker, and the candlestick maker. I believe that anyone can survive on 80 percent of his income if he absolutely has to.

Let me put it to you differently. The next time you arrive at work, you find out that you will have to take a 10 percent cut in pay. What will you do? I'll venture a guess: you'll manage somehow. It won't be easy; it may even seem impossible, but you'll make it.

If you have climbed on the credit carousel—spending all of your time trying to catch up with the bills while creditors spend their time trying to catch you—then you should seek professional counseling. Get your financial affairs in order before investing a dime in real estate. If you can't control your current income, it will be impossible to control a $10,000 cash profit from the sale of a property.

Setting up a budget isn't very hard; it's like setting up a diet schedule. It's after you've set up your budget that things get difficult. Bad habits can be killed, but they fight every step of the way, so you'll have to be well armed with determination. That means complete agreement with your spouse and at least a two-year commitment. But, as Robert Allen has said:

> If you will do for two years what most people won't,
> you can do for the rest of your life what most people can't.

Planning a budget is a three-step process. Step one is projecting your income and expenses; step two is designing a budget; and step three—the killer—is sticking to that budget like these letters are stuck to the page.

A budget can be as complex as a full accounting system, involving ledgers and a daily journal entry, or it can be as simple as a record of expenses and a loosely defined limit for each expense account. Hopefully, your budget will be as complete as possible without being so complex that you lose interest and give up after only a month.

If you own a home or personal computer, consider getting one of the dozens of home budget programs available, which will make budgeting an *almost* painless process.

If I were to attempt to explain a working budget in detail, this chapter might well turn into a small book by itself, so I will go through the basic steps and leave you to figure out a budget system that will work for you. For a more involved explanation, I recommend either Sylvia Porter's *The Money Book* or Jerome Rosenberg's *Managing Your Own Money.*

Plan out your expenses for an entire year. Remember to keep controllable expenses, such as entertainment and groceries, to a minimum. Use old bills for reference to get an idea of average monthly costs. Don't forget to count gifts and annual expenses, such as insurance premiums.

Break down all expenses into a monthly average, and compare that with your estimated income. (Break down occasional income, such as an annual bonus or a tax rebate, into monthly averages also.) If your income exceeds your expenses, there is no reason you shouldn't be putting aside a little every month. If your expenses exceed income, you'd better cut down on all variable expenses, such as entertainment, groceries, and clothes.

After estimating expenses and planning a budget to control spending, you must keep track of your expenses and compare your actual spending habits to your budget. You can pick up a ledger book at the nearest stationery and office supply store and track them in separate accounts, or you can sit down once a week with your spouse (or with yourself if you're single) and see how close you are to your budget. If you find yourself overspending, determine which needs to be adjusted—the budget amounts or your self-control.

If the thought of living for two years as a financial monk, locked up in a monetary monastery while all of your friends are living it up, is simply more than you can bear, take heart. I have no intention of advising you to give up entertainment and recreation. Instead, consider working toward a goal: a real vacation instead of allowing your "fun money" to be frittered away ten or twenty dollars at a time.

I work best under a reward system, so I set one up for myself and my family. We established a budgetary goal—so much saved, so much spent—and agreed that if we achieved that goal, we would reward ourselves. And the rewards can be great.

The first goal I set was to live within a budget and save $5,000 within an eight-month period. My wife and I agreed that if we could achieve that goal, we would treat ourselves to a trip. We would fly to the tropical resort of Mazatlán, Mexico, for eight fun-filled days in the sun, just like winning the Grand Prize on "The Price Is Right."

We did it. We lived below our income level, we reached our goal, and we took our trip. We lived like royalty: we parasailed, swam, burned ourselves to a crisp, and ate shrimp the size of your fist. It was a perfect second honeymoon. There was a new light in DeAnn's eyes when we returned home. She could hardly wait to start saving for the next trip, because she knew from experience that the reward was well worth the sacrifice.

We had so much fun, in fact, that the next summer we found ourselves once again in Mazatlán. It was even better than the first time, and when we returned we redoubled our efforts to save. Now it was fun seeing how much we could save and invest. And we planned for something exceptional: a trip to Europe.

We never imagined that we would be touring Europe so early in our lives, but there we were, traveling through fabled countries and cities only seen in magazines and dreamed about. Now we're looking forward to a month in Sweden. After that, who knows?

These trips are free, in a sense. It costs me the same to live at the top of my income level, eating Big Macs and wishing I could go to Europe, as it does to eat a few sack lunches, develop some financial self-control, and actually go to Europe. And the cost of the trips is only a fraction of the money saved, so I still have most of that money available for investing. Is it worth the sacrifice? You bet it is.

If you put this book down right now and never buy one piece of property, but turn this one key, your life will be changed permanently. You will experience an increase in marital happiness, you will feel better about yourself, you will be able to establish financial security, and when retirement time rolls around, it will be a time to treasure, not fear.

Well, the key is yours now. It might not look like much of a key, but it will open the strongest lock between you and success. Put it in the keyhole, and let's move on.

Key 4: <u>DO SET REALISTIC GOALS.</u>

> *Goals without plans are just dreams.*
> —JAMES E. GARRISON III

As a Southern California city-bred Boy Scout, I especially loved the hikes—getting away into the mountains, where there were live animals and no parents. One trip, a fifty-miler, stands out more than any other, because it is where I earned my fourth key. I may have earned a merit badge or two as well, but it's the key I really value. The same fourth key you're looking for here.

I must have been twelve or thirteen that year; my pack still weighed more than I did, and girls hadn't yet gained acceptance as full-fledged humans. We would be in the mountains for a week—pure fun for twelve-year-old boys, pure hell for a fifty-year-old scoutmaster. After we finally arrived in the mountains and hiked up to our base camp, a friend and I decided that we were going to go hiking up to a lake that we had heard about.

We started down a trail and had hiked for about a half hour when we came to a fork in the trail. Each of us turned to the other at the same time and asked, almost in unison, "Which way do we go?" Neither of us knew where we were going. Each of us had assumed that the other had brought a map. We knew we were on the right trail, but after getting started we were stopped because we had no way of knowing which way to turn. We had no way to reach our goal, so we turned and hiked back down the mountain, bitterly disappointed.

I've seen too many real estate investors stumbling back down the mountain for lack of a clearly laid-out path. They may have set a nebulous, long-range goal, "to get to the top," but they got to a fork in the road and had to give up in defeat. They may have stuffed their packs with knowledge and a sound budget, but they left their maps at home.

Your map will be a carefully laid-out plan of action. The most successful people are those who are capable of setting realistic goals and planning intermediate goals as stepping-stones to get them from the present to the future.

You want to retire to a thatched hut in the tropics in two years? That's fine: it's an achievable, if unorthodox, goal. But that goal without a plan is nothing more than a desire. Between now and then you will have to set and accomplish many intermediate and short-range goals. Let's take a few minutes here and analyze your goals.

I can't begin to estimate what might be realistic goals for you; only you can do that, based on your own personal situation. I can, however, give you some basic guidelines that you can use to determine goals for yourself. For me, an unrealistic goal would be to buy two houses a month while I am still in school. I would do poorly in both my schoolwork and my investing career. Your goals might be unattainable for me, and vice versa. So the first step is recognizing that your goals must be custom-tailored for you, by you.

My friend, Brent, is an excellent runner. He can run like a gazelle in his size-nine Adidas. I wear thirteens, and I can still run a fair race myself. But if we switch shoes, he flops all over the track like a drunken penguin and I can only lace his shoes to my feet if I'm willing to lose a couple of toes in the process.

Brent DeMille isn't Marc Stephen Garrison, nor am I he. In fact, I am not Robert Allen, or Ronald Reagan, or Buck Rogers. I can only please myself; I can't set goals that will be things *you* really want, nor can you set goals that will please me. If you want to spend your life on a tropical island, that's fine. You have to realize before you set any goals that we are motivated by different desires. We may be traveling the same pathway and going in the same direction, but our ultimate goals are different. Don't let anyone set your goals for you.

I'm expecting you to do more than read here. I want you to do some serious thinking and planning. This is meant to be an active course, not a passive one, so if you are not willing to set some major goals *right now*, then put the book down and turn on the TV.

You're still reading. Okay, next step: commit yourself to your goal, on paper. I'll even supply the paper. Run and get a pen. I'll wait right here.

If this is your own book, write at least one major goal in the spaces provided below. It should be something you want to do, such as taking a two-week tour of Europe or just quitting your job—unlocking the handcuffs. Include an objective and a completion date. Example: "I will quit my job—inserting widgets into wangles on the assembly line—no later than May 1, 19-."

If this is not your own book, ask to borrow it for a couple of years or, better yet, go buy your own copy so that you can write in it. You could even use a makeshift facsimile of the spaces below. (Drawing three lines on a piece of paper will work.) The key is to *do it now*. One characteristic of successful people is an ability to act and live in the present. If you've been meaning to join a procrastinators' club, but just haven't gotten around to it yet, then you probably didn't get a pen when I suggested it, and you are going to leave the spaces below blank and fill them in later. Good luck.

_____

_____

_____

So far so good, but don't put away the pen yet. Now set a dollar goal for your retirement income—a monthly cash flow that will allow you to leave your job in comfort. Nothing extravagant, but you should plan on a little more than they are paying you. No sense in giving up your current standard of living and slipping a few notches just so you can be an investor. Kind of defeats the purpose, doesn't it?

Goal: to have a monthly investment income of_____

There. You've set two goals—major goals—on paper, and it wasn't too hard, was it?

Now you must plan a time frame. Knowing you want to get to the top of the mountain won't help much without some idea of the distance involved. You need to know exactly how far away the pinnacle is from your present position. You need to take time into consideration and set intermediate goals. Furthermore, you will have to take inflation into account.

Your age at present_____

Your age when you want to achieve the financial goal you

have already set_____

How many years do you have to achieve that goal?_____

Your goal will allow you to retire at that level of comfort—if you retire today. However, if you are planning to retire at a future date, you will have to prepare for inflation. I don't have to repeat the first part of the book here, so we don't need to discuss the need to plan for inflation. To adjust your monetary goals, you will need to use your financial calculator.

To stay on the safe side, base your inflation projections on current trends. An average inflation rate of 8 percent is not out of line, as the rate is likely to fluctuate between 5 and 10 percent. With an 8 percent inflation rate, the value of your money will be cut in half approximately every twelve years. Now apply that factor to your goal, taking time and inflation into account. Update your goal below:

I will need $_____ in _____ years to reach my goal.

Now you have set a definite, worthwhile goal, adjusted for projected inflation—a financial goal for a monthly income that will allow you to enjoy doing whatever you enjoy doing.

For every great goal there must be a series of carefully planned intermediate goals, each of which are attainable. Just about anybody can get excited about setting the big goals, such as quitting a job and becoming a millionaire, but the daily grind of taking small steps to get there is about as exciting as a blood transfusion. Here again you will face the challenge of daily persistence.

I read *The Greek Treasure*, an excellent book by Irving Stone. I almost passed right by the best part of the entire book: a small, obscure quote buried in the text. Fortunately, my mind did a double take and forced my eyes back to the line that sums up my idea of success:

If you add only a little to a little and do this often enough, soon that little will become great.

A good way to look at this is to imagine the next few years as a hard climb up a very long ladder. One step at a time, very sure and safe, you will progress toward your big goal. Some of the steps may require you to stretch a little, but it will be worth the effort. You will be moving up. If you get bogged down, or reach an apparent impasse, you should get help from others who have been successful in that particular step. Be willing to share your problems with them so they can help you make the climb to the top.

Don't allow yourself to get so caught up in your financial success that you lose everything that is precious. The foundation for a happy life is not reaching a goal of $5,000 or $10,000 or even $100,000 a month. It is striving to reach a goal, keeping your priorities in order and well balanced as you work toward that goal. The joy is in running a good race, and knowing that you deserve the rewards, not what awaits you at the finish line.

Goal setting is the fourth key, and it might be the most important for your long-range success. But it will be a hollow victory if you reach your goals without key number five:

Key 5: <u>DO ESTABLISH A REPUTATION FOR HONESTY.</u>

> *You can shear a sheep every year,*
> *but you can skin it only once.*
> —ROBERT WALLACE GARRISON

We spend every waking minute in a world where taking advantage is the norm. Lying and cheating are accepted business customs. But as investors we must set a higher standard for success. If you choose to "skin" a few buyers or sellers now and again, you may make a quick buck; you may even make a quick thousand. But you will develop a reputation.

I recently got a phone call from a person living two houses down from a house that I had bought and resold within a week. That person knew how hard I had worked to improve that house. She knew how straightforward I had been in both buying and selling the home. She called to tell me that another house in the neighborhood was empty. She mentioned that the owners had tried to sell the home, couldn't, and had left it empty to move to where they had been transferred. The neighbor that called wanted to let me know that it was available. In fact, she even provided me with the forwarding address and phone number for the owners.

Thanks to her help I was able to get a good deal for myself, help out the people who had been forced to move, and help out the neighborhood as well. Before the deal was closed I had the home rented out and had arranged to have the overgrown lawn and messy yard cleaned up.

Problems do come up on occasion. There is nothing you can do about it. If you have a track record of honest dealings with people, you can avoid a lot of heartache and problems. Your reputation is branded on you and follows you throughout your investing career.

Two or three years ago I heard about an interesting concept in salesmanship, discovered by Joe Girard, who has earned the title "The World's Greatest Salesman." The essence of his success is what he calls the "250 rule."

His father was an undertaker, and as a boy it was his job to arrange for the printing and passing out of the funeral service cards to the mourners. After doing this for several years he noticed a remarkable statistic. He realized that the average number of people to attend a funeral was about 250. There seemed to be no discernible reason for this number, but it was consistent. When Joe Average died, it was time to order 250 more cards. Some time later Girard shared this statistical oddity with a friend who catered weddings. The friend told him that the same number of people were usually in attendance at weddings also.

Girard was a thinker, and now he had a riddle to solve. He spent some time thinking about it while he was in college, studying selling. Then he came to a startling—and obvious—conclusion: everyone has a circle of about 250 friends—friends close enough to attend a wedding or funeral. Now, some of us know more people and some fewer, but as a ballpark figure it will do. That means that when you buy or sell a home, you are establishing your reputation with about 250 people. One year from now, when it comes time to purchase another investment property, don't assume that you and the seller are total strangers. He or she may know someone with whom you have dealt, and your reputation will either make or break the deal.

Don't sell your scruples. You will sell them cheaply and pay dearly for them later—if it isn't too late. Honesty isn't just the best policy; it's the only policy for success.

If you develop a reputation as a good landlord or a fair dealer, the day may come when you can literally sit at home and have people call you to offer you excellent deals. Then you will be harvesting a crop that you planted at the beginning of your career—today.

That's the first five keys to success in real estate investing—everything you should do. If you can master this much, your success is almost guaranteed. But I have five more keys to offer in the next chapter—the don'ts of investing. Read them carefully, and avoid the stumbling blocks that trip most beginning investors.

CHAPTER 15

Pitfalls

I believe that genius is an infinite
capacity for taking life by the
scruff of the neck.
    —CHRISTOPHER QUILL

If you took the time to study the first five keys, and if you have made a commitment to yourself to apply them, you should be ready for the other five: the *don'ts*. *These keys are also power-ful, and essential for the real estate investor.*

Key 6: <u>DON'T BELIEVE EVERYTHING YOU HEAR.</u>

If you trust too much you may be
occasionally deceived. However, you will
live in torment if you cannot trust enough.
    —ANONYMOUS

Trust everyone, but cut the cards anyway.
    —BRUCE C. ERB

What a name for a key! And with the pride I take in having a posi-tive attitude, what kind of key am I offering here? Well, if there is one lesson that is usually learned the hard way, it's how not to trust. After living through several treacherous deals, I am almost inclined to say, "Don't believe *anything* you hear." I have found that things are rarely as they seem, and many people, eager to buy or sell, are willing to say or do whatever it takes to get a good deal.

There are sellers who will misrepresent both the monthly pay-ment and the interest rate on a loan just to make a sale. They must know that their lies will be discovered in due course, but

223

many buyers, after having made a commitment to such a seller, are inclined to hold on to the myth that this is a hot deal—when, in fact, it is nothing more than a hot potato that should be dropped. Maybe a seller isn't lying; maybe he's just made a mistake. But if you don't double-check his figures, you could find yourself tangled up in a nasty situation.

I was recently in the process of closing on a home that the owner presented as having no liens against it other than the VA loan, which I was to assume. In my earlier days as an investor I would have taken the seller at his word, but experience has taught me to check—just in case.

Unfortunately, this was just such a case. One way of avoiding costly entanglements is to be sure that you handle every closing through a competent real estate attorney or a professional title company, with a complete title search and the issuance of title insurance. In this case the title company with whom I dealt made a preliminary title search and found that there was a $2,000 thorn hiding among the roses. I almost kissed my title officer when she told me they had uncovered a tax lien against the property.

A tax lien is attached to the property itself, not the owner. Buying that property as is would have been like buying a car with a flat spare. Guess who would get stuck with the cost? Right. Yours truly, the new owner.

We managed to work out a deal. Or rather, I managed to work out a deal: the owner, who had somehow managed to forget all about the tax lien, agreed to pay the $2,000 to the IRS prior to closing.

I don't want to scare you away from investing, nor do I want to suggest that you should lose faith in humanity. Just take the time to check out the whole story. I've been told a few malicious lies motivated by greed; I've been told lies as innocent as a baby's breath; and I've heard hundreds of misrepresentations that live in the shadowy world of half-truths. Rarely have I been told the whole truth.

Truth itself is subjective, and my interpretation of it is likely not to agree with yours. When the seller insists that his house is perfect, and you can see it will take a week to make it habitable, he may simply have a new and unique definition for the word *perfect*.

Trust in another human being is a noble trait. And occasionally, it is a fatal flaw. John F. Kennedy trusted his advisers (or vice versa, as some historians say) and precipitated the Bay of Pigs fiasco; little old ladies allow con artists to bilk them out of every penny in their meager bank accounts; and an entire nation put their faith in a madman named Adolf.

There is another—possibly worse—type of trust. It's the trust in a friend who in innocence destroys your future. There has never been one successful person who was not told at least once—by a dear friend or relative—that he or she couldn't succeed. Wives tear down their husbands' ambitions (or husbands tear down their wives'); parents destroy their children's dreams; and best friends, perhaps sensing a permanent separation, deride lofty goals.

The reason this trust is especially insidious is that all the bad advice is based on truth—a narrow, uneducated truth. A few hundred years ago you would have been horrified to find out that your best friend was planning on taking a bath. Everyone knew that bathing induced all manner of sickness—even death. You would do whatever was necessary to prevent your friend from making a fatal mistake.

"Truth" may be false.

Key 7: <u>DON'T TRUST INSTINCT ALONE; USE EXPERTS IF NECESSARY.</u>

> *1 + 1 = 3 (definition of synergy)*
> —Dr. Robert Crawford

Leverage. A truly remarkable force. I remember my amazement when I first found out about the principle of leverage in real estate investing. I could control $50,000—even $100,000—with only a $2,000 investment. And we can use that incredible power every day as investors.

Then I learned another, possibly more important, use for leverage as an investor: *people* leverage. I could use the help of experts to multiply the effectiveness of every effort. I could leverage my knowledge by relying on the experts around me.

I recently heard a sad tale, related by the victim. He had bought a property without securing title insurance. Right off the bat he had failed to use key 6, "Don't believe everything you hear." It turned out that the title was as cloudy as a tropical rain forest. There were enough liens on the property to collapse it entirely. But he had taken the seller at his word, and now he was stuck with a very encumbered property.

If he had used the leverage that a title officer could have offered, he would have been able to avoid the heartache. The value of such help is worth many, many times the cost. Often the price of excellent advice is nothing more than a sincere thank-you or a nice lunch. Let me tell you about some of the most important real estate experts you will need to have on your team.

A *real estate agent* is licensed by the state to enter into a contractual relationship with a client to sell real estate. To sell the real estate, agents advertise the properties and show them to prospective buyers.

If you want to get some free education and develop good working relationships, try this: call any Realtor in your yellow pages. Tell the agent that you are interested in buying a home in the area. Describe what kind of property you are looking for, and how much you can afford to spend. That agent will take you to as many houses as you would like to see and give you a free seminar in home values and real estate principles. Continue going out with different Realtors; you will see how much difference there is among them, and you may find one who is not afraid to go out of his or her way to help you.

A couple of the characteristics that make a good Realtor good are personal investing experience and a willingness to work with creative financing techniques. If a Realtor tells me that the only way to buy a house is to put a large down payment on the property and to get financing from the bank, I tell that Realtor goodbye. I need someone who understands investors and who is willing to help me with my program.

Once you get to know an agent well enough to feel confident that he or she will work with you, begin asking any and every question that you need answered. They have taken special classes and have probably learned more about real estate than you are likely to learn in a year on your own, and that's real knowledge leverage.

The *state real estate commission* is charged with the regulation of real estate laws. Every state has one. Having the telephone number of your commission is essentially the same as having a staff of legal experts waiting on call. Imagine having a battery of lawyers, who charge no fee, waiting for your calls. As a real estate investor, you have the next best thing—your commission.

I learned the value of this source early in my investing career. I was involved in the purchase of a really nice duplex, which was being sold by two old-time real estate agents. The price and terms were almost too good to be true, which should have been my first clue that everything wasn't rosy.

The problem slowly surfaced, and as the closing date approached I became aware that the agents had made several misrepresentations. In fact, it was soon apparent that the misrepresentations could not have been unintentional; these people were out to skin me alive. When I confronted them with the facts I had unearthed, they warned me that if I attempted to withdraw from the contract I would lose all of my earnest money. (I hadn't yet learned to give earnest money in the form of a promissory note.)

Desperate, I called the real estate commission, as a friend had suggested. I was informed not only that I could recover my earnest money in full, but that the agents could lose their real estate licenses for willfully misrepresenting the property. When I called them the next day and informed them that I had been in touch with the commission, the agents quite suddenly experienced a change of heart. They were happy to give me a full refund, with a (sincere?) apology, and I got the distinct impression that they would have been happy to double that refund if I had asked.

An *appraiser* is a highly skilled professional who, based on years of schooling and experience, is qualified to render an opinion as to a property's value. When you are considering the purchase of a small two-bedroom house, how can you tell what its market price is? You can't look it up in *Consumer's Report*, can you? An appraiser, for $150 or more, will take a look at the house and render his or her opinion.

I prefer to appraise properties myself, based on my experience as an electrician and the property analysis system that I have developed. However, I have found a rather inexpensive way to leverage the expertise of an appraiser. Call an appraiser and offer to buy a nice steak lunch in exchange for letting you follow him or her around for a day. You can act as a secretary or helper all day, asking questions as you go along. That one day may pay greater dividends than a whole day of reading about investing.

A *title company* prepares an "abstract of title" for a property and provides title insurance. Despite its impressive name, an abstract of title is nothing more than the up-to-date history of a property. But they can't very well call it an "up-to-date history" and still charge $100, so why not call it an abstract of title?

When the title company searches the title (the rights to a property), they will find all easements, liens, and encumbrances that might be attached to the property. For example, if state property taxes are owed on a property, the state has a right to a portion of that property's value. You might not find out about that lien until six months after the sale, when a letter from the state tax board appears in your mail box. The title company would have discovered the problem and alerted you long before the closing date.

After the title company has prepared the abstract, they will offer insurance guaranteeing that according to all known information the property is being sold with only the liens and encumbrances listed in the abstract.

Now for the leverage. You have an expert waiting at a desk for your calls. This expert is a title officer, and he or she can save you hundreds of hours and dollars.

I have found myself at the desk of my title officer at least a hundred times, asking her whether the earnest money offer I am presenting says what I want it to say. I have actually had her write out complete earnest money forms for me. The boxes of chocolates and the flowers I have given her are nothing compared to the money she has saved me.

Recently I was closing on a property and needed some help in writing a special clause I wanted to include as protection. I called and talked to her for a few minutes, but she couldn't help me with it. Ten minutes passed and the phone rang. There she was calling to tell me that she had called several other title officers until she got the right answer. I wouldn't trade her for all the Porsches in Hollywood.

If you want to find a good title officer, pick up your yellow pages and start calling title companies. Explain that you are an investor, and ask the title officer what services he or she can offer. They are looking for loyal customers, so let them make a sales pitch to you. After all, investors are likely to buy more than one house in twenty years; active investors may buy four or five houses a month. When you find a good title officer, who will go out of his or her way to help you, then start calling and asking questions. Or stop by the office and have your officer help you write an earnest money contract. Then drop a thank-you note in the mail, or (you guessed it) take your title officer out to lunch.

A *real estate attorney* is just what the name implies: an attorney who specializes in real estate law. Such an attorney is often capable of handling all of the legal aspects of a real estate transaction, right through to completing the closing right in his or her office. Nurturing a relationship with a real estate lawyer will not necessarily give you access to free legal advice, but it will help tremendously as a source of bargain properties.

The reason is that real estate attorneys often handle foreclosure proceedings. People who are facing foreclosure will often call such a lawyer, looking for alternatives, and if they want to sell their house quickly, the lawyer can say, "I do know an investor in the area who can buy your house quickly and who will give you a good price."

A *property manager* is a professional who manages rentals. At least five out of every six people think that managing rental properties is a piece of cake, and all five of them are nuts.

Property management is a specialized skill that must be developed through years of training. It seems to require a certain personality type, and I'm too much of a softie to ever be a good manager. I always succumb to the first-of-the-month emergency stories, such as the tenant who had to spend the rent money on her cat, who desperately needed open-claw surgery.

Hiring someone who you know is competent to handle the special pressures that the job entails will greatly leverage your time and money. But if you insist on managing the property yourself, you can still use the skills of a professional manager. When you write an offer to purchase the property, include the phrase "offer is subject to the inspection of all rental records, and the satisfactory acceptance of their performance." With those records in hand, visit a professional property manager and ask him or her to render an opinion. You may need to raise the rents; find out what the going rate is for units such as the ones you are planning to buy.

This is one area of investing that I leave to experts. Actually, I have been forced by circumstance to become something of an expert in this field, but I thoroughly detest the job. So why not spend a little money to increase my free time for what I love to do—buy and sell properties?

A *real estate consultant* is a paid professional who can help you establish and carry out investing goals. Usually a paid consultant is an investor with extensive experience. He or she will charge a fee, with an initial retainer paid up-front and then an hourly charge for services rendered.

As a consultant, I have enjoyed helping new investors get started. It is something like a series of climbers working their way up the face of a mountain, each turning to help the next reach a new level. I am perhaps a quarter of the way up the face of the mountain, and it is with real pleasure that I turn and give a hand to people below me who are struggling.

There are two major advantages to having a consultant help you get started. First, as an experienced investor, the professional consultant can take a step back, away from the emotional engagement of a first-time investor, and clinically evaluate the pros and cons of an investment. Second, most would-be investors stay at the would-be stage all of their lives, too overwhelmed by the seeming complexity of the process to ever make a written offer. The experienced investor can take the novice by the hand and lead him or her through the process for the first time. Admit it; once you've been walked through a sale, you wouldn't have any trouble investing on your own, would you?

The consultant will often uncover defects in your best-laid plans, and by doing so may save you many times the consulting fee.

* * *

A *loan officer* represents a lending institution in processing a loan. As such, he or she wields more power than you might at first think. The position has grown in stride with the newly competitive nature of banking, as deregulation has thrown all lending institutions into the same ring to fight for customers. Today's loan officer is more than an order taker; the position requires a full customer service manager.

Many investors have an aversion to banks, rightly preferring to deal with the home owners themselves when it comes to arranging financing. But through my contacts at local banks, I have been able to put together some fantastic deals simply because I could secure financing with one phone call.

Home builders can evaluate the structural soundness of a property. One of the most common questions asked by beginning investors is, "How can I check a property for structural damage without having to pay for a full inspection?" Well, you could learn about construction as I did, installing electrical systems for eight years. But if that seems infeasible, try doing what a group of investors I met in California did. While I was working as an apprentice, my boss would be called in by this group to inspect a property before they would make an offer on it. They wouldn't pay for the inspection, but there was an agreement that if they bought the house and it needed electrical work, my boss would be the one to do it.

You can do the same thing with every home you are going to buy. If the work needs to be done anyway, you might as well pay a professional to do it right. And if that professional will give you a free structural inspection, what better way could you work together?

When you have the property inspected, or when you inspect it yourself, make sure to use the checklist provided in chapter 8.

Don't be intimidated by the expertise of someone who can help you. In school, were you afraid to ask your math teachers about math, just because they knew about a million times more than you? Of course not; that's why they were teachers. We often have the misconception that we will be imposing on someone else when we ask for help or advice. Usually nothing could be further from the truth.

Imagine for a moment that you are a Tinkertoy sculptor. A young man approaches and meekly asks you for a few words of wisdom. In fact, he will treat you to lunch at a fancy restaurant, such as Chef le McDonald's, if you will explain how to balance the little round blocks with the long green dowels. How would you respond? Chances are you would be very flattered, and you would be glad for the opportunity to expound on the virtues of Tinkertoy sculpting. (In the back of your mind, you also recall the old adage, "The teacher always gains more than the student.")

Why should a title officer feel any differently? They are bored out of their minds; they process these abstracts all day long, and nobody appreciates the knowledge they have spent years accumulating. Now they have the opportunity to get a nice lunch, and what does it cost them? Nothing, except sharing information they know as well as their own names.

It would be a good idea to start a special phone book, filled with the names and phone numbers of these contacts. It's like having a book of levers and pulleys that you can use to greatly increase your investing power. With this book by your phone, you can have almost any question answered in seconds. That's leverage.

Synergy occurs whenever the whole is greater than the sum of the parts. Combining an expert's knowledge with your own determination and hard work is synergy at its best.

If I were to describe this key, I would imagine that it is a very long key, capable of tearing the lock right out of the door. This key is an absolute must; the alternative is to open the lock without the help of a key, and that's never the best way to open a door.

Key 8: <u>DON'T WAIT FOR SUCCESS; MAKE IT HAPPEN</u>.

*The secret of walking on water is
knowing where the stones are.*
—HERB COHEN

If you want to succeed at drilling oil, you have to drill where the oil is. That advice may seem as helpful as "Buy low, sell high," but it is another overlooked fact of success. I often receive calls from beginning investors who can't wait to tell me about their "great deals." They may have found an $80,000 house that is selling for $2,000 under market value, on which they only have to put down $10,000 as a down payment. For some reason, they seem surprised when I am not impressed. Don't jump into the first property that looks good at first glance. It takes more than a glance to assess any property, and you may find yourself drilling where there is no oil.

You may have to investigate five or even ten houses before finding one that will be truly profitable, but persistence pays off. When it comes to making success happen, knowledge is useless without persistent effort, and all the work in the world is useless without knowledge.

We have reserved a name for the person who combines education with persistence until he or she achieves a goal. We call that person an entrepreneur. Webster's may have a slightly different definition, but mine really sums up the meaning of the word.

From Ogg Ooog, inventor of the wheel, to Thomas Edison, inventive genius extraordinaire, the true entrepreneur has been the person with creativity, intelligence, and the ability to see something through from beginning to end. The other 99.9 percent of the world's population may have the intelligence, but only one in maybe a thousand is willing to push beyond the threshold of despair.

Do you want success—as an investor, or as a parent, or just as a human being? Then you will have to do more than set goals and educate yourself. And you will have to do more than organize your time and your finances. You will have to commit yourself to success right up until the day of your first failure, and then one more day, and then another. You cannot quit if you want to succeed.

In 1858, Irving Spalding decided to create the ultimate soft drink. He combined soda water and natural fruit juices, and called his concoction 1-Up. It failed miserably in taste tests across the nation. Back to the laboratory went Irving and down the drain went 1-Up. Undaunted, Irving tried a new combination and called it 2-Up. It bombed miserably. Soon 3-Up followed, and then 4-Up and 5-Up. Each in turn followed 1-Up down the drain.

At the end of his patience—and money—Irving tried one last time, combining soda water, lime juice, and banana puree to make 6-Up. But it was a failure as well, so he gave up in despair.

He died three months later of a broken heart, never knowing how close he had come to success.

When you start (if you haven't started already) spending most of your "free" time investing, you will quickly find yourself discouraged. Your friends and family, if they aren't ridiculing you, are at least enjoying themselves while you are out there killing yourself. And overnight success is as rare as snow in Los Angeles. To maintain the necessary drive, take a look at the rewards and the alternatives.

The rewards are a wealth of time and money, and of the two a wealth of time is by far more valuable. The alternatives are grim, to say the least. I've thrown enough retirement statistics at you already, and you should have a pretty good idea of what lies ahead. This is it—now. You must make success happen.

A man from Florida whom I consulted with about his personal investments was just about to give up. He had been trying to find investment properties that he could afford, but with no luck at all. Discouraged, he called me one last time to say good-bye. I encouraged him to try a few more things; to find something that hadn't been done before.

He finally committed himself to investing several hundred dollars in putting a flier into one of those value-pack advertisements that are directly mailed out. You know the ones: they have coupons for all of the local merchants, like fifty cents off your next dry-cleaning bill. He paid to have 10,000 of them printed and mailed, saying, "I BUY HOUSES." It sounded like an awfully big investment for a person who was thinking about giving up, and I almost tried to stop him.

Several days ago he called me, out of breath. He told me about the first deal he got from the mailing. His telephone had hardly stopped ringing, and with his very first deal he was able to buy and sell a home and put $6,000 in his pocket. He said that was just a start; he had managed to buy nine homes in his area in less than two months. He was so excited he could hardly talk about it, and he said that he would have to call me back later, as he was late for a closing at a local title company.

The man is a success. Not because he is lucky, but because he persisted. He didn't quit after 6-Up failed; he kept trying, and the answer to his dreams was waiting just around the bend.

Try this tonight, just as an experiment. Stay home and watch TV, or lie down for a while and read *People*. But keep a pen and a noteboook handy. Now, every time someone calls you tonight and offers to sell his or her house to you—below market value, with little or no money down—be sure to make a note of it. Count all the calls you receive and send me the total. I'm really interested in seeing just how many people get more than three such calls a night.

If you don't receive any calls, don't you think you ought to do something about it?

This key is solid cast-iron. It is unbreakable. No matter how hard the lock seems to be, if you are willing to push as hard as you need to, for as long as you need to, the lock will eventually give way. There's no surer guarantee of success than this key, because it is virtually indestructible. The only way it will fail is if you give up.

Key 9: <u>DON'T EAT ALL OF YOUR PROFITS.</u>

If a man is wise, he gets rich. An' if he gets
rich, he gets foolish, or his wife does.
That's what keeps the money moving around.
—FINLEY PETTER DUNNE

There is an old fable about a man named Wong Li, who lived long ago in China. He was a very wise man who helped the emperor out of a tough situation. To thank Wong, the emperor insisted that he name his own reward; nothing was too much to ask.

"O great Chung Fou," said Wong, bowing low, "I have only one humble request. I would like to have only one grain of rice today, which shall be put into a storehouse. Every day for two full moons, whatever rice remains in the storehouse must be matched by an equal number of grains. If I leave my rice in the storehouse tonight, then there will be one added to it; if I leave those two again, then there will be two more grains on the next day. If I could only have this one wish granted, then I would be the happiest man in China."

The emperor, of course, thought he was getting a good deal, so he gladly granted the man's wish. By the tenth day, the emperor had to pay Wong only 512 grains of rice; hardly enough to fill a bowl. But by the end of the first month, he began to realize the full price of his agreement, so he called Wong into his castle.

"Wong," said the emperor, "you are very smart, but not very wise." And so saying, he called in his guards and had Wong Li put to death.

Just how many grains of rice would the emperor have had to pay on the last day of the second month? Well, if there were sixty-one days in the two months, he would have received a king's ransom in rice: 2,305,843,000,000,000,000 grains—almost two and a half quintillion grains. Literally more than all the rice in China. And that would be for the sixty-first day *only*.

That is an example of the power of multiplying the outcome of every equation; what mathematicians call a geometric progression. Now that we have such an amazing outcome, let's play with the figures a little and see what happens. First, what would have happened if Wong Li had eaten the first grain of rice on the first day? That one is easy; if you add zero to zero, you still get zero, and the emperor would have paid the full contract price.

Now what if Wong Li had waited until the second day to take a grain of rice, leaving one grain for the second night? That one is not too much more difficult: he would have shortened the entire contract period by one day, shortening the sixty-one days to sixty. He would then have lost his 2.3 quintillion grains for the sixty-first day.

Now for the real heart of my discussion. What would the result have been if he had always left one grain in the storehouse and always taken one to eat? The answer should be obivious: Wong would have been paid exactly sixty-one grains of rice.

As a real estate investor, you will share with other investors a unique opportunity: the chance to make 100 percent annual profit (and sometimes more) on your investments. Quite a few first-time investors will eat every grain of rice as they receive it. They will eat the first grain on the first day, taking the profit *and* the original investment to buy a new stereo system and a VCR to go with it. They have just cleared out the storehouse, and have thrown away unimaginable wealth.

But most people make just as serious a mistake: when they recover the original investment plus some profit, they immediately spend the profit and reinvest their original capital. And they think that they are investors, because they have a new VCR and it didn't cost them anything; it was "investment profit."

They may double their money again and again, taking the profit and buying another gizmo each time, but they will never create any wealth. They are taking away one grain every day and leaving one grain in the storehouse.

Success requires a willingness to forgo spending your profits. You must have the ability to delay the day of celebrating your wealth just as long as possible. The longer you wait, in fact, the more you will be able to afford to celebrate when you finally do. Obviously, had Wong Li waited until at least the end of the first month, he would have been able to take home a ton of rice without seriously affecting his wealth. He could have taken home the thirtieth day's pay—slightly over 1 trillion grains of rice—without sending himself to the poorhouse.

In the last chapter, I stressed the necessity of paying yourself first and of rewarding yourself. I have also suggested living below your income level for most of the year and then blowing a portion of your savings on an extravagant vacation. Now I am telling you not to spend your profits. "C'mon, Marc, which is it?"

I consider those vacations an investment. They are a reward that feeds the flame of success. But they are only a fraction of your savings. I'm suggesting that you eat a handful of rice on about the tenth day, when there are 1,024 grains in the storehouse. Then eat a bowlful on the twentieth day, and put off the day of real celebration—the trip around the world—until the end of the first month.

Translating that into more realistic terms, I would suggest that you build up equity *and* cash flow. Sit tight in a small house for several years; put off changing your style of living until you have amassed your second million in real estate and have developed a monthly income of several thousand dollars. Don't take a trip to Europe the first year; try something a little closer to home, something that will cost about one fifth of your real estate profits. And don't waste one penny of profit until at least your third successful investment.

A few years ago I opened my mailbox and found a $3,000 check—a very nice real estate profit. It would have been easy (oh, so easy) to spend all of it on a new computer, or as a down payment on a nice car. Instead, I took my wife out to a nice prime rib dinner. It's hard to track that $3,000, but I would have to estimate that that profit is worth at least $30,000 today. Now I can buy that $3,000 toy and have $27,000 left to reinvest.

This is an interesting key, because you will find that after you have finally opened the door to success, the landscape may surprise you. It is not a flat plane. There are hundreds of levels of success, and you can exist at any level you desire. But it is always an uphill climb, and you will face a new locked door at every level. This key opens every door. As long as you are willing to reinvest your profits and spend only a small fraction at each level, you will be able to unlock the door that opens onto the next level.

That's all but one key. Each one by itself is valuable, whether you invest in real estate or not. The last key is made specially for the real estate investor:

Key 10: DON'T BUY WITHOUT A GOOD PROPERTY ANALYSIS.

If only foresight were 20-20, we'd have no need for hindsight.
—JARED D. ERB

It's interesting watching the high jumpers in the Olympics as they prepare for their jump. By following the movements of their head and eyes, you can actually watch them go through every step of the jump in their minds before they take so much as one step.

You can do exactly the same thing when you prepare to make an offer on a house. It's possible, with a property analysis system, to plan every step of the process from the initial offer to the final sale. A failure to do so can often prove very costly. I have heard of many investors who, in their excitement at finding a nothing-down deal, have learned that the exit is every bit as important as the entrance. They don't realize until it is too late that the seller was simply unloading an alligator onto them, and the fact that there was no down payment does not mean it was a good deal.

One difficulty encountered in real estate investing is the mathematics of finance, which are complex. Figuring out the payments on a thirty-year fully amortized loan wasn't just a headache, it was an impossibility—until I learned how to use a financial calculator, a marvelous tool produced by the same computer technology that has given us everything from Pac-Man to space shuttles.

My very strong suggestion is that you invest in a good financial calculator, such as the HP-12C, made by Hewlett-Packard. I've had my 12C (for short) for a few years now, and it has paid for itself a thousand times over. I have compared it to all of the other financial calculators, and as an M.B.A., I can attest to the fact that it out-adds, out-divides, and generally out-everythings any other calculator on the market.

Unfortunately, when I first popped open the friendly *Owner's Handbook and Problem Guide,* I was sure it was written in Greek. I even had trouble figuring out how to add one and one.

It wasn't until I took a special course in graduate school that I finally figured out how to use the 12C, and then I really took off. The experience was comparable to taking flying lessons in a Lear jet. I knew I had a powerful tool, but I had no idea what it could really do until I learned how to use it.

This isn't meant to be an advertisement for Hewlett-Packard's calculator, but if you are serious about investing, the HP-12C comes highly recommended by me. It has saved countless hours and has increased the profitability of my investments. If you own an HP-12C, or if you plan on buying one, you may be interested in *The Real Estate Finance Tool Kit,* available through NCREI, P.O. Box 796, Provo, Utah 84603.

I think that the combination of a good calculator and a good system is essential, and I will not make a buying decision without first performing an analysis. It has allowed me to consistently pick a winner.

A word of caution: In every real estate transaction there are far too many factors involved to be plugged into any simple form. There is only one computer that can take that much information into account and come up with an answer: the human brain. The financial analysis will crunch through the numbers that would take a person a year to figure, but there is a point where instinct takes over.

* * *

Well, if you have managed to stay with me through all ten keys, and if you are willing to apply every one of those keys, there is no way you can fail. I defy you to fail.

That's the end of your basic training. You're ready to be certified as prepared for success. It's time to take your learning and put it to use.

If you are really ready for success, move ahead and put everything you've learned to work. Take your keys, open the door, and follow me. There is nothing holding you back from a bright future but your own insecurities. Conquer them, and achieve the success you deserve.

PART V

More than Wealth

CHAPTER 16

People Can Change the World

*The fragrance always stays on the
hand that gives the rose.*
                    —HADA BEJAR

A common complaint about the wealthy is that they only care about their money. The real problem is that a few selfish millionaires get all the attention because they flaunt their wealth. Who cares how much money Julie Andrews spends helping starving children around the world? We'd rather see Princess Caroline carousing on a royal yacht.

What do you think would happen if *People* magazine decided to concentrate on only the philanthropists, while *Us* continued to show off the playthings and pleasures of the idle rich? Which magazine would go out of business within two months?

I'd like you to meet a few people who have enjoyed tremendous financial rewards and tell you a little about how they chose to spend their fortunes.

Locked away in the history books is the fascinating story of Sir Moses Montefiore. Raised in seventeenth-century England, this man rose to wealth through hard work. After spending time as a stockbroker and as a lender, this man quit at the age of forty to devote the rest of his life to his dream: alleviating the pitiable condition of the Jewish people both in Europe and overseas, particularly in the Holy Land.

Montefiore could easily have spent the next sixty years of his life indulging in every pleasure imaginable, but instead he chose to devote himself entirely to his cause. His mission on behalf of the Jewish people generated universal concern for their cause and helped to free them of the discrimination that had been prevalent in Europe for centuries.

Would you like to do something along the same lines as the incredible accomplishments of Sir Moses Montefiore? Would you like to be able to actually change the world? Your friends will probably say that you would be crazy to even entertain such an idea. After all, they can hardly keep up on their bills and who won the last football game on TV. It's just too much effort—in their eyes—to do anything more than fend for themselves.

Robert H. Dedman began life with a natural desire for education. Within four years of leaving high school, he had finished three college degrees: one in law, one in economics, and one in engineering. He did all this while working full-time. That is impressive, but even more impressive is the full story of this man who has changed the world.

Mr. Dedman went on to become a successful lawyer. Noticing an investment opportunity, he began investing in building his own chain of country clubs.

His gamble paid off. But today he is not just living a life of carefree ease. This man, with his love for education, has granted $25 million to Southern Methodist University's undergraduate liberal arts and sciences college. He has also endowed the college with $1 million to establish a center for lifetime sports.

The attitude that he lives with is one that is almost common among the self-made millionaires of the world. He has worked hard for his success, but after providing for his family and his personal needs, he wants to share his wealth with those less fortunate.

This attitude may seem incredible to those who cannot fulfill their smallest dreams. But once you have a house to live in and enough money to cover all of your expenses, what else is there? All of the toys lose their luster when you can afford as many as you want, and you really can't take it with you.

Have you ever seen a hearse with a luggage rack?

When Harry Chapin lost his life to that all-American death, the car accident, he was a young, successful singer. His songs were popular for their haunting melodies and clear insights. He could have chosen the party life that has attracted so many pop singers, but instead he spent his entire career raising money for charities. It is estimated that before his death Harry Chapin had raised over $6 million in contributions for the humanities and the arts. Of the more than two hundred concerts he performed annually, half were benefit concerts.

Besides the benefit concerts, Harry served as founding trustee of World Hunger Year, and he served on the boards of many performing arts foundations. He once said, "Given this short opportunity we call life, it seems to me that the only sensible way—even if you have pessimistic thoughts about the 99 percent possibility that things are going wrong—is to operate on the 1 percent that our lives can mean something."

Life is fantastic, life is fun. These people did something more than just satisfy their physical desires. They went one step beyond and left a mark on the world. They weren't content to leave an estate for the inheritors and Uncle Sam to fight over.

I am inspired by these stories and the story of Paul Mellon, the great philanthropist whose contribution to the arts constitutes a gift to mankind that can never be tarnished. I also think of John Jacob Astor, founder of the Astor fortune, whose personal contribution of his book collection formed the cornerstone of the New York Public Library. Today, the great Astor legacy of helping others is carried on by Brooke Astor. In the last twenty-five years Ms. Astor has directed the distribution of over $130 million in philanthropic work.

These admirable men and women have left the world a legacy that goes far beyond anything left by billions of people who have passed through life with no other thought than to survive from birth to death. They were all willing to sacrifice, to work hard, and to change the world and the shape of history itself.

Let me give you just one more—although I could write an entire book about such people.

A story is told about Percy Ross, the Minneapolis tycoon. It is said that he invited over one thousand disadvantaged kids in Minneapolis to an all-you-can-eat Christmas Eve dinner at the Minneapolis Auditorium. I would give anything to see the expression on those children's faces when he pulled his grand surprise. The children were filled with a meal unlike any other they had had all year, and just as they were preparing to leave, the curtain went up in the auditorium, revealing a gleaming, brand-new bicycle for each of them.

Can you remember back far enough to have any idea what joy he must have brought to a thousand young lives? Why did he do it?

He did it because there is no joy comparable to helping others. We would all love to experience the same joy, but most of us can't afford it. Yet.

People like these leave more than just a tombstone. Because of them a child can smile, an illness can be cured, people can live in peace. I think that these people will rest in peace also.

Well, here it is. The end of the book, and the beginning of a new life for you, if you choose. In this last chapter I am going far beyond the reaches of any investment book I have ever read. I want to convince you to join the ranks of those listed above. Human beings have so much potential; most of them, however, operate on two cylinders in an eight-cylinder world.

Why not set a greater goal than mere money and toys? Why not set the ultimate goal: the wealth that comes with knowing that when you face the last day of mortality, the world will be a better place for your having been there.

I plan to change the world. I want to teach an entire generation of negative-thinking, failure-programmed people that success is possible. I want to see all people who have the desire and ambition succeed in whatever goals they set. I want to teach Success 101, and I want graduates from sea to shining sea.

Why should you be any different? If you can take off the golden handcuffs and provide for your own retirement, instead of relying on the government, you will be able to build a strong castle that you can call your own. And then you can make the changes in the world that you want to make.

Do you want to alleviate the hunger that claims hundreds of thousands of lives every year? Do you want to spend your days changing and influencing the way our country is governed? Of course, you don't have to change the world; you don't have to share my vision. Perhaps you want to spend your days in quiet worship, or with your children, nurturing them and spending the time with them that your own parents could never afford. That's every bit as important as what I may want to do.

The important point is that you are doing something that is valuable and important to you.

Financial freedom is not just a dream. It is real and can be achieved through real estate investing. Success requires no real financial genius, but it does require a solid knowledge of basic principles. This specific knowledge, together with your motivation, your personal plan, and *action*, will help you to realize your financial dreams.

It doesn't matter "how much," it just matters that you do something. For a reference, read Mark 12:41-44 and Luke 21:1-4.

Whatever you do, you will have changed the world, and with it made your investment plan and program something of great worth.

I wish you happiness on your journey. I pray that your worthy dreams become reality.

Epilogue

Jim Cooper slumped tiredly in front of the TV. Eight years as a foreman! He was due—long overdue—for a promotion; didn't anybody notice that he was working ten hours a day? He snapped his beer can open viciously, a warning to Heather and the kids that they damn well better tread lightly. He reached for the mail on the coffee table at his feet. Junk mail and bills—that's all they seemed to get anymore. The first two were bills, which he threw back on the table unopened. The third caught his eye—and, for a moment, his interest. It was one of those flashy fliers advertising a real estate seminar, crowded with pictures of supposedly successful people, boats, planes, and tropical islands. He was just tired enough to close his eyes and let his imagination run wild for a second. He even pulled out a few old dreams and dusted them off; he had once dared to hope for success. He laughed bitterly at the thought of driving around in a fancy car, or hopping onto a plane and flying to Europe.

He picked up the flier again and looked closely. It was filled with unbelievable promises of wealth and happiness that could be his if he would spend some time learning the tools for success. His heart quickened slightly. He knew better than to chase pipe dreams, but he also knew people who had made a bundle in real estate. Why not? He had almost nothing to lose, and everything to gain.

That was a little over two years ago.

It had been tough, thought Jim, as he dialed. Over two years of working full-time and investing on the side. Endless nights on the telephone, lunch hours spent clipping ads. For a while there, Saturdays required almost more work than weekdays. But Heather and the kids had pitched in, and he had grown closer to them than he'd been in years. He finished dialing and waited for the connection, reminiscing. The second year had gotten a bit easier. Though it wasn't quite a breeze, it still had its great moments, especially the day he realized he would never have to work for

249

someone else again. By then he had bought a half a dozen homes and had fixed up and sold four of them; his investments were making twice what he had—

"Good afternoon. United Airlines, may I help you?"

"Yes. I'd like to book tickets for my family to Paris, then on to Switzerland."

The American Dream is alive and well.

Glossary

Abstract: A short summary that contains the history of the ownership and title to a property, a listing of any conveyances and legal proceedings, and a description of the land and conditions of ownership. Referred to also as an *abstract of title* or an *abstracter's certificate*.

Acceleration clause (due-on-sale clause): A provision in a trust deed or mortgage that makes the balance owed due in full immediately, which accelerates the payment schedule. This acceleration could come as a result of failure to pay payments by a specified date or because of the sale or transfer of title. It effectively stops the assumption of the mortgage or trust deed, and most courts have upheld the enforceability of such clauses.

Acre: A plot of land measuring approximately 209 feet square, or consisting of 43,560 square feet, 160 square rods, 4,840 square yards, or 4,047 square meters.

Alligator: An investment that eats up an investor's capital because the cash flow from the investment is less than the amount of money required to pay the payments. So named because the minute you can no longer afford to feed it, it will eat you up.

All-inclusive trust deed (AITD wrap): A junior mortgage with a face value of both the amount it secures and the balance due under the existing loans. The mortgagee himself or through a trust company collects payments on its face value, then pays the payments on the underlying existing loans. The difference between the amount he collects and the amount he pays out in loans serves as his income. It is most effective when the underlying loans have a lower interest rate than what is being charged on the wrap.

Amortization: The process of paying a financial obligation through a series of payments on an installment basis. At the conclusion of the series of payments the financial obligation will be paid in full.

Appraisal: An estimate of quality, quantity, and value of an asset, as of a specific date, made by a qualified, unbiased, and disinterested person.

Assessed value: The value placed upon a property by a county tax assessor for the purpose of determining property taxes.

Assumption: The purchase of a property with the buyer taking over the existing mortgage and assuming liability for the payments.

Assumption fee: The loan institution's charge for the assumption report and paperwork involved in processing the assumption of a mortgage.

Bundle of rights: The rights that a person has to enjoy, use, and dispose of his real or personal property.

Closing costs: The fees required to finalize the purchase of a home or property. These fees may include the remainder of the down payment, property insurance, property taxes, title insurance, points, assumption fee, mortgage insurance premium, filing and recording fees.

Comparables: These are recently sold properties that are similar in location and type to a property that you are thinking of buying or selling. You would use the recent sales prices of at least three comparables to help you determine the sales price of the property in question.

Condominium: Condominiums are typically multi-unit housing complexes where individual apartmentlike units are bought instead of rented, and where each owner has his own deed or mortgage. Typically, owners of these housing units are required to pay a monthly common fee, which pays for all outside maintenance, lawn care, and common utility fees.

Cooperative (co-op): A housing unit physically similar to a condominium, but in which the owner buys shares in the corporation that owns the building. The cost of the stock is determined by the value of the unit. A common fee is usually charged to each cooperative member to pay for outside building maintenance, lawn care, and shared utilities. The cooperative is really a forerunner of the condominium, and is no longer commonly used, since there is no direct ownership of a single unit.

Deed: A written legal document, properly made out, executed, and under proper seal. Types of commonly used deeds are the administrator's, condominium, corporation, county, executor's, foreclosure, gift, grant, guardian's, mineral, quick claim, reconveyance, referee's, sheriff's, trust, warranty.

Deed of trust (trust deed, trust deed mortgage, or trust indenture): A form of deed on a mortgaged property where a third party (trustee) holds the deed. Upon payment in full of the note, the trustee delivers the deed to the property owner. The use of trust deeds in the U.S. is fast becoming the rule because of the ease of foreclosure in default situations and other advantages.

Earnest money: Payment made as evidence of a purchaser's good faith to go through with the purchase of real estate. It is given along with an earnest money (or binder) agreement, outlining the terms and conditions of the sale and payment for the property. An earnest money and offer to purchase form is available at most office supply stores.

Easement: The right of a person to use someone else's land for a particular purpose, such as access to their property. The right of easement is inherent with ownership of certain properties.

Encumbrance: Any claim against or attached to a property, such as a judgment, mortgage, lien, or easement.

Equity: The value a property has over and above the mortgage or mortgages against it.

FHA 203/203B: An FHA-sponsored loan program that features low down payments (5%) for owner-occupied loans. A feature of the FHA 203/203B loan program is that payments are level for the loan period. This loan is simply assumable without qualification or credit check.

Home owner's policy: Property insurance protecting a home owner against all expected perils, such as fire, theft, personal liability, and wind.

Independent contractor: A party who has complete charge of and responsibility for the work he does. He in essence is working for himself. The hirer of an independent contractor is not legally responsible for the independent contractor's acts.

Individual retirement account (IRA): A government-established retirement saving plan. Individuals and spouses may invest money in numerous savings instruments, ranging from IRA bank accounts to money market funds. The actual deposit is tax deductible. The gain from the investment is tax exempt. There are certain restrictions and penalties on how much you can deposit annually and on withdrawing and using these funds before age fifty-nine. For more information on IRA savings accounts, seek competent tax advice or visit a reputable local bank, savings and loan office, or stockbroker in your area.

Inflation: An increase or expansion of an economy beyond its normal growth. Monetary inflation is *always* caused by an increase in the supply of money. In the United States that supply is determined by the Federal Reserve Board, and the money supply is increased through the actions of the Federal Reserve Open Market Committee.

Inflation rate: The rate of decrease in the real value of money expressed as a percentage of a base year.

Interest: 1) Money or consideration received for the use of money or assets. 2) A share or right in an asset, idea, or property.

Interest income: The money received as interest on a loan. An example of interest income would be the $10 received on a one-year loan of $100 at 10 percent interest.

Interest-only loan: A loan without any specific amortization schedule. The borrower is required only to keep current on the interest charged.

Interest rate: The annualized percentage rate that is charged for the use of a sum of money. An example would be a $100 loan due in one year with 10 percent interest. At the end of the year both the $100 principal and the $10 interest would be due in full.

Investor: An individual who puts money, time, or his possessions into an idea or project in anticipation of future benefits for either himself or others. Examples of investments that investors make would be stocks, bonds, real estate, or even education. Any person who sacrifices money and time for education is making the best investment possible.

Joint tenancy: Property held by two or more parties with each having the legal right to assume full title upon the death of the other. Under joint tenancy, probate is avoided. See *tenants in common* for another form of property ownership by two or more parties.

Junior lien: A lien subordinate (junior) to another lien against a property.

Land: the surface of the earth and the area under each parcel to the center of earth, including all natural things that grow on it and any mineral or air rights inherent with property ownership.

Landlord: The owner of a property or his agent who has a legal right to rent a property, building, dwelling, or office space to another. An example of a landlord would be a property owner's son who is given the position of managing his father's apartment complex. The son becomes the landlord. The son then leases a unit to his friend. The friend insists on having the right to sublet included in the rental agreement. Several months later the friend moves and sublets his unit to a sister of his. The friend now becomes a landlord to his sister in that he holds legal right to rent out the unit.

Lease: A written contract between a property owner or his representative and a tenant specifying the terms of a lease agreement. Some states allow oral leases.

Legal journals: Daily newspapers, found in most major areas, that carry legal recordings and notices. Examples of real estate legal notices would be the legal notices of default filed against property owners for nonpayment on a mortgage or trust deed note, and the notices of foreclosure sale on properties.

Leverage: The use of borrowed funds (OPM, other people's money) to purchase an asset. An example of leverage would be purchasing an investment property for $50,000 with $1,000 down. The $1,000 would be leveraging $49,000 of other people's money. The magic of leverage becomes clear when you realize that for $1,000 you are getting $50,000 worth of appreciable property (given that you bought the property at market value) and $50,000 worth of income property tax benefits.

Lien: The claim one party has on the property of another as result of a legal judgment or as security for a debt. Some types are tax liens, mortgage liens, and judgment liens.

Listing agreement: The legal agreement that a property owner enters into with a real estate agent or agency to sell, lease, trade, or rent a property. The listing agreement specifies a time period of the listing and a sales commission percentage.

Market value (fair market value): The price at which a property can realistically be sold. The highest price a buyer will pay and the lowest price a seller will take for a property when both are acting free from any compulsion and collusion.

M.B.A. (master of business administration degree): Two years of full-time graduate study that teaches you only how little you actually know.

Multiple Listing Service (agency): A membership organization for Realtors who share certain property listings and sales commissions with other members.

National Committee for Real Estate Investment (NCREI): A national company that promotes the concept of financial freedom through real estate investing. NCREI sponsors workshops and seminars across the country and markets resource materials for investors. For further information, contact NCREI at P.O. Box 796, Provo, Utah 84603.

Offer: A written document signed by a buyer offering to purchase a specific property at a specific price under a specific set of terms. When a seller signs and accepts the terms of the offer, the written document becomes a contract.

Open listing: A contractual relationship enabling the owner(s) of a property to use as many real estate agents as they desire. A real estate commission is paid upon closing with the first agent who presents an acceptable purchase offer to the owner. An open listing is the opposite of an *exclusive right-to-sell listing* that an owner may give a single Realtor. Since it creates a condition wherein the commission on the sale is free game for any agent, Realtors do not like open listings and are less likely to actively sell such properties.

Option: The right to purchase a property at a certain price, during a certain period of time, under some set of specified terms. To conform with legal requirements, an option must contain the following things:

1. Some consideration (something of value given in exchange for the promise) to bind the agreement
2. A legal description of the property involved
3. Specified conditions and terms
4. Specified time period for exercising the option

The entire option must be in writing, and in many cases witnessed.

Ordinary income: Income taxed at the "normal" income tax rates. Examples of ordinary income would be remuneration from employment, tax dividends, commissions, and gains from the sale of real estate held for less than six months.

Point: One percentage point. The typical use of the term *points* is in reference to discount points that a lender charges a buyer for the "right to borrow money."

Qualifying: The process of determining whether a buyer is financially able to assume the responsibility of ownership of a property and paying the required debt service. This process may include checking credit, employment, past landlords, and other sources of financial history that may help determine the capability of the buyer.

Real estate: The land and everything built on it, attached to it with the intention it would become a permanent part of the property and pass with it upon sale, or growing on it.

Real estate commission: A state agency that regulates and licenses real estate brokers and salespeople. Many state agencies are also responsible for making the local state's real estate rules and regulations.

Realtor: A licensed member of a local real estate board affiliated with the National Association of Realtors.

Refinancing: Obtaining a new loan to pay off the existing financing. People usually refinance to get the equity out of their homes.

Rehabilitation (rehab): The restoration of a property to a habitable condition. Many government programs help property owners rehabilitate and modernize run-down properties with low-interest government loans.

Second mortgage/trust: A mortgage junior to the first or original mortgage on a property. A property may have a first, second, third, fourth, or even more mortgages. Each subsequent mortgage is junior or behind the senior mortgages in legal standing.

Subject-to clause: A clause contained within or added to a purchase agreement that makes the offer subject to the performance of an act or some other event. Subject-to clauses are also known as *weasel clauses*. Examples of two subject-to clauses are:

"Offer subject to partner's approval."

"Subject to buyer's approval of appraisal."

Subordinate: To make a senior lien junior to another lien. An example would be if you held a first mortgage against a lot, and the owner needed to get a construction loan for it. You would most likely be asked to subordinate or move your first-position mortgage into second position behind the construction loan. This changing of positions in the line of title is called *subordination*.

Subordination clause: A clause contained within or added to a purchase agreement that refers to the subordination of existing financing. Two examples of subordination clauses are:

"Seller agrees to subordinate seller's equity to buyer's new mortgage."

"Seller hereby agrees to subordinate said note and trust deed to buyer's new loan; both parties agree that the loan amount of the new deed of trust or mortgage will not be greater than the increase of the value of the property as a result of, but not exclusively from, the new improvements made by buyer from the proceeds of buyer's new loan."

Supply and demand: The underlying premise behind all market exchange in a free market economy. As the quantity of a product supplied increases, while the quantity demanded remains the same, the price will decline. If the quantity supplied decreases, the price will rise. As buyers demand less, competition among sellers increases, and the price drops.

Survey: The physical determination and marking of the measurement and area of a property.

Tenant: One who occupies or uses another's property in exchange for some financial payment or other consideration to the property owner.

Tenant at sufferance: A lessee who stays in possession of the leased property after the lease has expired.

Tenants in common: Two or more parties who own equal shares of a property. If one partner dies, his share goes to his estate. For another form of joint property ownership, see *joint tenancy*.

Termite inspection: An inspection of a property by a licensed pest control company, which then issues a written statement of whether the property is free from termite damage or not.

Title: The formal document that establishes a legal right to ownership or a lien against a property.

Title company: A private company that prepares real estate title abstracts, helps in property closings, and provides title insurance.

Title insurance: Insurance protection sold to the purchaser of a property by an insurance company to cover any loss from undiscovered defects in title.

Variable rate mortgage (VRM): A mortgage wherein the borrower allows the lender to alter the interest rate and monthly payments under prespecified criteria. Most variable rate mortgages contain "caps" that limit both the annual interest rate increase and the total interest rate increase by which a loan may jump over its lifetime.

Veterans Administration: A government agency that administers benefits to qualified veterans. The VA guarantees conventional loans. These loans, called VA loans, are originally given to veterans only; however, they can be assumed by subsequent buyers without restriction.

Wrap-around mortgage (wrap): See *all-inclusive trust deed.*

These definitions have been excerpted from *The Real Estate Greenbook* by Marc Garrison, copyright 1985, published by the National Committee for Real Estate Investment.

Index

Driveway, 126
"Due-on-sale clause," 99, 184
Dunne, Finley Peter, 235

Earnest money, 108–9, 171, 227, 228
Earnest Money Receipt and Offer to
    Purchase (sample), 177–78
Easements, 54
Edison, Thomas, 233
Educated persistence, 163–64
Education, importance of, 207–10
E. F. Hutton, 93
Electrical system, 127
Eminent domain, law of, 54
Employment information, 152
Empties, 81–85, 160, 184
    locating, 82, 84–85
    and neighbors, 83
    and owner location, 83–84
Equity, 237
    buildup, 44–45
    instant, 105–6
Erb, Bruce C., 223
Erb, Jared D., 238
Escape clauses, 106–9, 148, 160, 171,
    176, 194
Estate
    freehold, 54
    less-than-freehold, 54–55
Eviction, of tenants, 131–32
Exclusive agency listing contract,
    143–44
Exclusive right-to-sell contract, 142
Exclusive right-to-sell multiple list-
    ing contract, 142
Exterior (fixing up), 121–22
    see also Outside
Exterior walls, 126

Family, two-income, 152
Farmers Digest, 207
"Farming," 79–81, 147, 160, 187
Features, selling, 145, 146, 150
Federal Housing Administration, see
    FHA
Fees, at closing, 109–10, 140
    see also Finder's fee; Inspection
    fees: Mortgage fees; Origination
    fee; Processing fees
Feldstein, Martin, 34

FHA (Federal Housing Administra-
    tion)
    foreclosures, 94–96, 160
    loans, 66, 98–99, 108, 184
    repossession lists, 77, 187
Finances, organizing personal,
    210–15
Financial analysis, and property
    analysis system, 171–75
Financing, 62, 145
    offer subject to satisfactory, 108
    see also Owner financing
Finder's fee, 146–47, 153
First impressions, while negotiating,
    112
Five-year profit potential
    of affording today and tomorrow,
    188–89
    for full-time investing, 194–95
    and investing for cash flow, 185
Five-year summary
    of affording today and tomorrow,
    189
    for full-time investing, 195–96
    and investing for cash flow, 185–86
Fixing up, 62, 121–28, 160, 192
    exterior, 121–22
    inside, 126–28
    interior, 122–24
    outside, 125–26
    work, 124–25
    see also Seller's Checklist to Maxi-
    mize Sales Price
"Fixity," concept of, 62
Fix-up expenses, returns on, 118–20
Fliers, 72–74, 146
    sample, 73
    see also "I sell houses" fliers
Flipping, 175, 194
Floors, 126–27
Forced sales, 66, 67
Ford, Henry, 197
Foreclosures, 86–88, 229
    after auction, 87, 93–96, 160, 186
    at auction, 91–93, 160
    before auction, 88–91
    and bank, 87, 91–94, 160
    and cure date, 88
    FHA, 94–96, 160
    from home owner, 160

About the Author

At the age of twenty-two, Marc Stephen Garrison began investing part-time in real estate to pay for a college education. His success as an investor paid for several undergraduate degrees and an M.B.A. Since then he has achieved complete financial freedom through his real estate investments. Motivated by his own success, he has dedicated himself to teaching others how to achieve the same level of freedom. Marc is on the *Financial Freedom Report's* national board of advisers and is chairman of the board of the Freedom Foundation. Today he writes a nationally recognized column, "Real Estate Across the USA," and lectures at investment seminars and conventions across the country. He is the author of several books on real estate investing, financial planning, and time management.

Marc lives in the Wasatch Mountains with his wife DeAnn and their three children, Ryan, Kelly, and Hunter. He is currently working on his next book, *The American Dream*.